THE ANTI-EMILE

Other books of interest from St. Augustine's Press

Aristotle, *Aristotle – On Poetics*, S. Benardete & M. Davis, trans.
Aristotle, *Physics, Or Natural Hearing*, G. Coughlin, trans.
St. Augustine, *On Order [De Ordine]*, S. Borruso, trans.
St. Augustine, *The St. Augustine LifeGuide*
Thomas Aquinas, *Commentary on Aristotle's Nicomachean Ethics*
Thomas Aquinas, *Commentary on Aristotle's Posterior Analytics*,
    R. Berquist, trans.
Thomas Aquinas, *Commentary on Aristotle's De Anima*
Thomas Aquinas, *Commentary on the Epistle to the Hebrews*,
    C. Baer, trans.
Thomas Aquinas, *Commentary on St. Paul's Epistles to Timothy, Titus,
    and Philemon*, C. Baer, trans.
Thomas Aquinas, *Disputed Questions on Virtue*, R. McInerny, trans.
Thomas Aquinas, *Treatise on Law*, A.J. Freddoso, trans.
Thomas Aquinas, *Treatise on Human Nature*, A.J. Freddoso, trans.
Henry of Ghent, *Henry of Ghent's* Summa of Ordinary Questions:
    Article One: *On the Possibility of Human Knowledge*, R.J. Teske, S.J.,
    trans.
Karel Wojtyła [John Paul II], *Man in the Field of Ressponsibility*, K.W.
    Kemp and Z.M. Kiero, trans.
John of St. Thomas, *Introduction to the Summa Theologiae of Thomas
    Aquinas*, R. McInerny, trans.
Josef Pieper, *In Tune with the World: A Theory of Festivity*
Josef Pieper, *The Platonic Myths*
Josef Pieper, *Scholasticism: Personalities and Problems of Medieval
    Philosophy*
Peter Kreeft, *Summa Philosophica*
Peter Kreeft, *The Philosophy of Jesus*
Peter Kreeft, *Jesus-Shock*
Plato, *The Symposium of Plato: The Shelley Translation*, P. S. Shelley,
    trans.
Servais Pinckaers, O.P., *Morality: The Catholic View*, M. Sherwin, O.P., tr.
James V. Schall, *The Regensburg Lecture*
James V. Schall, *The Modern Age*
C.S. Lewis and Don Giovanni Calabria, *The Latin Letters of C.S. Lewis*
Edward Feser, *The Last Superstition: A Refutation of the New Atheism*

THE ANTI-EMILE

REFLECTIONS ON THE THEORY
AND PRACTICE OF EDUCATION
AGAINST THE PRINCIPLES OF ROUSSEAU

H. S. Gerdil
(1718–1802)

Translation, Introductory Essay, and Notes
by
William A. Frank

ST. AUGUSTINE'S PRESS
South Bend, Indiana

KH

Manufactured in the United States of America

1 2 3 4 5 6   16 15 14 13 12 11

Library of Congress Cataloging in Publication Data
Gerdil, Giacinto Sigismondo, 1718–1802.
[Reflexions sur la théorie & la pratique de l'éducation. English]
The anti-Emile: reflections on the theory and practice of
education against the principles of Rousseau / by H.S. Gerdil;
an English translation, with introduction and notes by
William A. Frank.
p. cm.
Includes bibliographical references and index.
ISBN 978-1-58731-036-2 (clothbound: alk. paper) 1. Education –
Early works to 1800. 2. Rousseau, Jean-Jacques, 1712–1778. 3.
Rousseau, Jean-Jacques, 1712–1778. Emile. I. Frank, William A.
II. Title.
LB575.G43 2011
370.1 – dc22   2011013871

∞ The paper used in this publication meets the minimum requirements of
the American National Standard for Information Sciences – Permanence of
Paper for Printed Materials, ANSI Z39.48-1984.

ST. AUGUSTINE'S PRESS
www.staugustine.net

11/26/12

To

Paolo Guietti

TABLE OF CONTENTS

Note on the Text   ix

Preface by Rocco Buttiglione   xi

Acknowledgments   xiv

Introductory Essay   xv

Reflections on the Theory and Practice of Education against the Principles of Rousseau's *Emile*

Preface   1

Part One.
Reflections on the Basic Principles of the Theory of Education

1. Rousseau's seductive rhetoric   4
2. Emile is an unreal abstraction   5
3. Whether contrariety is part of man's original nature   7
4. Whether the self is ordered to other selves from the beginning   11
5. Whether self-interest is a sufficient foundation for moral social relationships   17
6. Love of honor and the attraction to an idea of perfection are natural inclinations   18
7. The attraction to moral virtue is a natural inclination   21
8. Whether society corrupts man's natural goodness   24
9. Whether society invents the fear of death and makes men cowards   27
10. Whether laws and society reduce man to a servile state of dependency   30

11. On the natural love of order and origins of society   34
12. Man's reason, the natural analogue to animal instinct, requires education   38
13. Whether children are capable of understanding moral categories   43
14. On the importance of the fear of God in the moral education of children   48
15. On the authority of fathers and the obedience of children   51

Part Two.
Reflections on Particular Educational Practices,
and Most Especially on Matters of Curriculum

16. On reasoning with children   58
17. Rousseau's dialogue misrepresents how to reason morally with a child   62
18. On a child's capacity for handling ideas   67
19. On teaching fables   71
20. On the study of languages, and especially Latin   85
21. On the study of history   96
22. On the study of geography   104
23. On the study of geometry   107
24. Francis Bacon's observations on studying and reading   110
25. The intellectual temperament of Rousseau's student   119
26. On the native climate of the ideal student   122
27. On the ideal student's physical constitution   126
28. On the social status of Rousseau's student   129
29. Insufficiency of philosophy for forming a national ethos   133

Conclusion   139
Endnotes   143
Index   165

NOTE ON THE TEXT

The French edition used for this translation is: *Reflexions sur la théorie, & la pratique de l'education contre les principes de Mr. Rousseau* (Geneva: Chez Em. Du Villard, 1764). The 1765 English translation, *Reflections on Education; Relative both to Theory and Practice in which some of the Principles attempted by Mr. Rousseau, in his Emilius, or Treatise on Education, Are occasionally examined and refuted. Written in French by Father Gerdil, Barnabite: Professor of Moral Philosophy in the Royal University of Turin: Preceptor to his royal Highness the Prince of Piedmont.* 2 vols. (Holborn: L. Davis and C. Reymers, 1765) proved helpful. In fact, what began as an attempt to put an earlier English translation into contemporary idiom evolved into a distinct translation. The number and quality of revisions, additions, and corrections to the Davis-Reymers edition have been extensive, even though the debt to the earlier work remains large. Two modern Italian translations have proved helpful: *L'Anti-Emilio, ovvero Riflessioni su la theoria e la pratica dell'educazione contro i principi del Rousseau. Aggiunte le Considerazioni sopra gli studi della gioventù*, translation and introduction and notes by G. L. Arrighi (Firenze: Sansoni, 1924) and *Riflessioni sulla teoria e la pratica dell'educazione contro i principi del signor Rousseau*, introduction, translation, and notes by Carlo Corsetti (Rome: UNITOR, 1990). I am indebted to the scholarship of the two Italian translators who have identified the sources of many of Gerdil's references. Section divisions and subtitles, italicized and set within brackets, have been added to Gerdil's continuous text. All citations of Rousseau's *Emile* are to Allan Bloom's English translation (n.p.: Basic Books, 1979). In the absence of a standard rubric for citing the *Emile* by "chapter and verse," the following convention has been adopted: *Emile* 1. 2 (B, 37) which signifies *Emile*, Book One, paragraph 2 (Bloom trans., page 37). Gerdil's own notes to the text are indicated by an asterisk and placed as footnotes; other notes and references are numbered and included as endnotes.

PREFACE

The idea of translating Gerdil into English is brilliant, the translation is very good, and William Frank's introduction is precise and inspiring.

Gerdil has a significant place of his own in the history of philosophy. A disciple of Malebranche, he is an outstanding example of Christian Cartesianism and represents the tradition of ontologism after Rousseau, recapitulating it in the light of different adversaries and a different spiritual atmosphere. It would be incorrect, however, to consider him just as a follower of Malebranche, for he has a historical dimension that is thoroughly missing in the great French Oratorian. In the case of Gerdil, we have the continuation of a Christian philosophy *within* modernity, one that is wholly coherent with the critical acceptance of tradition, history, and authority. His philosophy does not arise as a criticism of modernity from the point of view of the Middle Ages.

Rousseau proposes a complete break with tradition. As he conceived it, a new man will arise who is severed from the whole heritage of the past. With him the history of mankind begins anew. In a certain sense we have here a transposition of the Cartesian *cogito* into the field of philosophy of education. The subject begins with himself. Against this philosophical and political project, Gerdil insists on the idea of tradition. We have not made ourselves. Our parents have procreated us. Parents not only procreate their offspring, they also introduce them into the realities of nature and society, which is to say, they educate them. No education is possible without a lively dialogue with history and society. Since the beginning man stands in a close relationship to others; he is made for the human society. To belong to others in a relationship of friendship and love means to be freer than to be isolated and to belong only to oneself. A metaphysical idea of tradition stands as the background to Gerdil's position. Not only have our parents procreated us, but we have also been created by God and received the gift of being through his creative act. Another great Savoyard, Joseph de Maistre, will develop this idea of tradition later. The metaphysical idea of tradition is derived, of course, from Malebranche. The historical reading of this idea, which Gerdil gives us, depends, however, upon the Italian environment in which Gerdil is active. In this respect the reader can feel the presence of Giambattista Vico. It becomes apparent that in taking up Gerdil's thought we find ourselves at the confluence of the French and the Italian philosophies.

The second fundamental error of Rousseau is that he does not recognize and accept the idea of original sin. Neither men nor children, for that matter, are good or bad by nature. They are capable of good but prone to evil, and this is the reason why they need to be educated. Original sin is not just a theological doctrine; it is at the same time an anthropological explanation of the real nature of man. Through tradition parents and educators pass on to the next generation the results of their struggle for truth and offer the starting point for a further development. The new generation has the right – and the duty—to put to trial in their own life experience the heritage of the past to see what in it is really of permanent value and what is linked only to the historical circumstances of the past. When, however, tradition is refused *en bloc* and without this critical dialogue, then a generation regresses to barbarianism and denies itself creative and innovative power. The impulses and desires of the child need to be organized and subjected to the power of reason, and therefore we must acknowledge the legitimate role of authority in the educational process.

Another of Gerdil's criticisms is of a more methodological nature. Where are we to find the pedagogue who will teach Emile? The educator must in his turn have been educated. How is it possible if society is so thoroughly corrupted that in it the prophet of a new social order may arise? The young Karl Marx will repeat this objection in his *Theses on Feuerbach*, although with an intention thoroughly different from that of Gerdil. But that is another story.

In these our times one form of modernity – that based largely on Rousseau – is collapsing and the mood of the day is an unclear postmodernity that in some of its versions could well be a return to barbarianism. All the more important it is then that another form of modernity be rediscovered and brought to the attention of the American public.

Rocco Buttiglione

ACKNOWLEDGMENTS

The Introductory Essay, published as "Hyacinth Gerdil's *Anti-Emile*: A Prophetic Moment in the Philosophy of Education" in *The Review of Metaphysics* 61 (December 2007): 237–61, is used with the generous permission of the editor, Jude P. Dougherty. I wish to acknowledge the generosity of the Confraternity of the Scuola Grande di San Rocco for permission to use Tintoretto's image of the Temptation of Adam on the cover of this book. Much of the translation and research for the notes was supported by a sabbatical grant from the University of Dallas in Fall 2001.

I gratefully acknowledge the assistance that my colleague, Valeria Forte, provided in securing permission to use Tintoretto's image. It has been gratifying to receive from my editor, Bruce Fingerhut, enthusiastic support for this project of introducing of Gerdil to the American public. Two friends have been instrumental in my work in the philosophy of education. My colleague, Cheri Clodfelter, longtime chair of the Department of Education at the University of Dallas, for many years provided ongoing encouragement and the opportunity to teach teachers in an ideal setting. It was in conversations with Jack Paynter, of beloved memory, that I came to appreciate the significance of Rousseau's *Emile*.

It is fitting to dedicate this book to Paolo Guietti, who introduced me to Gerdil and his distinctive tradition of philosophy.

INTRODUCTORY ESSAY

> "The past is never dead,
> it is not even past."
> – William Faulkner

To say that the publication in 1772 of Rousseau's *Emile or On Education* was controversial would be an understatement. Published in Paris, it was immediately denounced at the Sorbonne. The French Parliament condemned the book, had it confiscated, and ordered its author arrested. In Rousseau's native city, Geneva, the *Emile* was burned. It is in the context of such controversy that one of the most accomplished philosophers in Northern Italy, Hyacinth Sigismond Gerdil (1718–1802), was asked to review Rousseau's book to determine whether there was to be found in it anything "contrary to the principles of religion and sound morality."[1] In the process of devising what was originally intended as a modest evaluation of Rousseau's work, Gerdil found himself articulating the elements of his own philosophy of education. The result is the work at hand, first published in Turin in 1763, which he entitled *Reflections on the Theory and Practice of Education against the Principles of Rousseau.* The little book, much reprinted and translated, soon picked up the popular title, *Anti-Emile*, by which it largely has been known ever since. It is reported that Rousseau himself considered Gerdil's critique of his book to be principled and thorough, traits that he found rare among the widespread criticism of his works.[2] Gerdil's rhetorical style is marked by

---

[1] *Anti-Emile*, § 1.

[2] According to Gerdil lore, Rousseau is supposed to have remarked: "Among the very many opuscula published against me and against my writings, it is

a tone of elevated civility; despite its polemical intent, his tone never strays far from the detachment of philosophical inquiry. Apart from historical considerations of its contribution to the hot polemics over Rousseau's book, Gerdil's *Anti-Emile* has contemporary relevance. *Emile's* principles of education are still with us. They have, however, become conventional instead of controversial. Gerdil's *Anti-Emile* is a book for anyone who would like to cast back the mind's eye to a moment in history when the profound potential of Rousseau's book for transforming Western culture and casting the minds and hearts of men in a revolutionary spirit was seen for precisely what it proved to be.

Despite the efforts of Allan Bloom to elevate Rousseau's treatise to the status of "a book comparable to Plato's *Republic*,"[3] the *Emile* is not well known outside of limited academic circles. This neglect, however, should not be taken as a sign of its minimal importance or weak influence. One hundred years ago the French educationalist, Gabriel Compayré, wrote about Rousseau's influence in America:

> Without our suspecting it, Rousseau's pedagogical spirit has insinuated itself into and penetrated the methods of teaching and the educational practices. . . . Wherever discipline has become more liberal, where active methods are supreme, and where the child is kept constantly in a state of interest, lively curiosity, and sustained attention, his dignity being at the same time respected, there we may say Rousseau has passed by.[4]

only the work of Father Gerdil that I have had the patience to read to the end. It's disappointing that this estimable author has not understood me." Quoted by Corsetti in his introduction to *Riflessioni sulla teoria e la pratica dell'educazione, contra i principi del signor Rousseau*, introduzione, traduzione e note by Carlo Corsetti (Rome: Unitor, 1990), 19.

[3] "Introduction" to Jean-Jacques Rousseau, *Emile or On Education*, Introduction, Translation, and Notes by Allan Bloom (n.p.: Basic Books, 1979), 4.

[4] Gabriel Compayré, *Jean Jacques Rousseau and Education from Nature*, trans. by R. P. Jago (New York: Burt Franklin, 1907; reprinted 1971), 109–10.

John Dewey's progressive, child-centered theory of education was a major conduit of these ideas in American schools.[5] Their influence continues today in pedagogical practices such as discovery methods, group projects, interactive and manipulative methodologies, and the appeal to different learning styles, which are staples in contemporary teacher training programs and the practice of their graduates. Rousseau's Emile is the prototype student.

If, as a matter of principle, the rationale behind pedagogical practice follows from an understanding of the nature of the human person, we might wonder about the philosophical presuppositions at the Rousseauan origins of today's liberal, progressive movements in education. Allan Bloom identifies the fundamental issue:

> Rousseau is at the source of the tradition which replaces virtue and vice as the cause of man's being good or bad, happy or miserable, with such pairs of opposites as sincere / insincere, authentic / inauthentic, inner-directed / other-directed, real self / alienated self. . . . [His] analysis supersedes that based on the distinction between the body and soul, which in turn has activated the quest for virtue, seen as the taming and controlling the body's desires under the guidance of the soul's reason. It initiates the great longing to be one's self and the hatred of alienation which characterizes all modern thought.[6]

As Bloom sees it, Rousseau radically transformed the very meaning of moral virtue. Instead of the classical notion of inducing the curbing restraint of reason into inclinations, Rousseau reconceived virtue as liberating innate inclination from the restraints or exploitations

---

[5]   What Compayré calls liberal discipline and active methods is especially evident in Dewey's early, influential essays, "School and Society" (1900) and "Child and Curriculum" (1902), John Dewey, *The School and Society and The Child and Curriculum*, with Introduction by Philip W. Jackson (Chicago and London: University of Chicago Press, 1990).

[6]   Ibid.

of alien authorities. Plato and Rousseau can agree that moral virtue is the great end of education. But they mean something very different by their words. Education, if we can put it thus, is soul-craft, and souls are crafted with different ends in view: perfection of the inherent sociability of the classical human soul versus perfection in the spontaneous autonomy of the modern self. The different ends call for different systems of education. They equally proceed from different starting points, as we shall see below. In this connection, it is interesting to observe that philosophy and educational theory spring from the same source. Plato understood the connection, so did Rousseau. In the twentieth century John Dewey saw it clearly.[7] It is not a strong point of contemporary thought that critical, professional attention to the theory and practice of education is carried out within the methodologies of the social sciences that have largely liberated themselves from the speculative reason of philosophy.

It is with these ideas in mind that I think it behooves one to reflect on the original ideas and ideals that give rise to the theory and practice of the education by which the next generation is brought to maturity. Gerdil's *Anti-Emile* is, therefore, of contemporary relevance inasmuch as it returns us to a moment in the development of Western culture when some of the deepest convictions of modern philosophy about the nature of man and the meaning of human existence acquired the transformative power of educational theory and practice. His book helps us to see what was – and continues to be – at issue in the pedagogical ideals and practices we adopt.

The following introduction has two parts. In the first part I offer an interpretive essay that aims to set out Gerdil's philosophical achievement. He saw in Rousseau's *Emile* a fearful genius, a source of ideas forceful enough to radically transform critical aspects of Western culture. His understanding of the book's potency materializes as he sets Rousseau's views in contrast with the living tradition

---

[7] J. J. Chambliss, Introduction to *Philosophy and Education in Their Historic Relations* by John Dewey, transcribed from his lectures by Elsie Ripley Clapp, ed. by J.J. Chambliss (Boulder, San Francisco, Oxford: Westview, 1993), 4–7.

of classical education. Ultimately at issue are radically different views of human nature and what counts as the final achievement in the work of education. These ultimate philosophical views become the principles that govern the practical matters of curriculum and pedagogy. My essay mainly aims to bring out philosophical principles, though I shall conclude with comments illustrating some of Gerdil's pedagogical wisdom. In the second part of the introduction, I introduce Gerdil as a historical figure with a distinctive place in the history of philosophy. It is an interesting fact that Hyacinth Sigismond Gerdil is now little known in the English-speaking world. Accordingly, I give a brief chronology of his life; I also place the *Anti-Emile* within the context of his other significant philosophical works and situate his thought within an account of the history of modern philosophy.

I. Interpretive Essay

Whether Gerdil is pursuing the theoretical or practical side of his reflections, he reads the *Emile* as a pedagogical treatise. He addresses his *Anti-Emile* to elders responsible for education, be they parents, teachers, or political authorities, who might find themselves swayed by the powerful rhetoric of Rousseau's *Emile*.[8] If today we postmoderns are swayed by Rousseau's proposals, it is more likely that the influence has been mediated by established institutions and common opinions whose origins have been pretty much filed in the history

---

[8] In the Preface he explains that his review of *Emile* "provides us with an occasion to develop and publish certain ideas that may not be altogether useless for those who are occupied with the education of youth." In the Conclusion, directly addressing parents warning them against Rousseau's seductive rhetoric, he writes: "Fathers and mothers, do not be seduced by the deceitful attractions of brilliant novelty. Be wary of subjecting your children to the perilous experiment of a method that is not yet warranted by any success. . . . Take care that mistaken vanity does not induce you to sacrifice these innocent victims to a deadly desire for singularity and that the unhappiness into which you will have cast them does not constitute your shame and despair."

books. I imagine that most who today take up the *Emile* are likely to read it as an influential moment in the history of philosophy or as one of the great books worthy of the "careful reader."[9] For many, reading it might be an exercise in *ressourcement*. Not so with Gerdil: he wrote for the public, not the academy, and he was looking forward prophetically to the future, not backwards in search of a historical turning point. This is not to deny that he was a careful reader or that his reading lacks justice or insight with respect to the text. In fact, I think it is especially penetrating in its recognition and evaluation of principles that govern the *Emile*. In part, the penetration derives from his practical point of view. He sees the social consequences latent in Rousseau's ideas. As noted above, what began as a simple review to determine for some person of authority the suitability of *Emile* for public distribution[10] grew into a systematic exposition of the principles that informed his own considerable experience as a teacher. It is the vantage point of this philosophy of education that provides the wind tunnel, as it were, for testing Rousseau's revolutionary ideas. The results are twofold. First, one has a sober assessment of the ethical and social consequences one might expect if the principles of the *Emile* are taken to heart by educators. Secondly, the elements of Gerdil's own philosophy of education are laid out in a systematic and accessible fashion.

What does Gerdil foresee as the practical effect of the *Emile*? He thinks that the book aims "to prepare souls by means of a total revolution in their thinking," to form citizens suitable to the revolutionary social order that Rousseau has proposed in his *On Social Contract, or Principles of Political Right*. Toward this end, Gerdil thinks that Rousseau's pedagogy would succeed in inspiring "that vexation with and aversion for religious and social institutions, which animate

[9] Allan Bloom is the most notable example of the latter sort of reader; see his introductory essay and notes to his translation, Jean-Jacques Rousseau, *Emile or On Education*, introduction, translation, and notes by Allan Bloom (n.p.: Basic, 1979).

[10] The identity of this person has not been passed along with the treatise, and he still remains unknown to contemporary scholarship.

him and which breathes forth from all his writing. . . . [H]e will make bad Christians and bad citizens" [Preface]. The connection between religion and politics is crucial for Gerdil. The ends of civil society are ruled and measured by the providential order of the natural law. In the concluding argument of his treatise [§ 29], he rejects the enlightened notion that philosophy is sufficient for forming the habits and convictions requisite to citizenship. He insists on the irreplaceable role of religion in the formation of a national ethos. This is a point at odds with contemporary common opinion committed to the exclusion of religion from the public sphere. Yet there is a serious issue here that ought to give common opinion pause. Gerdil argues that the natural reason of philosophy fails to win broad commitment in a civic community to the personal order of virtue or to the public order of justice. The appeal of erudite and abstract reasoning is insufficient for mobilizing the unity of public spirit, constancy in motive, and firmness in conviction necessary to form the character of the citizen. As religion retreats to subjective interiority or even disappears into irreligion, public spiritedness will necessarily weaken. Despite postmodern claims for irreligious commitments to solidarity, it is hard to see in the assertions much more than enlightened self-interest.[11] Gerdil's main idea is that religion provides the broadly acceptable reasons for commitment to personal habits of benevolence and the claims of intrinsic goodness (*bonum honestum*) which are essential to civic order. In his view of human nature, there is an innate or natural appeal to doing what is right or good, just because it is right and good, just because of the simple beauty of such an act, indifferent to self-interest. Such a sentiment, however, does not arise unmixed in a person's soul; it is compounded with other powerful self-seeking inclinations. It is the chief work of education to bring from out of this original contrariety of the soul's desires some greater effective prominence to the appeal of the *bonum honestum* and the

---

[11] In this context I think of Richard Rorty's argument in his *Contingency, Irony, and Solidarity* (Cambridge University Press, 1989) as a particularly acute formulation of the postmodern alternative.

unmediated care for the good of others into the moral order of persons and society. Although philosophical thought can arrive at an understanding of these truths, its reasons lack the rhetorical force to broadly overcome the soul's self-interested inclinations. Like philosophy, religion insists on acts beyond self-interest, but its power of suasion touch more broadly distributed, deeper affections of the soul.

"Intrinsic goodness (*bonum honestum*)," "benevolence," and "order" are central notions in Gerdil's anthropology and social philosophy.[12] They have in common the fact that they are spiritual realities, irreducible to baser categories of utility or pleasure and pain. Civic society is inconceivable without their operative presence in human affairs. The human person is perfected to the extent that these principles govern one's thought and action. What is evident in these principles is their intrinsic social characteristic. The exemplary primacy they hold in human life is predicated on the fact that man is essentially a social being. It is on this point – the essential social being of the human person – that Gerdil focuses much of his theoretical criticism of Rousseau.

It will be useful to review the main narrative line of development in the *Emile*. It is a point of pride, a measure of success, that the tutor, Rousseau, can introduce the 15-year-old Emile with these words: "The child raised according to his age is alone. He knows no attachments. . . . He loves his sister as he loves his watch, and his friend as his dog."[13] In other words, one of the main achievements of the early

---

[12] See esp. § 11 on the natural love of order at the origins of society that operates in addition to and overarching with respect to the roles of fear, utility, and benevolence in disposing men to assemble in civic society. Gerdil had developed a remarkable analysis of these ideas in the first work of his intellectual maturity: *On the Origin of the Moral Sense, or Demonstration that there is in man a natural criterion for approval (praise) and disapproval (blame), with respect to the intrinsic moral difference between the just and the unjust: which, together with the ideas of order and beauty, originates with the faculty that man has for knowing truth.* In the *Anti-Emile*, for notion of *bonum honestum* (*honête*) see §§ 3, 7; for the notion of order see §§ 4, 10, 11, 20

[13] *Emile*, Book IV, paragraph 35; Bloom trans., p. 219.

stage in Rousseau's pedagogical project is to prevent the introduction of social, interpersonal categories into the life of reason. The youth Emile is formed into an isolated individual.[14] He feels pleasure and pain related to his own body. He lives in a world of other things which he knows by perception and to which he is tied only by use-relations. Other people are no more than things, and he has become adept at manipulating them to serve his own interests of curiosity and the pursuit of pleasure and avoidance of pain. Within the logic of the *Emile*, the atomic, isolated character of Emile represents a necessary, if temporary, moment in the development of the complete man and citizen, which Emile will become when he is properly socialized from the ages 16–24, which is the tutor's work in Books IV–V.

In his *Reflections*, Gerdil repeatedly returns to the fictional status of the boy, Emile, who from birth to age 15 years is raised with no intrinsic relations to other persons. Perhaps he can be criticized for his inattention to the principles and tactics Rousseau employs in Book IV–V to introduce the category of "the social" into the mentality and conduct of Emile. However, I think he might also be excused for not doing so, as there is a vexing, even profound tension in the relationship of the two major moments into which Rousseau divides the process of education. Within the fictional logic of the book, Rousseau would have us imagine raising a child to the age of 15, preserving in him an absolute and uncompromised self-interest. It is a practical, realistic impossibility. But Rousseau uses the mechanism of an extended thought experiment (namely, Bks I–III) to introduce a natural principle of individual autonomy which he believes all historically constituted societies have aimed to undermine. As he conceives it, historical man has always been caught in the contrariety between being a Man and being a Citizen. A person must diminish himself, he must alienate himself, when he enters society and

---

[14] Gerdil construes the achievement thus: "[Rousseau] intends to form an *abstracted man*, having no relationship to social institutions of any kind. . . . Emile must learn to be nothing other than a man, in case the dissolution of society should prevent his being any longer a citizen" [§ 2].

civilization. The institutions of society are historically constituted as instruments for that diminishment and alienation. The person formed in the practice of the *Emile*, however, will arrive unalienated and undiminished at the moment when he enters into the society constituted according to the principles of *On Social Contract*.[15] It is important to see here that for Rousseau it is the institutions and practices of historical societies that set up the conflict between personal self-interest and interpersonal communion. There is no basis for such natural contrariety. By contrast, Gerdil thinks that the tendencies to incivility or unabated egoism are inborn, and that it is the business of civil society and its institutions to moderate, if not overcome, these inclinations. As Gerdil would see it, Rousseau's thought-experiment, if we might so call it, causes us to yield to a false imagination. Pedagogical practices that would follow its logic would prove morally and politically disastrous.

Gerdil's own positive theory of education is capsulated in the formula: "through reason man is man. Reason is by nature a social faculty. To make a man reasonable is to make him sociable." [§ 4] A person's reason reaches its perfection in the extension of the person as fully and completely as possible into the order of reality. This order of reality extends not only to the vast regions of nature and the many eras of history, but particularly to the intelligible order of one's immediate relations to social and moral realities through which we are attached to other persons. The measure of a man's education, the mark of reason's cultivation, is therefore his participation in a common existence. The following passage is helpful for understanding what Gerdil means by a cultivated reason:

[15] The condition he describes in the memorable first sentence of Book I, namely, "everything is good as it leaves the hands of the Author of things, everything degenerates in the hands of man," (Bloom translation, p. 37) in principle can be overcome. It is the literary experiment with Emile that shows the conditions for the possibility of an individual who is not denatured by his entry into society. The suspicion, even hostility, with which Rousseau views the governing principles of actual societies is even more striking than the optimism with which he regards the innate goodness of the unsocialized child.

No man can be educated for himself unless his reason is cultivated. Consequently one cannot properly form reason except by practices that are relative to the state of society. Therefore no man can be educated for himself, without being educated for others. A man detached from all society who would enrich his understanding by deep study might indeed become a prodigy of learning, but I do not know that he would be a man of strong reason. We have seen men most cultivated in their books, yet altogether inept in their lives. [§ 4][16]

We notice that Gerdil distinguishes "a man of strong reason [*un homme fort raisonnable*]" from "a prodigy of learning [*un prodige de savoir*]." He also directly targets the former as the essential end of education. Finally, he holds that the isolated or detached condition of the self is inconsistent with the "strong reason." When these ideas are applied within the thicker actualities of human life, it follows that the measure of reason's perfection is the intelligent care for, and enjoyment of, life with others. Cast in classical ethical terms, it means that by living out the virtues of justice and love a man most becomes himself precisely inasmuch as he advances the due good of his fellow men and enjoys communion of mind and heart with them. These are not novel ideas, nor would Gerdil claim they are. In fact, one could say that he does no more than make the case for the venerable tradition of classical education. Gerdil understands himself as a teacher transmitting a living tradition shaped by Plato, Aristotle, the Bible, Cicero, Augustine, the medieval schoolmen, renaissance scholars, and modern mathematicians and natural scientists. His own broad learning in the humanities and sciences, both classical and modern, exhibited in the rich details of his *Reflections*, are ready resources for

---

[16] Put differently at § 12: "Reason was not given to a man so that he might supply his own partial wants. It was given to men so that they might learn to unite and in a mutual commerce of reciprocal duties and assistance find everything that would be necessary to live in a manner suitable to the dignity of their nature."

his understanding of the cultivated reason. It is this living tradition that gives definition to the potentiality of reason, specifying its range and penetration.

By contrast with Rousseau's educational practice which counts victory in the achievement of the unalienated self,[17] Gerdil's practice aims at what we might call the "connected self."[18] In the final analysis, as I implied in my introductory comments above, the theoretical dispute between Rousseau and Gerdil is conducted at the level of anthropology. Rousseau sees the perfection of man, if only in the ideal, in terms of individual autonomy and self-sufficiency.[19] A telling passage from his *Emile* captures the point: "A truly happy being is a solitary being. God alone enjoys an absolute happiness."[20] Sociability is therefore essentially compensatory or medicinal; it makes up for the

[17]   See Bloom above, fn. 6.

[18]   The language of the "connected self" is my own formulation. Within the contexts of Gerdil's anthropology and pedagogy, I believe the expression accommodates the basic concept of a unified providential order uniting all reality, an order in which man participates within his developed reason, The concept makes appearances throughout his *Reflections*, most notably at §§ 4 and 11. It is a major if not the central theme of his remarkable study *On the Origin of the Moral Sense*. The proximate philosophical origins of his idea can be traced to his study of the system of ideas in Malebranche's philosophy and his own understanding of divine providence at work in nature and history.

[19]   He maintains an "equilibrium theory of happiness," according to which he is happy whose powers are equal to his desires, and he whose desires exceed his powers is unhappy. In accordance with this formula, the task of education is to achieve self-sufficiency by maintaining equilibrium through increasing capacity to meet desires and suppressing desires that would exceed capacity. See esp. *Emile* 2. 16–21 (B, 80). With respect to Rousseau's uncritical identification of happiness with self-sufficiency, a remark by the medieval Franciscan, John Duns Scotus, is apt: "nec est mirum quod ad maiorem perfectionem sit capacitas passiva in aliqua natura quam eius causalitas activa extendat (nor should one be surprised that there be in some nature a passive capacity for a perfection greater than that to which the nature's own active causality extends)" *Ordinatio* Prologue, Q. 1, n.75 (Vatican, 1950, p.46).

[20]   Book IV, paragraph 45; Bloom trans., p. 221.

ontological flaw in human nature. It is Rousseau's genius that sets in motion through the *Emile* forms of education aimed at achieving in the midst of society, indeed as the goal of society, the greatest possible measure of self-expression. What I think is the genius of Gerdil is his recognition of that fateful moment. He clearly envisioned the character of souls that would be crafted by the principles of the *Emile*.

Up to this point, I have spoken of the theoretical dimensions of Gerdil's quarrel with Rousseau. It is instructive to note several concrete teaching practices that Gerdil recommends in the second part of his *Reflections* devoted to particularities of curriculum and teaching methods. In a unit devoted to the topics of study and reading [§ 24], he distinguishes two goods to be derived from study. "The first is simply to embellish the mind with the knowledge we acquire. The second is to form our manner of thinking by the exercise of our intellectual faculties and amplify the force and range of the intellect." The distinction between intellectual embellishment and capacity for thinking is especially important inasmuch as Gerdil thinks the chief work of education is to increase the capacity of the intellect by extending its range, subtlizing its discriminations, and solidifying its judgments.[21]

---

[21] § 20: "There are others in whom reason, wisely cultivated, is strengthened little by little through the knowledge they acquire in the course of their education. The range of their vocabulary, that is to say, the multitude and variety of their ideas, enable them to perceive a greater number of relations between objects, to determine them with greater precision, and consequently to combine them with more judgment. What is the good sense of peasants and even the acuity that can show in the pursuit of their small interests when compared to the extensiveness and preciseness of thought, which is generally characteristic of persons who have cultivated their minds by solid studies and who have exercised themselves in the employment of civil life? It would be to compare the rough technique of the simple laborer to the intelligence of a skilled machinist. It is not at all through the scarcity of ideas that one succeeds in perfecting reason. It comes through the order we bring to these ideas."

In another remark he talks about encouraging in children the habit of reading. He begins with a comment on the larger good served by the habit of reading. It is clear that he has in mind here what we would consider recreational or leisure reading.

> No weight is so oppressive as that of a fatigued spirit buried under itself. There are many people who strive to avoid themselves. Such people avoid themselves even more than the world avoids them, because they cannot even endure themselves, for they have failed to develop a habit of reading and thinking.

The idea that reading serves to restore the self in moments of rest, that reading and thinking are a pleasure and result in self-knowledge, elevates reading beyond utility and mere entertainment. Gerdil concludes that "we must therefore strive to inspire young people with a taste for reading." In an account of how this is done we see an example of Gerdil's wisdom and charm as a teacher. To begin with, he wryly comments that "it is a charming speculation to pretend to lead children through the whole course of their studies by always amusing them." But such a "nice thought" is quickly corrected with the sober realization that "the most necessary studies require hard work and self-denial. We may partially mitigate the coercive quality of study, but we cannot entirely remove it and still hope to make solid progress." Here Gerdil's realism, born of experience in conducting children in their studies, is evident. However, we might wonder what the onerous quality of serious study has to do with inculcating the life-long habit of thoughtful reading. To which he responds: "and therefore it is not by means of these kinds of studies that we will inspire children with a love for reading. But we will succeed with reading that is amusing and instructive, so long as we take care not to propose it as part of their studies, – for the very word will ruin everything, – but rather as a reward for applying themselves to their studies. Selections from history, strange accounts of travelers, dialogues, a series of prints, medals, natural curiosities of various kinds, and so forth, – these can all serve this purpose." No doubt particular selections will vary widely, but the main point is to distinguish the kind of thinking that requires the hard work of study from the sort of thoughtfulness that attends freer, unnecessary mental activity. Pleasure, entertainment, and individual curiosity motivate the latter. Thoughtfulness, however, does not automatically attend such reading, at least not in the beginning with children. Gerdil requires that the contents of this liberal reading be the medium of conversation with the teacher, with the purpose of introducing a measure of order to ideas that have been more properly the subject of hard study. Reading thereby becomes attached to the habits of learning "to compare the objects, to form combinations, and to connect them to principles in order to deduce the consequences." Reading and conversation become habits settled in childhood and youth that serve beyond the considerations of scholastic studies to enlarge reason throughout a person's life.

Gerdil also devotes reflections to the practicalities of teaching of languages, especially Latin, the study of history, geography, and mathematics, especially geometry. In the case of geometry, he agrees with Rousseau on the merit of a young student learning to confect geometrical notions through observational and manipulative experiences: "Nothing can be of greater service than to make exact figures, to combine them, to place one upon the other and to examine the relation they bear to each other" [§ 23]. But whereas Rousseau would suppress any subsequent move to treat these ideas with the formal rigor of "the definitions, propositions, and demonstrations that naturally follow," Gerdil insisted on conceptual mastery of a synthetic system of elementary geometry. Adept at mathematics himself, he pointed out three different methods employed by geometers. Euclid's geometry, for instance, is notable for its rigor in demonstration. A second method is distinguished for its orderly "progression from the simple to the compound, from lines to angles, from angles to surfaces, and so forth," a method that particularly "contributes to the enlargement of mind and makes us think with precision." The third method, which "appears best adapted to rouse or nourish a spirit of invention," develops the propositions of geometry in response to a natural need to know or to a spontaneous order of inquiry. Gerdil himself prefers no one of the three approaches; he thinks it best to "consult the genius of the student . . . and the purpose for which he is being instructed." Any of these three systems increases the student's capacity for reasoning, for understanding ideas, which properly understood are "notions determined by relations" [§ 12]. Indeed, elementary reasoning is a matter of combining ideas, of comparing objects within one's grasp, and arranging them according to some design. It is "nothing more than the faculty of arranging, *facultas ordinatrix*" [§ 16]. Reason's search for order naturally stretches toward judgment and standards of measure and proportion. The desire for order leads to the ideas of truth, goodness, and beauty.[22]

Gerdil's student will early on begin to learn history [§ 21]. His studies will stock the memory with historical facts and chronology, but necessary though the details may be, the main purpose for the study of history is to enlarge reason: even young children, he thinks,

> are capable of penetrating up to a certain point the relations that determine historical facts, of understanding the connection between cause and effects, of recognizing the resemblance and opposition of characters, and of seeing those events in which character either bears up or gives way.

Rousseau's Emile would also learn history, but not, however, until he is well into his adolescence. Whereas Rousseau thinks the relations that determine historical facts are exceedingly complex, Gerdil thinks they can be simple enough, especially when the telling of them is enriched by poetry:

[22] § 16 devoted to countering Rousseau's injunction that one should never reason with children concludes with an interesting essay, replete with examples, on how one can and should reason with children.

"what reading can be more wonderful to a philosopher or more fascinating and instructive to children than the entire sequence of the history of the people of God? What an abundance and variety of events! What a mixture of grandeur and simplicity in the lives of the patriarchs! Never was man more truthfully depicted. . . . In the hands of the Sacred Historian, it is nature that speaks and acts. . . . [The determining] relations in sacred history are of the utmost simplicity. Children easily comprehend them. Moreover, they learn to love God and to fear him. They learn to recognize and distinguish deep-seated, primitive dispositions of the human heart."

In our day, the renowned neurologist and man of letters, Oliver Sacks, observed that a child learns the Bible before Euclid.[23] Under the guidance of Gerdil's pedagogy, history brings the child more fully into the world he inhabits. He gains the capacity for insight into the human springs of action and culture; he learns to compare, to weigh, and to order reality in terms of moral and civil categories. Through the enlargement of his reason in this way he comes to inhabit a moral cosmos.

I have paused at geometry and history; Gerdil has equally

---

[23]   Contrasting "two wholly different, wholly separate, forms of thought and mind," schematic, abstract conceptual thought and symbolic, narrative thought, Sacks writes: "though equally natural and native to the expanding human mind, the narrative comes first, has spiritual priority. Very young children love and demand stories, and can understand complex matters presented in stories, when their powers of comprehending general concepts, paradigms, are almost non-existent. It is this narrative or symbolic power which gives a *sense of the world* – a concrete reality in the imaginative form of symbol and story – when abstract thought can provide nothing at all. A child learns the Bible before he follows Euclid. Not because the Bible is simpler (the reverse might be said), but because it is cast in a symbolic and narrative mode." Oliver Sacks, *The Man Who Mistook His Wife for a Hat and Other Clinical Tales* (New York: Summit, 1970, 1981, 1983, 1984, 1985), 174–75.

interesting thoughts on other curricular matters. It is clear throughout, however, that he thinks a child can think and should think; that he can and should gain a facility with ideas. There is undoubtedly hard work here, on the part of the student studying, and on the part of the teacher holding to standards and engaging the child's mind in an orderly, methodical fashion. Throughout Gerdil's practical considerations, the pedagogical values identified by the Italian scholar, Carlo Corsetti, are evident: self-conscious respect for the rhythms of natural growth, a sure sense of what are the indispensable tools of the intellect, a pedagogy and curriculum that respects gradualness and continuity in systematic development, and an unmistakable seriousness of educational purpose.[24]

Even if we must agree with Roberto Valebrega's judgment that, when viewed as a literary work as a whole, the *Anti-Emile* lacks proportion in the development of its parts and that its elements settle one after another in a somewhat fragmentary fashion,[25] its value does not rest upon its formal literary structure. Gerdil is not writing an essay or a dissertation. He does not see himself as a poet fashioning a work of art. In an interesting way, Gerdil's philosophy of education is not even *his*. He indeed speaks from his own experience as a teacher. Yet when it comes to understanding the work of pedagogy, he does not cast himself in the role of an inventor, experimenter, or visionary. In his reflections he speaks on behalf of a living intellectual tradition. For him reason is preeminently social. And if I can put words into Gerdil's mouth, he sees the teacher as one who mediates

[24] Corsetti, *Riflessioni*, 19. In a different vein, G. L. Arrighi in his introduction to G. S. Gerdil, *L'Anti-Emile, ovvero Riflessioni su la teoria e la pratica dell'educazione contro i principî del Rousseau*, traduzione, introduzione e note (Florence: G. C. Sansoni, 1924) justly observes that Gerdil's approach to the ends of education is preeminently realistic; he considered studies to be "the means for action, as a torch in the hand of those who advance to win the good" (p. x).

[25] Roberto Valebrega, "Gerdil e la critica alla cultura dei Lumi," *Barnabiti Studi. Rivista di ricerche storiche dei Chierici Regolari di S. Paolo (Barnabiti)* 18 (2001), 193.

his student's always increasing entry into the life of society. Against Jean-Jacques Rousseau, one of the most powerful rhetors of his day, Gerdil's civil reasoning makes a convincing case that education is the essential means to the chief end of society, namely, man's perfecting sociability. In opposition to reductive contractarian accounts that inform enlightened, liberal philosophies, social institutions cannot be reduced to tools in the service of individual goods. Rather, they embody and express the communion or social interrelationship which is an ingredient in the essential good of human persons. [26]

Given the inherent social nature of man, Gerdil advances principles and practices of education that cultivate capacities of thought and judgment suited to the truth of man's essential social nature. [27] He fears that men and women, whose the judgments of the heart and reasons of the mind were to be formed in accordance with the principles and practices of Rousseau's *Emile*, would stand unfeeling and unknowing before aspects of reality that make up our common life. Gerdil and Rousseau can agree that education enlarges and intensifies the capacities of human reason and that human reason is ordered to achieving the full human life. They differ in their views of what that life is. Rousseau's Emile, as Bloom has shown, may well be sincere, authentic, inner-directed and wholly unalienated, but can he love and serve both God and neighbor? If, in the final analysis, religion and patriotism – two premiere forms of sociability – call for self-sacrifice, then is self-love, even Rousseau's unalienated *amour propre*, strong enough cause? If not, then religion and patriotism

[26] "[Gerdil] is intent on demonstrating the full 'naturalness' of social life; his argument establishes some key points: the necessity of 'reciprocal communication among men,' without which they could not sufficiently provide for their own sustenance, nor could they cultivate their intellectual faculty; and so it follows that such 'communication is not a purely arbitrary establishment' but a means fixed by nature for the conservation and felicity of human kind." Valebrega, 136, quoting Gerdil, *Discours philosophiques sur l'homme considéré relativement à l'état de nature e à l'état de société.*

[27] As such, Gerdil insists that formal education ought to be widely available to any capable child; it ought not be the luxury of the few nor the recreation of the privileged classes.

must alter their meaning. They can no longer call men and women beyond themselves.[28] Gerdil envisioned just such a transformation of the meaning of fundamental social institutions when, in the first paragraph of his *Anti-Emile*, he foresaw that the chief effect of Rousseau's system of education would be to "inspire . . . vexation with and aversion for religious and social institutions. . . [H]e will make bad Christians and bad citizens."[29]

II. Situating Gerdil

Gerdil's place in the history of modern philosophy

Gerdil is now little known in the English-speaking world. Yet he produced a large body of work, and he exercised a broad intellectual influence, a measure of which is the fact that his complete works, edited and unedited, were published by five different houses in the 18th and 19th centuries.[30] His *Anti-Emile* was quickly diffused throughout Europe in its original French as well as in English, German, and Italian translations. "For almost a quarter of a century Gerdil represented a point of reference in the Italian intellectual culture, whether in his capacity as holding the university chairs of Moral Philosophy and Moral Theology or as a founding member of the Academy of Science of Turin."[31] John Henry Newman knew of him and his work.[32] David Hume scholar Laurence L. Bongie cited him

[28] Gerdil argues against the sufficiency of self-interest in §§ 5–6.

[29] Preface.

[30] Bologna: P. Toselli, 1784–1791 (six volumes); Rome: Poggioli, 1806–1821 (twenty volumes); Naples: Diogene, 1853–1856 (8 volumes); Florence: Celli, 1844–1851 (seven volumes); and Paris: Migne, 1863.

[31] Roberto Valebrega, "Gerdil e la critica alla cultura dei Lumi" in *Barnabiti Studi. Rivista di ricerche storiche dei Chierici Regolari di S. Paolo (Barnabiti)* 18 (2001), 191

[32] John Henry Newman, *The Idea of a University*, introduction and notes by Martin J. Svaglic (Notre Dame, Ind.: University of Notre Dame Press, 1960), xl, 148, 359. Also see his *Apologia Pro Vita Sua*, Note G (New York and London: Norton, 1968), 264.

liberally in his treatment of Hume's antipathy to revolutionary thought.[33] In his comprehensive history of philosophy, Frederick Copleston gave two passing references to our subject.[34] Such scholarly references can be multiplied, but not by many times. Contemporary scholarly interest continues in Italian and French studies of pedagogy and 18th-century ecclesiastical history. For the last twenty-six years of his life, he served as cardinal bishop and worked in Rome as a theological advisor to Popes Pius VI and Pius VII.[35] From a political perspective, these were times dominated by the French Revolution and Napoleon Bonaparte's European conquests. The Church's ecclesiastical integrity was assaulted by the forces of Jansenism, Febronism, and Josephism.

Three broad intellectual-ideological trends in the 18th century set the conditions for most of Gerdil's work: *moral libertinism*, against which he insisted on the *bonum honestum* and the primacy of virtue; the *secularism and empiricism* of modern thinkers, which he countered with a metaphysics that embraced the personal immortality of the soul and a theistic First Principle; and *liberal philosophies of civil society* that undercut the natural finality and proper authority of societies such as the family and Church, which he corrected with the enduring insights of premodern political philosophy. Italian scholar Massimo Lapponi captures the animating spirit of Gerdil's thought in the following passage:

---

[33] Laurence L. Bongie, *David Hume: Prophet of the Counter-revolution* (Oxford: Clarendon Press, 1965), 36–38.

[34] Frederick Copleston, S.J., *A History of Philosophy. Volume 4. Modern Philosophy: Descartes to Leibniz* (Garden City, N.Y.: Image, 1960), 182, 210.

[35] See the bibliographies of Antonio Lantura, *Giacinto Sigismondo Gerdil, filosofo e pedagogista nel pensiero italiano del secolo XVIII* (Padua: CEDAM, 1952), 7–22 and Massimo Lapponi, *Giacinto Sigismondo Gerdil e la filosofia cristiana dell'età moderna* (Rome: Spazio Tre, 1990), xi–xiv. For an overview of Gerdil's philosophical thought relative to the main problems of epistemology, metaphysics, and ethics, see Silvia Fasciolo Bachelet, "Il pensiero filosofico di Giacinto Sigismondo Gerdil," *Barnabiti Studi. Rivista di ricerche storiche dei Chierici Regolari di S. Paolo (Barnabiti)* 18 (2001): 29–96.

The thought of Gerdil is animated by a strong metaphysical tension that aims to lead man to recognize the proper spiritual superiority in the faculty for knowing truth and for conforming oneself to it. This objective truth in its turn, precisely because connatural to the immaterial intelligence of man, is demonstrated to have its origin and its end in the infinite wisdom of God, the communion with whom constitutes the end of man's moral life. Descartes, Malebranche, and St. Thomas are harmoniously united in this perspective. In its light, the great danger of atheism and of the Epicureanism that necessarily follows from it is the negation of objective values of intelligence in the field of metaphysics and morality, and by consequence, the negation of the category of *honestum* and its normative authority. The result of these negations would be for man to retreat to himself alone and to seek there for the satisfaction of his own sensibility and of his own utility, with consequent disappearance of virtue, and especially the disappearance of social virtue, which is essentially founded on the same order of the true and the *honestum*. Therefore only on a solid transcendent metaphysics which finally arrives at the communication of one's intelligence with God, and not on fragile pragmatic premises, can one build the moral and social order.[36]

Gerdil defends the prerogatives of religion, the claims of a metaphysics of transcendence, and the natural goodness of civil society and the authorities that direct it. Yet he is a modern philosopher, whose inspirations are Malebranche and Descartes. However much one finds in him the Cartesian penchant for clearly and distinctly ordered ideas, one also sees these thoughts enriched by broad literary and historical erudition. Gerdil's appropriation of modern thought finds no need to break with the past. One should probably say that

[36] Ibid, 123.

his modernity is not "modern" in the conventional sense of a philosophy with self-conscious new beginnings. In his philosophy of society and culture, he draws heavily from the classics of antiquity, most especially Cicero, but he learns as well from Hume and Bacon. Gerdil knew well the early Christian theologians and especially in the later decades of his career he accorded a special weight of authority to Thomas Aquinas. It would not be accurate to characterize his work as eclectic. Conceptually it enjoys an open sort of coherence based on a consistent philosophical point of view, even if many of his individual works are occasional pieces, prompted by historical events of the day.

Gerdil's adoption of Descartes's philosophical point of view needs to be carefully qualified. He appropriated Cartesian influences under the guidance of Malebranche. There is a distinctive philosophical tradition that moves from Descartes through Malebranche and Gerdil. Identifying this development in modern thought has been a major contribution to the history of philosophy by Augusto Del Noce.[37] As he observes, the canonical historiography of philosophy draws a rationalist line of thought that begins with Descartes, passes through Spinoza, and culminates in Hegel. In this movement, philosophy departs from within the Cartesian *cogito* and arrives at Absolute Reason. The guiding thread in the modern rationalism and enlightenment is "reason as rule,"[38] according to which, truth, the

---

[37] See especially his *Da Cartesio a Rosmini. Scritti vari, anche inediti, de filosofia e storia della filosofia*, ed. by Francesco Mercadante e Bernardino Casadei (Milan: Giuffrè, 1992) and "Problemi del periodizzamento storico: l'inizio della filosofia moderna," *Archivio de Filosofia* (1954): 187–210; also Luca Del Pozzo, "La 'metafisica civile' de Augusto Del Noce: ontologismo e liberalismo," http://mondodomani.org/dialegesthai /ldp01.htm ; accessed Jan. 22, 2007.

[38] Francis Slade develops this thesis in a set of articles: "Rule as Sovereignty: The Universal and Homogenous State" in *The Truthful and the Good*, edited by John J. Drummond and James G. Hart (Dordrecht, Boston, London: Kulwer, 1996): 159–80; "Rule and Argument in Political Philosophy," in *Ethics and Theological Disclosures*, edited by Guy Mansini and James G. Hart (Washington D.C.: The Catholic University of America Press, 2003):

very intelligibility of reality, be it nature or history, is the work of human mind. Truth lies in the conformity of human mind to the rule of its own reason. Reason itself establishes itself as the measure and source of truth, not to be confused with the classical idea of mind that discovers and perfects itself in its identity with its intelligible objects. This "enlightenment" strain of modern philosophy constitutes itself in establishing the autonomy of human reason. Apart from the determinations of the self-legislating reason, the human world is of itself indeterminate. Societies and their institution become "arbitrary 'social collectives,' and 'special interests,' and for its part the [modern] State is free to deal with them as it finds convenient."[39] Personal freedom and individual autonomy are limited by no governing norm of law, custom, or tradition not subject to rule of sovereign reason. And this reason, it must be emphasized, recognizes no rule or measure outside or above itself. The inner logic of modern enlightenment rationalism annuls any putative natural claims to society and its institutions.[40] For our purposes it is important to note that within this rationalist tradition, truth and the intelligibility of the world are essentially conditioned by the subjective interiority of the human mind. One, as it were, never escapes the confines of *cogito*. The egocentric predicament[41] seems inescapable, and with it comes

149–61; and *"Was ist Aufklärung?"* in *The Common Things: Essays on Thomism and Education*, edited by Daniel McInerny, introduction by Benedict M. Ashley (Mishawaka, Ind.: American Maritain Association, 1999): 48–68.

[39]   Slade, "Rule as Sovereignty," 176.

[40]   It is worth emphasizing that Gerdil is particularly keen to check this reductive vaporizing of the social reality. As he sees it, Rousseau develops foundational principles that connect his "system of politics and his theory of education. There he presents social institutions in the most odious light. He establishes the following maxims: . . . [2] We were born to be men, but laws and society plunge us back into infancy. [3] The dependency upon other men that is the consequence of laws and society is repugnant to nature and the source of all vices. [4] It is impossible to educate man for himself and for others."

[41]   The expression was coined by Ralph Barton Perry, *Journal of Philosophy, Psychology, and Scientific Method* 7 (1910): 5–14.

the inevitability of moral and epistemological relativism and a politics polarized between libertarian claims of personal autonomy and the realities of impersonal totalitarian State sovereignties.

Gerdil cannot be situated along this developmental line. Del Noce shows how one can depart from Descartes's *cogito* in a different direction, as did the influential Oratorian priest, Nicolas Malebranche (1638–1715). For the purposes of this introduction we can put aside the complex and highly charged issues of ontologism and occasionalism. It will suffice to observe that in the hands of Malebranche these special doctrines develop resources for acknowledging a transcendent being as a first principle to which human mind conforms itself. Moreover, they privilege the human experiences of freedom and interiority in the genuine encounter with the illuminating exemplar being of Truth itself. In effect, Malebranche's development of Cartesian impulses leads to a recovery of Augustinian Platonist modes of thought. From within the optic of Augustinian Platonism and its doctrines of illumination and exemplarism, Gerdil accommodates both the truth of nature manifest in modern scientific inquiry and the humanistic truth expressed in art, history, and politics. It is this line of philosophical development that Gerdil advances. The existence of this second tradition of modern philosophy has been largely neglected since the middle of the 18th century, which is unfortunate, since it possesses an attractive wisdom. The tradition represents a coherent Christian philosophy, distinct from either Christian existentialism, Aristotelian Thomism, or transcendental Thomism, which have been dominant models of Christian philosophy in the 20th century.

Situating the Anti-Emile *within the body of Gerdil's works*[42]

For our purposes it is useful to divide Gerdil's works into an earlier

[42] As noted above in fn. 30, Gerdil's published and unpublished works have been collected in five different editions. In his ample bibliography Arrighi (pp. xliv–liii) selects sixty-three works, which he annotates and classifies under the categories of metaphysics, morality and law, theology and apologetics, and pedagogy. Lantura (pp. 8–19) names sixty-five titles among the philosophical works. In his monograph, *Giacinto Sigismondo Gerdil*, 98–100,

half, which embraces his academic writings, and a later half, which largely includes his ecclesiastical writings. The academic writing can be divided into earlier youthful studies in which Gerdil searches for a consistent philosophical point of view and later works that represent his mature, settled thought.[43] Chief among his earlier works are the two studies of Locke and Malebranche, namely, *L'immatérialité ed l'âme démonstrée contre M. Locke par les memes principes par les quells ce philosophe démonstre l'existence et l'immatérialité de Dieu; avec des nouvelles preuves de l'immatérialité de Dieu et de l'âme tirées de l'Ecriture, des Pères, et de la raison* (1747) and *Défense du sentiment du père Malebranche sur la nature et l'origine des ideas, contre l'examen de Mr. Locke* (1748). Five of his later works deserve particular mention, as they form a coherent line of development. His mature thought first emerges in a systematic work on the metaphysics of knowledge, *Della Origine del Senso Morale, o sia, Dimonstrazione che vi ha nell'uomo un naturale Criterio di approvazione e di biasimo, riguardante l'intrinsica morale differenza del giusto e dell'ingiusto: il quale unitamente alla nozione dell'ordine e dell bello nasce della facoltà, che ha l'uomo di conoscer il vero,*[44] which he appends to his treatise on the philosophy of religion, *Introduzione allo studio della religione* (1755). Precisely against the backdrop of these first two mature works, Gerdil levels his critique of the *Emile*. His *Reflections on the Theory and Practice of Education, against the Principles of Rousseau* (1763) is soon followed by two treatises on anthropology and the political philosophy, namely, *Discours*

Massimo Lapponi lists thirty-seven titles with significant developments of Gerdil's philosophical thought.

[43] Lapponi, ibid., 97; and Bachelet, "Il pensiero filosofico," 41.

[44] *Demonstration that there is in man a natural criterion for approval (praise) and disapproval (blame), with respect to the intrinsic moral difference between the just and the unjust: which, together with the ideas of order and beauty, originate with the faculty that man has for knowing truth –* what begins as kind of conceptual analysis of basic concepts develops into something like a phenomenology of the moral sense. In the end, the reader is left with a concept of reason enlarged by its grasp of the unavoidable truths of the immaterial soul and the infinite spiritual being of divinity.

philosophiques sur l'homme considéré relativement à l'état de nature e à l'état de société (1769) and *De l'homme sous l'empire de la loi, pour servir de suite aux Discours philosophiques sur l'homme* (1774). Both these works follow up in a systematic way the critique of liberal social theory which was begun in the *Anti-Emile*.

Chronology

Jean-François Gerdil was born June 23, 1718, at Samoëns in the Haute Savoie to a family with a history of civil and ecclesiastical service.[45] On making his religious profession in 1735 in the Congregation of Regular Clerics of St. Paul, more popularly known as Barnabites, he took the name Giacinto Sigismondo (Hyacinth Sigismond). After three years of studies at the University of Bologna, he taught philosophy at the Barnabite college at Macerata 1738–39 and at Monferrato 1739–48, where he was professor of philosophy and prefect of studies, during which time he was ordained to the priesthood (1741). In 1749 he was appointed professor of Moral Philosophy at the University of Turin; four years later he assumed the chair of Moral Theology. By 1759 he had withdrawn from university teaching, not long after Victor Amadeus, duke of Savoy, nominated him to the office of preceptor of his sons, Charles Emanuel IV, prince of Piedmont, and Victor Emanuel I, duke of Aosta. Pope Clement XIV designated Gerdil cardinal *in pectore* in 1773. In 1776 Pope Pius VI elevated him to the office of cardinal bishop and called him to Rome where, until his death in 1802, he served in various capacities, most notably as consultor to the Holy Office. He was widely admired for his vast learning, his prudent judgment, and his humble, pious life.

---

[45] For particulars of Gerdil's biography, see Lantura, 23–35 and Pietro Stella, "Appunti per una biografia di Giacinto Sigismondo Gerdil," *Barnabiti Studi* vol. 18 (2001): 7–29.

[Preface]

In his *Emile* Rousseau proposes a new plan of education closely connected with his new plan of legislation. The goal of his *On Social Contract* is a universal overthrow of civil order; the goal of the *Emile* is to prepare souls by means of a total revolution in their modes of thinking. It seems likely that Rousseau's legislative ideas will remain simply ideas. His political paradoxes, more singular than all the reveries of the good Abbé de Saint-Pierre,[1] are better made for astonishing the world than for winning it over. But if we can make ourselves easy on this score, it seems there is reason to be alarmed at the consequences of a mode of thinking which, though it may not lead men to the goal that Rousseau would have wanted, it may nevertheless cause them to gradually estrange themselves from that end toward which one must tend for the good of humanity. Our philosopher will not succeed in totally overturning present society, but he will easily inspire that vexation with and aversion for religious and social institutions, which animates him and which breathes forth from all of his writings. He will not make savages, but he will make bad Christians and bad citizens.

It is especially in Books 1 and 2 of *Emile* that he devotes himself to developing those principles that serve as the foundation and connecting link for his system of politics and his theory of education. There he presents social institutions in the most odious light. He establishes the following maxims:

[1] The condition of man living in the state of nature is for him to be self-sufficient and to be happy.

[2] We were born to be men, but laws and society plunge us back into infancy.

[3] The dependency upon other men that is the consequence of laws and society is repugnant to nature and the source of all the vices.

[4] It is impossible to educate a man for himself and for others.

[5] A father himself has no right to command his children in that which is not ordered to their good.

From these maxims, which serve as the foundation for the system of his social contract, he deduces in this volume the practical rules for the conduct of the first stage of life which determine the whole course of education.

It is to an examination of these principles and rules that the present book is dedicated. In challenging the paradoxes advanced by Rousseau we have tried to establish the theory and practice of education on principles that are more solid, more consisteint with the spirit of humankind, the peace of families, the tranquility of states, and the general advantage of all men. We do not attempt to refute everything that is reprehensible in the *Emile*. To criticize this book is not even our chief purpose. Rather, it provides us with an occasion to develop and publish certain ideas that may not be altogether useless for those who are occupied with the education of youth. Initially I had intended only to respond to a question proposed to me, namely, whether there was anything contained in the first volume of *Emile*[2] contrary to religion and sound morality? But then on reviewing my reflections, I noted that they tended to be interconnected and were capable of being ordered. This is what gave rise to the composition of the present work, in which I try to suitably extend and unify the subject of the treatise as it is announced in the title. If it ever falls into the hands of Rousseau, we would ask him to read it. He will see his opinions attacked without animosity or bitterness, and perhaps upon recollection he will be able to recognize that, since he has not always been consistent with himself, he cannot always have been in the right.

I have only one word more to say to those who may attempt to vindicate Rousseau. It is not enough to show that he has asserted things contrary to what are imputed to him, since that would only demonstrate that he frequently contradicts himself. But ignoring for the moment that natural inconstancy of some minds, there are still others that have good reason to be contradictory. And so it will be necessary to prove either that he has not said the things that are imputed to him or that what is imputed to him is properly said.

[PART ONE
Reflections on the Basic Principles
of the Theory of Education]

[1. *Rousseau's seductive rhetoric*]

You have honored me, sir,[1] in asking whether I had found anything in the first two books of *Emile* contrary to the principles of religion and sound morality. I had only perused the work lightly, but now I shall re-read it with greater attention, and I shall take note of those passages in which the author abandons himself so much to his own particular view of things that one is forced to the extreme of choosing between him and the rest of mankind. It is above all in *Emile* that Rousseau develops that style of reasoning I would say is not only singular, but of such original singularity that it has won him great celebrity. Indeed, so much so, that D'Alembert reproves him with as much charm as truth:

> Your philosophy is characterized by the firmness and inexorability of its progress. Once your principles are laid down, the consequences fall out as they will. So much the worse for us, if they are disagreeable; and regardless of how unfortunate, it would never suffice to induce you to take a second look at your principles. Far from fearing the objections one can raise to your paradoxes, you forestall these objections by responding with new paradoxes.[2]

I do not intend to undertake a systematic refutation of this famous work. One needs eloquence in order to contest successfully with the reputation of eloquence. Rousseau knows the taste of his age; he

4

understands the value of a strength and energy of expression. Does he threaten Europe with approaching destruction? His prophecy seems almost fulfilled: "[Europe] will be peopled with ferocious beasts. The change of inhabitants will not be great."[3] Rousseau knows quite well that many of the honest people he has lived with are neither bears nor wolves, but a new, bold, lively thought has a much more powerful effect than the cool monotony of reason. It is rare today that a regularity in the plan, a correctness or, to say it better, the truth in the design, and a justness in the proportions would decide the worth of a work among the better part of the public; what is decisive is the brilliance of the colors. A reader struck with one of these spirited and passionate expressions, which seizes his imagination, which penetrates and exalts his soul – will he patiently allow us to prove that that which fascinates him is nothing but an illusion and that he is wrong to applaud what so pleasantly enchants him? I shall therefore content myself with a simple exposition of the reflections which the reading of the book will give rise to in my mind. I aim at no virtues other than justice and good sense, qualities that are not brilliant, but not useless.

[2. *Emile is an unreal abstraction*]

I begin my reflections with the general remark that Rousseau acknowledges that his plan of education embraces many articles that cannot be realized in the world as it now is. This is an objection that he raises himself, and to which he responds that it is not his fault if men have corrupted everything through their bad institutions. Very good, grant that men have ruined everything and that Rousseau would reestablish everything; this would not be relevant to the question at hand. While we await the reform of the universe, of what use is a plan of education, which perhaps is good for the world as it should be, but which on so many counts is impractical for the world as it is?[4] In order to bring about this strange reformation will it not be necessary for Emile to spring forth already formed from the brain of Rousseau, just as in earlier times Minerva was born from the head of Jupiter?

Rousseau acknowledges that in the state in which things now are a man, who was abandoned to simple nature from his infancy and who had not been raised as others had been, would find himself strangely displaced in the world.[5] Now given the avowed impossibility of reconciling the author's plan with the actual state of things, do we not have reason to fear a comparable ill consequence? Do we not run the risk of doing nothing by aiming at the whole program, or of doing harm by embracing it only in part?[*]

It seems that Rousseau's plan consists in considering in his student only the human condition; he intends to form an *abstracted man*, having no relationship to social institutions of any kind. Emile is not to be raised with a view toward the army, the church, or the bar, but solely to fulfill the purposes of human life.[6] Our author imagines that his abstracted man will be more certainly adapted to various states of life to which he may be called. It is much as though we were to attempt to form a generic or abstracted artist, without having in view either painting, sculpture, or architecture. Would such an abstracted artist ever rival a Raphael, a Michelangelo, or a Palladio? I believe that however much may be said for Rousseau's *abstracted man*, we should find it a difficult matter to make of him a good soldier, a good priest, or a good magistrate. Rousseau does not deny that on some occasions it may be proper to educate a child for the position he is to occupy in society; but who knows whether he may be able to keep this post, "given the unsettled and restless spirit of this age which upsets everything?"[7] He must accordingly be ready to meet every eventuality. Emile must learn to be nothing other than a man, in case the dissolution of society should prevent his being any longer a citizen. Would not one imagine that we were at the brink of being overrun by the Tartars, just as he prophesies in his *On Social Contract*?[8] It

---

[*] This is also the author's opinion in his Preface where he says, "in this alliance the good is spoiled, and the evil is not cured. I would prefer to follow the established practice in everything than to follow a good one half way. There would be less contradiction in man" (*Emile* Pref. 6; B, 34). [Gerdil's note.]

is all too true that the world is not so good as it should be, yet in all probability, Europe will long continue in its present state. And in order to prevent greater harm, nothing would be better than to educate children for the various positions of society, for one man properly placed may do a great deal of good and prevent much evil.

Rousseau writes:

> Someone of whom I know only the rank had the proposal to raise his son conveyed to me. He doubtless did me a great honor; but far from complaining about my refusal, he ought to congratulate himself on my discretion. If I had accepted his offer and my method were mistaken, the education would have been a failure. If I had succeeded, it would have been far worse. His son would have repudiated his title; he would no longer wished to have been a prince.[9]

If Rousseau had intended to entertain us with satire, I would readily acknowledge that the passage would stand up well against those of Juvenal. But to speak seriously, had he been called upon to educate Titus or Marcus Aurelius, would we applaud him for successfully depriving mankind of the fruit of their examples, their virtues, and their good deeds?

[3. *Whether contrariety is part of man's original nature*]

It is time to take up Rousseau's principles. Here is his beginning:

> We are born weak, we need strength; we are born totally unprovided, we need aid; we are born stupid, we need judgment. Everything we do not have at our birth and which we need when we are grown is given us by education.[10]

Let us grant this principle. The consequence that results is that men are made one for the other. The ways nature takes to preserve its works are no doubt a part of nature's plan and its finality. Infants would perish without the aid of adults; therefore this assistance is in nature's plan, and furthermore, adults are destined to aid infants. The need of help on one side and a capacity for helping on the other – these constitute a relationship intended by nature to connect men one with the other and to lead them into society. I concede, then, this opening principle, but I believe myself to be right in drawing the consequences. Men have natural relations that bind them together. Therefore, the solitary man is not the man of nature.

Our author continues:

> This education comes to us from nature or from men or from things. The internal development of our faculties and our organs is the education of nature. The use that we are taught to make of this development is the education of men. And what we acquire from our own experience about the objects which affect us is the education of things. Each of us is thus formed by three kinds of masters. The disciple in whom their various lessons are at odds with one another is badly raised and will never be in agreement with himself. He alone in whom they all coincide at the same points and tend to the same ends reaches his goal and lives consistently. He alone is well raised.[11]

But this end toward which the three educations must converge is nothing other, according to our author, than that of nature. For he says that since the agreement of these three educations is necessary for their perfection, then one that is not within our power must regulate the other two.

It remains now to explain the nature of nature. Rousseau correctly refutes the indefensible opinion of those who say that nature is but custom, and he elaborates his conviction in the following terms:

> We are born with the use of our senses, and from our birth we are affected in various ways by the objects surrounding us. As soon as we have, so to speak, consciousness of our sensations, we are disposed to seek or avoid the objects

which produce them, at first according to whether they are pleasant or unpleasant to us, then according to the conformity or lack of it that we find between us and these objects, and finally according to the judgments we make about them on the basis of the idea of happiness or perfection given us by reason. These dispositions are extended and strengthened as we become more capable of using our sense and more enlightened; but constrained by our habits, they are more or less corrupted by our opinions. Before this corruption they are what I call in us *nature*.[12]

According to Rousseau there are then three inclinations or three natural principles for our decisions. Agreeable or displeasing sensations, the fitness or unfitness of the objects, and lastly, the ideas that reason gives us of perfection and happiness. This is approximately what the ancients had already designated as the agreeable, the useful, and the intrinsically good.[13] And these three inclinations or dispositions, prior to any alteration of them, is what he calls the nature of man.[14]

It is necessary, therefore, that he recognize in the nature of man, independently of its being in any way adulterated by opinion or prejudice, that contrariety, which so much astonished the wisest among the pagan philosophers. It is a truth of experience that agreeable sensations often incline us to seek objects which are by no means fitting for us, and the pursuit of which is contrary to the ideas reason has given us of perfection and happiness. It is this which caused Plato to say that pleasure is the source of many evils and that it is a bait by which men are taken like fish with hooks.[15] This judgment of Plato reflects the experience of the ages that had preceded him, and those that have followed have only served to confirm it.

We must note, moreover, that according to Rousseau these dispositions extend and solidify themselves to the degree that we become more sensible and more enlightened. Thus the simple development of the organs, of which he had before spoken, suffices to increase men's sensibilities but not to make them more enlightened. Under the sway of the first stage of life, man finds himself possessed of the greatest degree of sensibility. Can anyone say that at this age reason has acquired a sufficient light and strength to restrain these excesses of sensibility and to direct it properly in accordance with the ideas that reason gives us of perfection and happiness? From this it follows that nature, if left to itself, must become vicious by the inequality of the increase of those dispositions or inclinations that are the motive powers of our decisions. The inclination that takes its rise from agreeable sensations quickly asserts its power to the highest degree; and this inclination is capable of plunging a man into utter ruin. To the contrary, the inclination that takes its rise from the real fitness of the objects or from the ideas that reason gives us of perfection develops itself slowly, even though it may be the disposition that is most necessary for the conduct of man.

In short, the natural state of first stage of life is much sensibility and little judgment. This vicious inequality, the cause of almost all the disorders of vice, thus points out to us the remedies which education ought to provide: to prune the one and supplement the other, it is to this that the cares of a wise instructor should tend. Cicero considered the art of philosophy as the medicine of the soul.[16] In this sense we may say that education is nothing else than the proper application of this art to the needs of infancy.

There is, then, a real contrariety in the inclinations of man. This contrariety ought to be one of the principal objects of education. This contrariety derives from the primitive dispositions, which, according to Rousseau, constitute the nature of man.

When he tells us that "it must be laid down as an undoubted maxim, that the first motions of nature are always right, and that there is no original evil in the human heart,"[17] we answer that this maxim is contrary to revelation, contrary to experience, and that it hardly agrees with the principle he has established. For in fact the inclinations that arise from agreeable or disagreeable sensations develop with all of the vigor that those sensations are capable of giving them. And because they cannot be restrained or moderated by reason, which is too weak in the first stage of life, habits will be acquired, which reason, when more enlightened, can only disapprove of, and which she will overcome only with the great difficulty.*

As to the practical consequences that Rousseau derives from this maxim for the purposes of directing education, I will speak about them later. At this point it suffices to observe that there are very few good men who do not rejoice that they have been contradicted and corrected in their infancy.

[4. *Whether the self is ordered to others' selves from the beginning*]

It is, then, to these original dispositions that everything must be related; and that could be done if our three educations were only different from one another. But what is to be done when they are opposed? When instead of raising a man for himself, one wants to raise him for others? Then their harmony is impossible. Forced to combat nature or social institutions, one must choose between making a man or a citizen, for one cannot make both at the same time. . . . Natural man is entirely for himself. He is numerical unity, the absolute whole is relative only to itself or its kind. Civil man is only a fractional unity dependent on the denominator; his value is determined by his relation to the whole, which is the social body.[18]

[*First objection – a matter of logic*] This conclusion appears to me very extraordinary, and I do not understand how it can be deduced from the initial principles. The primitive dispositions he mentions are

* Rousseau does acknowledge in a subsequent part of his work that children, even while at the breast, have a "disposition . . . to fury, spite, and anger [that] requires extreme attentiveness" [*Emile* 1.153; B. 66)]. This disposition is not the fruit of a vicious education; infants are born with it, yet the disposition is vicious. Does not, then, this observation of Rousseau contradict his favorite maxim, that "all the first motions of nature are right"? (*Emile* 2.63; B, 92) [Gerdil's note.]

founded, first, on agreeable or disagreeable sensations, secondly, on the fitness or unfitness of the objects, and thirdly, on the ideas that reason gives us of happiness and perfection. What is there in all this to prevent us from educating a child for himself and for others?

[*Second objection – natural man's need implies innate sociability*] The solitary man is not the man of nature. This has been proved above, following Rousseau's own principles, which demonstrate that man cannot provide for his own needs, procure the conveniences of life, or perfect his judgment without the help of the knowledge and strength of other men. Nature has bestowed on man no particular instinct, but she has given him reason as the foundation of arts, which make up for the want of instinct. By his reason man subdues the other animals and makes the whole earth serve his needs. But reason cannot effect any of this without the help of society; the civil state only adds the necessary order to natural society. If man is made for society, it follows that he cannot be raised well for himself unless he is also raised for others. In fact, education should assist the natural development of the human faculties. But these faculties, having a natural relation to other men, can only be developed adequately within society. To take a man from society and require him to exercise his natural faculties is like taking the light from the eye and then requiring it to exercise its functions.[*]

[*Third objection – human beings develop in a moral environment*] Everything in the universe is connected. From this it follows that everything depends not only upon its interior constitution but also on the relation of action and reaction which connects it with the neighboring objects. Cut off the communication which connects one part of the universe to the other, and you immediately denature it. In the

[*] What is said in this place with respect to the advantages of society will by no means count against those religious who retreat from the world. Those who would flee from the corruptions of the age are still united to the society of the faithful whom they edify by their examples. [Gerdil's note.]

vacuum of an air pump fire is extinguished, plants cease to vegetate, and animals are deprived of motion, respiration, and even of life. The world is not a collection of an infinity of natures formed without relation one to the other, assembled together by chance. Everything is a part of a whole and is tied to the whole; it is the work of Providence. Now just as in the physical world corporeal substances lose all activity when they lose the relations that tie them together, so intelligent natures, made to fill a place in the moral world, which is nothing other than the order of society, cannot break the ties which attach them, without denaturing themselves and depriving themselves of the exercise of their most noble functions, namely, those that derive from their relationships or their obligations in regard to other intelligent beings. In educating a man for himself, therefore, he should be educated for others.

[*Teaching as a ministerial art*] But "one cannot make both at the same time," Rousseau says. I should rather have said, one cannot make one without the other. The works of nature are not like certain works of art. The sculptor cannot at the same time make the legs and arms of a statue. But the operation of nature, as its works take shape, extends itself simultaneously through the whole. Education may be termed an art, if you wish to so call it, but it is one that is simply ministerial, for it creates nothing. The gardener, charged with cultivating a young plant, carefully transplants it into the most suitable spot, waters it, defends it from everything which may injure it, from the heat of the dog days and the winter's frost. If it bends in its growth, he straightens it with force, and he does not hesitate to use the knife to cut off useless branches that would only divert the course of that precious sap needed to nourish it and to make it fruitful. The gardener creates nothing: all he does is keep at a distance everything that would interrupt nature in its operations. It is nature that causes the young plant to grow, and its action extends to all the parts that compose it.

[*Reason is social*] This comparison with the gardener, as commonplace as it is just, aptly indicates the care that the educator must take for the development of a man's faculties from the time of his infancy. No man can be educated for himself unless his reason is cultivated, for it is through reason that man is man. Reason is by nature a social faculty. To make a man reasonable is to make him sociable. Consequently one cannot properly form reason except by practices that are relative to the state of society. Therefore no man can be educated for himself, without being educated for others also. A man detached from all society who would enrich his understanding by deep study might indeed become a prodigy of learning, but I do not know that he would be a man of strong reason. We have seen men most cultivated in their books, yet altogether inept in their daily lives.

[*Fourth objection – anthropological evidence from the New World natives*] It is scarcely possible to raise men more for themselves and less for others than are the Indians in the Province of Quito, according to the description given of them by Don George Juan and Don Antonio de Ulloa in their excellent account.[19] These Indians are natural men; they live only for themselves and take notice only of physical needs. The dignity of office holds little attraction for them: an Indian will receive with the same indifference employment as a justice of the peace or a hangman. Profit has no sway over them, for they refuse to do the smallest services in exchange for the greatest compensation. The Indian seated by his little fireplace undisturbed watches his wife at work. The traveler who has lost his way will never succeed in persuading him to quit that posture in order to guide him even a short distance. The only thing they never refuse is to entertain themselves, but then they must have drink. When they are drunk, they all lay together without distinction, men and women, with little concern whether the one beside them is another man's wife, their own sister, or daughter; on these occasions every duty is forgotten.[20]

Wouldn't one say that this is more or less the natural man, mentioned in Rousseau's *Discourse on the Origin and Foundations of Inequality among Men*?[21] Yet according to the account of our learned Spaniards, these men, who have not been spoiled by civil education, these men formed uniquely by nature in the development of their faculties, have gained no advantage if we consider them simply as men.

If considered a part of the human species, the narrow limits of their understanding seem to clash with the dignity of the soul; and such is their stupidity, that in certain particulars we can scarce forbear entertaining the idea that they are really beasts, and even destitute of that instinct we observe in the brute creation.[22]

Perhaps one will attribute this depravation to vices of the climate, and I do not doubt that it may be a partial factor. But it is as equally unreasonable to attribute everything to the influence of the climate as to attribute nothing to it. Only in recent times have we given the dispute a certain novelty by casting the question as an option between these two extremes. The issue is one that is dealt with in every age. But whatever be the power of the climate over the dispositions of the Indians of Peru, their case will provide a proof of the extent to which a civil education can correct its influence. For Don George and Don Antonio have observed that the children of the Indians of this same province of Quito when they are raised in the city become as reasonable as other men and appear of a nature quite different from the rest of the nation. On the other hand, they have also remarked that in the various and vast provinces through which they passed, the uncivilized Indians differed not at all from one another. Those of Quito were not more ignorant or stupid than those of the Valles or of Lima; nor were these last more intelligent than those of Chile or Arauco.[23] Yet what a difference of climate there is among all these people! We see therefore that the lack of a civil education has an equal influence on entire peoples in very different climates, and that in the same climate education has the power of elevating those who receive it above the general brutishness of the people who are deprived of it.

These authors further observe that the children who are taught the Spanish language profit greatly by it. They do not think it is because this language can inspire them with understanding, but because it enables them to converse with the Europeans, and thereby profit from their understanding.

> Do we not often see among ourselves a child, without any assistance other than his mother tongue, acquire every day some new knowledge by conversing with intelligent persons? But do we not at the same time see what advantages another child, who applies himself to the study of other languages, possesses over the former? How much greater the understanding and knowledge he must have beyond the other, and only because his education has been better.[24]

[*Fifth objection – evidence from ancient Greeks and Romans*] The ancients simply did not know the distinction that Rousseau makes between educating a man for himself and educating him for others. They did not think that the natural man was the "numerical unity" and the citizen the "fractional unity."[25] Nevertheless they did not fare badly in educating both men and citizens. Where shall we find, to limit ourselves to the pagans, a man more worthy of this name than Socrates? His character was marked by a sober view that represented to the mind objects as they really were, a quality more rare than one might think, an imperturbable equanimity, and a universal beneficence toward all men. When I say universal beneficence, I do not mean the abstract love of humanity, which people praise so much. It costs nothing to love humanity in general. I speak of the love of men taking them as they are, with all their faults accompanying them. Such were the qualities of the man in Socrates, and these qualities made him a perfect citizen. Aristides caused a scheme of Themistocles to be rejected because it was unjust, even though it was most advantageous for his country. Here is an example of integrity with respect to mankind in general, and this man deserved to be called a just man. Aristides, forgetting himself, runs to the aid of Themistocles when the welfare of his country was in question; here he proves himself a good citizen.[26] Fabricus rejects with horror the proposal made him by the physician of King Pyrrhus, who offered to poison that terrible enemy of the Romans: Fabricius was an honest man. He refused the presents offered him by that prince: Fabricius was a Roman.[27] The ancients believed that to form a man it was necessary to make him virtuous, and the virtuous man could not but be a good citizen. They were therefore far from imagining that one could not make at the same time both a man and a citizen.*

[*Sixth objection – against the teaching of Christianity*] Finally, Rousseau's idea appears contrary to the principles of the institution of Christianity, which teaches us to educate children in the practice of the duties that they ought to exercise toward other members of society.

[5. *Whether self-interest is a sufficient foundation for moral social relationships*]

"Good social institutions are those that best know how to denature man."[28] This maxim would seem to be a natural consequence of a system of philosophy that is not at all to Rousseau's taste.[29] If physical sensibility were the sole foundation of our soul, – if this were the motive for all our actions, – if avarice, vanity, and even ambition had

---

* Rousseau in one part of his work, says that "the love of one's nearest [is] the principle of the love one owes the state; . . . [it is] the good son, the good husband, and the good father who makes the good citizen" [*Emile* 5.23; (B, 363)]. Might not this be produced as an argument against Rousseau? A man cannot be properly educated for himself without endeavoring to make him a good son, a good husband, and a good father. This gentleman admits that to educate a man for himself is to try to make him a reasonable man; and this cannot be done without cultivating in him the dispositions which are first to make him a good son, and in due course of time, a good husband and a good father. These dispositions are also, according to our author, what serve to form a good citizen. If so, then, a man cannot be educated for himself, without being also educated for others; and the assertion, that "a man and a citizen cannot at the same time be formed" must of course have no foundation. [Gerdil's note.]

no other power than what they borrow from the love of carnal pleasures, – if the valor of heroes had no other motive than the desire to please women, – if personal interest were the only tie which attached men to society, – if justice consisted only in a disposition to be useful to that society to which we were not otherwise connected than from motives of one's own advantage, – if independent of personal advantage all actions were in their nature indifferent and became afterwards virtuous according to the exigencies of that society founded on self-interest, – if, consequently, it were a matter of indifference whether a man murdered his friend or crushed an insect, – in a word, *if there were absolutely no moral integrity relative to human nature in general*, – then it would surely be necessary to denature a man in order to make him a citizen. The citizen is obliged to give his life for his country. How can one reconcile this obligation with a system that in the final analysis reduces everything to sensual pleasures? In what manner can self-preservation or the love of pleasure induce a man to sacrifice himself for a society, the preservation of which cannot be of any benefit to him after his death?

But Rousseau believes in virtue. According to him, virtue is not a word devoid of meaning, a Platonic idea. It is a real perfection of the soul, the possession of which is essential to the happiness of mankind. The basic dispositions, which he lays down as so many natural principles of our action, are founded not only on agreeable and disagreeable sensations but also on the ideas that reason gives us of perfection and happiness. If he had confined himself to agreeable and disagreeable sensations, I confess a man would have to be denatured in order to make him a citizen. But what he adds respecting the ideas of perfection and happiness prevents this consequence from being deduced. To make a citizen, virtue alone is necessary. But virtue is a perfection of man, and man naturally loves his perfection.

[6. *Love of honor and the attraction to an idea of perfection are natural inclinations*]

It is well said that man is not only attracted by sensual pleasures and coarse interest, as is currently the fashion to claim. The idea of intellectual perfection is capable of moving him with greater vivacity. Man loves genius, learning, penetration, and memory. Those who are not possessed of these qualities wish to have them, and if fools are not inclined to wish for them, it is because they think themselves already possessed of them. Great men who are blessed with them wish to have them to a still higher degree. D'Alembert, with reason on his side, says that the study of geometry would give the sweetest satisfaction to a man who would occupy himself with it on a desert island, as he could not but perceive the gradual improvement of his mind.[30]

This idea of perfection is far from being a chimera. The sentiment of honor, which depends on it, or, one might say, is even a form of it, sufficiently proves its reality. The sentiment of honor derives from those qualities that make us estimable in our own eyes and that render us worthy of the esteem of others. A man may derive satisfaction from sensual pleasures, but he does not look upon them as qualities capable of gaining him the esteem of his equals. And assuredly, in all countries of the world, that man would be considered extravagant who would judge himself worthy of honor and to have merited the esteem and respect of others on the basis of his having a sensation of pleasure. This certainly proves that men only affix the idea of honor to those qualities which they deem estimable because they render those who possess them better than those who lack them. Some barbarous or depraved nations have made a merit of tolerating a large quantity of wine; but this honor had no relation to the sensation a man experiences when he relishes the liquor which wets his palate. On the contrary, they thought a capacity for drink was a sign of a vigorous constitution, proper for bearing the greatest fatigues of war. A voluptuary prides himself in being a good judge of the table. But this must not be attributed to wanton gluttony, for the object of his childish vanity is a delicacy of taste. And thus, not withstanding the depravity of manners and opinions, the sentiment of honor can only be tied to those qualities that bear by some means or other a relationship to the perfection of man.

This sentiment of honor is susceptible of a greater degree of vivacity than any other sentiment. It seems as though nature has conferred upon it so much power, in order to cause men to take a more lively interest in their own perfection, and to induce them on occasion to sacrifice on its behalf the desire of conveniences, pleasures, and even life itself. The main thing is not to be mistaken regarding the idea of perfection that we must form for ourselves.

Consider the learned man who wears himself out at his books: is it the attraction of sensual pleasure or the hope of gain that makes him read so much? Far from it. He often studies at the expense both of his health and fortune. The interior satisfaction he feels in contemplating the truths he discovers and, if you will, the desire for recognition are the motives that encourage and sustain him. Not even for a crown would such a man trade his right to any of his discoveries. Corneille well knew what he might expect from the generosity of a minister who had the soul of a king. But Corneille's sublime soul took greater pride in the possession of the *Cid* than the treasures and honors, which were offered him in exchange for it.[31] The eagerness of the minister and the inflexibility of the poet sufficiently disprove the principle of a modern philosopher to the effect that all the desires of mankind are centered in sensual pleasure and that whatever we wish beyond it we only desire as a means to sensual pleasure. Corneille knew quite well that money was much more useful for gratifying his senses than a piece of poetry. And Richelieu, at the pinnacle of greatness and fortune, respected by all Europe, France at his command, a throne the only thing above him, did he not have, in the full splendor of his power and reputation, all that could interest men to flatter him in every path of taste he might choose to tread? But Corneille could by no means be induced to give up the most illustrious monument of his genius, and the Cardinal, obliged to admit to himself the superiority of his rival in this kind of talent, was humiliated by Corneille's refusal to confess the share he flattered himself to have had in a piece so worthy of admiration. I do not believe that Richelieu wished to call the *Cid* his own like a plagiarist, who attributes to himself the verses of others, or a priest who preaches sermons he has not composed. It is more probable that

Richelieu, who sometimes conversed with Corneille on the subject of poetry, imagined he had furnished him with ideas, which might give him some right to the pieces he composed. Be this as it may, however, this circumstance seems to prove that the attachment a man has for objects that contribute to his intellectual perfection, that the satisfaction he feels from the good opinion he forms of this perfection, and that the pleasure that results from seeing his opinion in this matter confirmed by that of others, – these are all sentiments founded originally in nature and the satisfaction that they give immediately touches the soul, independently of any sensual pleasure or civil interest.

[*7. The attraction to moral virtue is a natural inclination*]

If the possession of talents, genius, learning, and indeed, all the qualities that perfect the human understanding can give such exquisite pleasure, what satisfaction must the good man feel who is possessed of virtue? What pleasure can equal the peace he enjoys? What treasure is of equal value to the conscience of the just? Let us stop a while at beneficence. This word, so frequently repeated by the Abbé de Saint-Pierre,[32] is too beautiful for us not to adopt it. Is there a more pleasing sensation than that of having the power of doing good? Observe that man whose soul is clouded with disgrace and who feels the neediness of indigence; his languid eye and downcast look reveal the blackness of the grief that oppresses him and gnaws at him. Your liberality is about to raise him from the depths of suffering. You dissipate his grief. A sweet sensation of joy floods into, awakens, and enlivens his soul. His eyes, which before were languid, regain their splendor. The drawn lines of his face relax, and the dignity of man reappears in his countenance. The man has new life from your beneficence. Is there any happiness comparable to yours? It is beautiful, says Cicero, to see a man who by the charm of his eloquence can so captivate a large assembly that he alone seems worthy of being heard.[33] But it is even more beautiful for a man to dedicate his care, his talents, his labor to the safety, the tranquility, the happiness of his family, his neighbors, his country, and to expose his own person to preserve them from impending danger. Hercules and Theseus deserve to be called heroes less because of their exploits than because of their good deeds. It is useless vainglory that bestows this title on the conquerors who only ravage the face of the earth. Achilles, who knew nothing except how to fight, is not a hero. This august title is reserved for the benefactors of mankind.

Virtue, then, can produce in the soul a sentiment of pleasure and satisfaction capable of making itself beloved, independent of every other consideration. Cicero justly reproaches the Epicureans for their unwillingness to distinguish the delight a virtuous action causes through the mere satisfaction that we find in doing it from the pleasure resulting from the anticipated advantages which the exercise of and reputation for virtue may win us.[34] This is the case with those who deny the intrinsic morality of human actions and who consider all things with an indifference to their natures.

It is not possible, therefore, to approve of those who fear running counter to certain ideas unhappily already too acceptable. They do not dare to deviate from the way of speaking they hear from certain brilliant spirits who base the worth of virtue on the fact that, when all is said and done, it procures more advantages than vice, and it exposes us to fewer hazards. This makes the same case for virtue that a merchant makes for arithmetic; he prizes it for its utility, for it keeps his accounts in proper order and governs his trade. On the other hand, the mathematician, in addition to the utility of arithmetic, which may be of equal advantage to him as to the merchant, recognizes in the theorems of arithmetic a real beauty, inherent to the truths they contain, and he applies himself to it for the satisfaction that he finds in the nourishment of his spirit. Virtue is not less estimable than arithmetic. It offers us resources in all conditions and situations of life. Its utility is undisputed, but to limit its merit to the advantages we derive from it fails to do justice to its worth. He who only practices it with this intention loves virtue no more than the merchant who keeps regular accounts loves arithmetic. The one no more merits the name of a virtuous man than the other does the title of a mathematician. He who is attached to virtue with a sentiment analogous to the satisfaction a mathematician feels in solving a theorem is disposed to be virtuous.

It is a deplorable sight to behold Christian philosophers who, in laying down the principles of virtue, hardly dare mention its intrinsic goodness. Consider this unanswerable argument of its intrinsic goodness for all who believe in God. Tell me, philosopher, can God make lying, perfidy, treason, perjury, pride, ingratitude or impatience to be intrinsically good actions or qualities? You answer, No. But why? Because they are repugnant to the order of God's wisdom, and God cannot contradict his own wisdom. Very well then, I say, this repugnance stamps on vice an intrinsic deformity. And for the contrary reason, the conformity of virtue to the order of supreme wisdom is a source of the intrinsic goodness of virtue. Cicero understood these truths, and he expounded them in a most illuminating way in his *On the Laws*:[35] They are held sacred in the tradition by all the Doctors of the Church. And you, Christian philosopher, scarcely dare speak the language of your teachers! What do you fear? Of not being ranked in the list of thinking beings? Of passing for a pedant? These reproaches are inevitable. But from whom? Are you afraid of those who pride themselves on their irreligion? No: then it must be the murmuring of those indistinct echoes that repeat what they do not understand. This alarms and frightens you! What weakness!

In this section I have said nothing regarding either the intrinsic goodness of virtue or the sentiment of honor that is repugnant to Rousseau's principles. One can only say that, within this author's system, virtue and honor are qualities that are born from the state of society rather than the state of nature.[36] But it is certain that society could not give blossom to these sentiments of honor and virtue if nature had not put their seeds in the heart of man, seeds that wait only for the occasion to develop themselves. Moreover, Rousseau admits that the family forms a natural society.[37] Is this natural society not sufficient, in many respects, for exciting these sentiments and developing them up to a certain point? It must then be admitted that man is naturally ordered to honor and virtue, and that virtue is a disposition of the soul most befitting his nature and which greatly contributes to his perfection. And so in no way does it denature a man to make him virtuous. But the virtuous man is the well-formed citizen. One need not, therefore, denature a man in order to make him a citizen.

[8. *Whether society corrupts mankind's natural goodness*]

It is true that in this volume, Rousseau does not make much of a case for the state of society. "Society," he says, "has made man weaker not only in taking from him the right he had over his own strength but, above all, in making his strength insufficient for him."[38] He compares the imperfect liberty of children even in the state of nature to that which men enjoy in a civil state. "No longer able to do without others, each of us becomes in this respect weak and miserable again."[39]

In what state, then, can one man do without being assisted by others? Was there ever such a state? Or can we have any idea of it, unless we trace mankind to that pretended primitive state in which men crawled upon their four feet? I could confute this proposition by means of other contradictory propositions taken from his political principles,[40] but I prefer to avail myself of what Bossuet has said before Rousseau wrote, and which no one says better.

> By the government each individual becomes stronger. The reason is that each one is secured. All the powers of the nation center in one, and the sovereign magistrate has the right to combine them. . . . All strength is transferred to the sovereign magistrate: every one strengthens him to the prejudice of his own, and renounces his own life in case of disobedience. The people gain by this; for they recover in the person of the supreme magistrate more strength than they yielded for his authority, since they recover in him all the strength of the nation reunited to assist him. Thus an individual is at ease from oppression and violence, because in the person of the prince he has an invincible defender,

and much stronger beyond comparison than all those who may undertake to oppress him. . . . Proud and violent men are enemies to authority, and their normal language is, "Who is Lord over us?" . . . In willing to give everything to force, each one finds himself weak in his justest claims, by the multitude of concurrences against which he has to be prepared. . . . [No state is worse than one] in which everyone would do all that he wills; no one will do that which he wills; where there is no master, everyone is master; where everyone is master, everyone is a slave.⁴¹

This is what the great Bossuet has drawn from the sources of revelation. Have we really found anything superior? And would we be wise to abandon the straight way along which our fathers marched in order to turn into obscure and remote paths, the end of which nobody has yet seen, and which will lead us we know not where?*

---

* In all parts of his work, Rousseau represents in the most odious light the civil state, laws, and social institutions. In the fourth book we find the following remarkable passage. "In the civil state," he says, "there is a de jure equality that is chimerical and vain, because the means designed to maintain it themselves serve to destroy it, and because the public power, added to that of the stronger to oppress the weak, breaks the sort of equilibrium nature had placed between them" [*Emile* 4.99 (B, 236)]. And in a note, he adds, "The universal spirit of the laws of every country is always to favor the strong against the weak and those who have against those who have not. This difficulty is inevitable, and it is without exception." [B, 236 fn] That the strong will sometimes makes a bad use of the protection of the laws to oppress the weaker may sometimes be the case, because men often abuse the best things. But that this is the universal spirit of the laws of all countries is a proposition our author can by no means support and can never prove. "All our wisdom," says this writer, in another place, "consists in servile prejudices. All our practices are only subjection, impediment, and constraint. Civil man is born, lives, and dies in slavery." [1.34 (B, 42)] And in another part we find the following passage: "Everything is only folly and contradiction in human institutions." [2.25 (B, 82)] We frequently meet

Rousseau continues, "We were made to be men; laws and society have plunged us once more into childhood."[42] He says that "we need to have [our heads] fashioned on the outside by midwives and on the inside by philosophers. The Caribs are twice as lucky as we are."[43]

Unless knowledge and virtue degrade mankind, I cannot see that Lycurgus, Solon, Aristides, Socrates, or, if you will, Turenne, Newton, and D'Aguesseau[44] were reduced to a state of childhood by education and the assistance they received from laws and society. Can anyone show me outside of the civil state men who were more men than these? Rousseau seems to envy the lot of the Caribbean natives, whose heads are not fashioned by philosophers or midwives. I do not know the particulars regarding the Caribbeans, but in general the savages do not lag behind the Europeans in the singularity of the ways they have for fashioning the bodies of their children, either by pressing their heads to make them flat or long like a grenadier's cap, by pulling out their ears to make them flap on the shoulders, or by perforating the lips and nostrils to ornament them with rings and feathers. Our midwives have not yet acquired this dexterity. It is true that the heads of these people are not fashioned by philosophers. If our author means to speak of those philosophers who inspire "the unsettled and restless spirit of this age which upsets everything in each generation,"[45] he is right to caution us against that kind of philosophy which has yet produced no notable effect, other than to agitate many persons against religion, against government, and against the duties of society, without rendering them either wiser for themselves or better for others. But let us have heads fashioned by philosophers such as Cicero of *On Duties*, Epictetus, and Marcus Aurelius, or especially such as the orthodox Christian philosophers, and our heads would not be the worse for it. Rousseau may find among the Caribbean cannibals stronger stomachs, but he will not find better heads.

with exaggerations such as these in Rousseau's works; but whenever he forms axioms, he expects we should implicitly believe them. [Gerdil's note.]

26

[9. *Whether society invents the fear of death and makes men cowards*]
One of the disadvantages Rousseau finds in society is that it weakens
courage and instills a fear of death.

> Do you want to find men of a true courage? Look for
> them in the places where there are no doctors, where they
> are ignorant of the consequences of illnesses, where they
> hardly think of death. Naturally man knows how to suffer
> with constancy and dies in peace. It is doctors with their
> prescriptions, philosophers with their precepts, priests
> with their exhortations, who debase his heart and make
> him unlearn how to die.[46]

This is to say that true courage is only to be found among those ignorant, stupid people who, according to the accounts of travelers,
live almost like the beasts of the field, without art or without culture,
wholly occupied with the present, without any anticipation of the future. These men, if such there are, can bear their suffering without
murmuring, because they resemble children who only feel the present evil, without attending to consequences. Death is not terrible to
them, because they cease to live, without knowing they are about to
die. Does courage, then, consist in not fearing a danger of which one
is not aware? A man is peacefully walking along the street, a maga-
zine of powder he knows nothing of takes fire and blows him up into
the air. Can it be said that this man has confronted death with
courage? Take a man from that state of brutishness and stupidity,
which is not natural to man (if it is true that man is not made to always be an infant), give him some glimmer of reason, some thoughtful ideas; in a word, take human nature as it is, and I say that the
prospect of death has naturally something terrifying to every man
who is capable of thinking and reflecting. It is a difficult thing to entertain the idea of one's own destruction.[47]

Add to this that the proofs that Rousseau brings forward, following the lead of some celebrated philosophers, to reveal the weakness
and absurdity of materialism, adequately demonstrating that nothing
is more natural to man than the sentiment of the immortality of one's

own soul. The impression that moves men to regard death as a passage from one life to another is too universal not to be natural. This conviction has manifested itself at all times and in all places, in Europe, in Asia, in Africa, in America, among cultivated nations, among savages, and even among the Caribbeans. A reason sound and enlightened, free from passion and prejudice, told Socrates that death could not be the same to the good and the wicked man.[48] Now even Rousseau recognizes these things,[49] so is it not strange that he should situate the idea of true courage in men who are ignorant of the consequences of diseases or who are altogether unmindful of death? To be ignorant of the consequences of diseases and of what will follow after death is to live in a state of infancy or in a stupidity worse than infancy. The indifference which results from it is not courage. To have a well-considered understanding of the nature of death and not to be apprehensive about what follows, to be easy with respect to the fate of a life to come by not giving it any thought – the sentiment which Rousseau thinks is natural to man[*] – is to will oneself insensate, or rather, to blind oneself to set purposes, in the manner of the insensible world.

Yet Rousseau establishes the principle of true courage, the source of our peace of mind and happiness, in this brute stupidity, born of ignorance and nonchalance. "Savages as well as beasts," he says again, "struggle very little against death and endure it almost without complaint."[50] Such are the models, o wise men, that a philosopher proposes for teaching you how to live in peace and to die with tranquility! The desire of self-preservation is natural to man. In vain

[*] "[The materialists]," says Rousseau, "are indeed deaf to the inner voice crying out to them in a tone difficult not to recognize. A machine does not think. . . . No material being is active by itself, and I am. One may very well argue with me about this; but I sense it, and this sentiment that speaks to me is stronger than the reason combating it" [*Emile* 4.262–63 (B, 280)]. And further: "whereas I can conceive how the body wears out and is destroyed by the division of its parts, I cannot conceive of a similar destruction of the thinking being. . . . I sense my soul. I know it by sentiment and by thought" [*Emile* 4.284–85 (B, 283)]. [Gerdil's note.]

will Rousseau contest this principle: nature, stronger than him, has engraved it on every heart. Therefore the prospect of an evil, the consequences of which may be fatal, cannot but excite some disquieting sentiments. To be convinced that death is only a passage from one life to another, and yet to disregard it, is to act contrary to nature and to reason. The thought of death, considered from this point of view, should be the rule of life. Only a convinced materialist can, consistent with his principles, remain tranquil at the thought of what follows death, secure in the hope of a total destruction. But the security of a materialist depends more on the efforts he makes to reassure himself against fear than on any reason he has not to be afraid. I dare to say that not a single materialist, who upon examining his own self, would be able to find within himself evidence for a total conviction in the mortality of his soul. What a frightful uncertainty must arise within the heart of the unbeliever from this lack of evidence. Accordingly I conclude (from the author's own principles, but against him) that every reasonable man ought to govern his life with a view toward what follows after death. To ignore this thought and not to reflect on it is equally against nature and reason.

But the thought is terrible. I agree. Yet the object is of itself terrible, and it will not cease to be so by our not attending to it. There is then but one single method of arming ourselves with courage at the prospect of death. It is by considering the order of religion and profiting from the means it alone furnishes to render death not only sufferable, but even desirable. Would Rousseau like an example of such heroic courage? Let him recall the great apostle of Christianity, who having eternal happiness in view, sighed after the blessed moment which was to deliver him from the bonds of the body and reunite him forever with his Divine Master.[51] The history of the Christian religion will furnish him with comparable examples in every century. Without having recourse to books, let him only ask men of integrity who are still living. They will tell him with what edification they saw fervent religious come from all parts at the first news of the plague at Marseilles and joyfully shut themselves up within the walls of that unfortunate city, dedicating themselves to the service of the sick, in the hope of gaining a heavenly crown by sacrificing a perishable life in the service of their brothers. Such men, with no disrespect to Rousseau, are of more value than savages or beasts. I myself saw on his death bed a venerable old man with whom I had familiarly lived in my early youth. This virtuous man, far removed from the busy world, had passed an obscure but innocent life, tasting in his retreat and in such works of piety as were suited to his station that peace of mind, that sweet tranquility, that inward joy, which the pomps and pleasures of the age seem to promise but never to bestow. The purity and calmness of his soul appeared in the simplicity of his discourse and manners. His last illness did not alter his disposition. A sweet serenity colored his countenance. Approaching his bed, I asked him how he felt. He answered with his accustomed tranquility, half in Latin, half in French, "J'attends Regnum Caelorum." A few hours later, he expired in this happy expectation. Are such men debased in their hearts?

As to what Rousseau says with respect to physicians,[52] it is no concern of mine. But it seems likely that his book will not detract from their practice.

[10. *Whether laws and society reduce man to a servile state of dependency*]

Another deprivation of society, according to the author, is that born from dependency:

> There are two sorts of dependence: dependence on things, which is from nature; dependence on men, which is from society. Dependence on things, since it has no morality, is in no way detrimental to freedom and engenders no vices. Dependence on men, since it is without order, engenders all the vices, and by it, master and slave are mutually corrupted.[53]

To say that the dependence of men established in all governments of which history takes any notice is a disordered dependency that gives rise to every vice overtly contradicts Holy Scripture, which authorizes and recommends in a thousand places this kind of dependency. "Be obedient," says St. Peter, "for the love of God to the order which is established among men: Be obedient to the king, as being possessed of the supreme power, and to those to whom he gives his authority."[54] St. Paul speaks the same language. I know that Rousseau considers vile slaves those who have not the so-called courage to think as he does. Yet we dare to say that the first apostles of Christianity did not lack courage and that they were by no means possessed of that flattery and cowardliness that Rousseau makes the mark of slaves.

This dependence is inevitable and cannot be avoided even in our author's ideal system. By the social pact "each of us puts his person and all his power in common under the supreme control of the general will. . . ."[55] Yet Rousseau at the same time is obliged to acknowledge that every individual can have, as a man, a particular will contrary to the general will.

> His private interest may speak to him quite differently from the common interest; his absolute and naturally independent existence may make him envision what he owes to the common cause as a gratuitous contribution, the loss of which will be less harmful to others than its payment is burdensome to him, . . . injustice that would bring about the ruin of the body politic, were it to spread. In order, therefore, that the social pact may not be an empty formula, it tacitly includes the commitment, which alone can give force to the others, that anyone who refuses to obey the general will shall be compelled to do so by the entire body; this means nothing else than that he will be forced to be free. . . .[56]

Thus in a system imagined precisely for the maintenance of liberty, a man is obliged to be dependent and submit to the authority of a body that can force him to obey despite himself. It is true that Rousseau has found an admirable expedient to remedy this inconvenience. The City, in constraining a man to obey despite himself, makes no attempt upon his liberty, but to the contrary, it forces him to be free. The fact is clear. As Rousseau understands it, liberty consists in doing what we want. Therefore to force a man to be free, by compelling him to obey despite what he wants, is to force a man to do that which he wants, precisely while compelling him to do that which he does not want to do. Who does not understand such a claim? But besides the City which limits itself to making laws, it is still necessary in Rousseau's system that there be a magistracy charged with all the particular acts of government. Here, therefore, there is a particular body, or sometimes a single man, on whom it is necessary to depend.[57]

The dependence of men is not contrary to the nature of man. Nature did not make men in order to live alone, and therefore they were not made to live independently. Society and dependence are correlative ideas, for no society can subsist without order, and there can be no order without dependency. Sick persons submit to the prescriptions of their physician, travelers to the directions of their guide, and soldiers to the orders of their commander. They are persuaded that the physician, the guide, and the general know better than they what is to their advantage. Men know by nature that it is necessary for them to live in society, and they must certainly know it naturally, since everywhere they are established in societies; the multitude also know it must be governed. The people who have been the most jealous of their liberty have seen that they cannot do so without a leader authorized to maintain the laws and armed with the public strength to oppose those whose particular interests set them against the general interest. Rousseau says that the multitude desire what is good, but do not know it. He admits that the best and most natural order is that in which the multitude are governed by the wise. Upon this principle, the Medes, worn out by anarchy, voluntarily submitted themselves to be governed by Deioces, whose wisdom and integrity they knew well.[58] In doing this, they followed the impulse of nature, which requires order in society as well as in everything else. The savage, whom Robinson Crusoe saved from death (I cite an instance to which Rousseau can have no objection), delivered himself up without conditions to his benefactor, not only out of gratitude for the benefit he had received from him, but because he recognized that Robinson was superior to him in wisdom and could teach him to be a better man.[59] One has never seen a dependence more absolute than that of this man in regard to the master that he had given himself. Yet this man was a savage, that is to say, one of those wild souls in whom Rousseau so complaisantly admires the original independence of nature. In sum, because men must live together, it is necessary that some should command and others obey. One might try to evade the fact, but after a few twists and turns, we must either come back to this conclusion or say with Rousseau that when the city or its magistrates commit a man to prison, it is that they want him dependent, but they force him to be free. The Egyptian, with good reason, said, "O Hellenes! Will you always be children?"[60]

Rousseau represents neither the state of nature nor the state of society in their true light. He says that "we were made to be men; laws and society have plunged us once more into childhood."[61] He adds that "whoever does what he wants is happy if he is self-sufficient; this is the case of the man living in the state of nature."[62] First of all, it does not occur to him that without laws and society there would be no education, and without education men would be either simpletons or ferocious, or both the one and the other, according as their passions were calm or agitated. Rousseau paints the state of nature as his imagination represents it to him. A more solid writer will depict it according to nature with features drawn from the testaments of history. This writer is the author of an excellent treatise *On the Origin of Laws, Arts, Science, etc.* There was a time, he says, when almost the whole world was plunged in an extreme state of barbarity. Men were then seen to wander in the woods and plains, without laws, without regulated order, without any leader: here is the state of nature, properly characterized. Their ferociousness became so great that in some cases it brought them to the point of eating one another. They so far neglected even common knowledge that some even forgot the use of fire.[63] It is these unhappy times the profane historians refer to when they relate the miseries that the world labored under in the beginning. We shall find no difficulty in believing these accounts, if we turn our attention to the state into which the ancient historians say that several countries had fallen in their own times, conditions the reality of which we find confirmed by modern studies. Travelers tell us that even at this day in some parts of the world there are men so cruel and ferocious in their nature that they enter into neither society nor commerce with one another; they wage perpetual war, seeking to destroy and even to eat each other. Devoid of all principles of humanity, these people live without laws, without regulated order, without any form of government. So little different from the wild beasts, their only shelter is in rocks and caverns. Their food consists in a few fruits and roots, which the woods supply them. For want of knowledge and industry they are seldom able to procure more solid nourishment for themselves. Deprived of even the most simple and commonplace notions, these people are men only in their appearances.

Here are two pictures drawn from quite different testimonies. On one hand, Rousseau affirms that the law and society have returned men to a state of childhood and that the condition of man in the state of nature is to be sufficient unto himself and to live happily. This he asserts, but he does not provide the least proof. On the other hand, the author of *On the Origin of Laws* affirms that the want of laws and government plunges men into the most horrible barbarity, and he proves it with the facts. With which of these two should we agree?

[11. *On the natural love of order and origins of society*]

We must not, however, imagine that men are born wicked, as Hobbes thinks.[64] If this were the case, the sum of unjust actions of every people would infinitely surpass the sum of humanly just actions. Instead, however, the sum of just actions is incomparably superior to the evil, or else no society could possibly subsist. This would be easy to verify in particular cases. What usually convinces us to the contrary is that ordinary acts of justice and goodness are little noticed because they are in the natural order of things. We do not feel the pulse of the heart and the arteries so long as they occur in conformity to that state of health that is natural to man. But we acutely feel every displacement of the parts that run contrary to the natural condition. Every particular motion in bodies is determined by the general order and tends toward this order. It is the result of the combinations of all the moving forces of the universe, and it tends to maintain the harmony between all the moving forces. Whatever is done in nature is directed by those principles ordered among themselves and tends toward the maintenance of the order in these principles. The regularity of the primitive combination of the whole system has determined a regular course in all the movements of the parts, and this regular course holds together the regularity of the system. In organic bodies, which have a principle of sensation, their preservation and well-being depend on the natural harmony of their parts; pain and misery is tied to the derangement of parts that disrupts this harmony. Such is the plan of nature.

If we turn our attention from sensitive to intelligent beings, we shall find that the idea of their order is in some way natural and common to the species, and that it is a powerful inclination, which induces them to act in a manner consistent with their perfection and happiness. Man is naturally a friend of order, and wherever he finds it he approves it and delights in it. He can know nothing except because of the order discerned in his perceptions; he can do nothing except because of the order that he puts into his operations. The more disposed he is to seize the order and perceive it in the different intelligible objects, the greater is his genius and his talent. It is from the order of our affections that a calmness and serenity of soul proceeds; the contrary condition, which consists in the disrupted harmony, produces disquiet, rage, and despair. If a given number of men find themselves assembled for a purpose of some sort, a certain impression of order will immediately lead them to arrange themselves in a manner suitable to the object for which they gathered.

Thus it is neither fear alone, nor utility alone, nor benevolence alone, which has disposed men to assemble in social bodies. Each one of these causes is in itself inadequate, and it is this that renders defective those systems that pretend to establish the foundation of society exclusively on either the one or the other. It is then necessary that all three should be held together, since they naturally tend toward the same end. We must join to them the ruling impression of order, which serves as their common bond, and then we shall have the true principle of every civil society. Benevolence is in effect the first sentiment which connects men to each other, as seems evident from the state of the family, from the pleasure we take in the fellowship of our friends, from the satisfaction we feel when we are able to oblige others, and from the gratitude we express to those who oblige us. These sentiments may be opposed or even overpowered and smothered by selfishness, but they are not on that account less natural. Utility is the second motive that inclines individual men and families to join together. Without this assembly, they would often want for necessities. By virtue of it, however, they are able to provide for themselves not only indispensable needs but also the more agreeable things of life. Fear is the third motivation for associations. For cupidity, in the process of breaking the first bonds of nature, arms wicked men against those who are good, and so requires these latter to unite their forces in order to repel the attacks of the former.

These are the causes that bring men to assemble. But they are no sooner gathered than the impression of order prompts them to give an arrangement, a suitable form to their association. This arrangement requires the rules, which are called laws. The establishment of laws leads to the establishment of the authority charged with their maintenance. Such is the origin of the civil order.

Thus man, naturally a friend to order, is not by nature wicked, but becomes so by rivalry and by the clashing of interests which stir up his passions. At first sight it might seem as if society by increasing interests increases the causes of this clashing and thereby the sources of evil, but in this matter there are two obvious considerations. The first is that in the state of society the division of interests does not proceed from the first needs of life. With respect to things necessary for life, the civil state furnishes sufficiently for all and even an abundance for many. In the state of nature, on the contrary, or in those states that approximate it, men are frequently exposed to all the horrors of hunger and famine. It is to these severe extremities that the author of *On the Origin of Laws* attributes the horrid barbarism into which men can be plunged by the state of nature, for it can provoke them to destroy and even to devour each other. The civil state, by securing for men the sure means of subsistence, has banished the horrid custom of devouring each other, which for want of such a state, still subsists in certain savage and barbarous nations. Let the clashing of civil interests in a state of society be ever so great, it can never excite passions comparable to that which carries men to the extremes of cruelty and ferocity. The second observation to be made is this: It is true that society multiplies interests by increasing wealth and the conveniences of life. Yet it lessens the clashing and the effects of this clashing by the laws, which set limits to pretensions and fix the rights of each man. Men living in the state of nature will have greater contests about a little wild fruit than the greatest interests are capable of exciting in well-ordered states.

To this we may add that by virtue of their natural constitutions some men have from birth limited spirits and calm passions, others have spirits more lively and passions more ardent. If uncultivated, the first will remain imbeciles, and the other sort become ferocious if they are not governed or restrained. There are others who are born with a physical disorder of their organs, a derangement which does not produce an absolute folly, but which causes an irregularity of ideas which gives rise to uneasy, bungling, turbulent characters that delight in disorder and mischief making. People of such dispositions can only be kept in order by the natural fear they have of the chastisements and corrections, which alone can restrain the impetuous sallies occasioned by the confusion of their brains. Now the assistance required in order to rear and guide men in conformity to their respective characters is only to be found in the state of society. Therefore, it was only from caprice that Rousseau took it into his head to say that laws and society again reduce men to a state of childhood. Does he himself not acknowledge that men are indebted to their education for all that which they lack when they are born and which they want when they are grown up?[65]

Now I am absolutely certain that no reasonable plan of education can be formed that does not have some connection or other with laws and society. Rousseau would not have been able to outline his new system, except by virtue of the insight he acquired from society, and which he abused in order to undermine that same society. He pretends that society debases man. He apparently imagines that men in the state of nature would generally have those elevated sentiments which people of birth find within themselves, and furthermore, that they would be able to give them freer rein if they were to live in total independence. But this is sheer illusion. That nobility and generosity of sentiment that characterize well-born souls scarcely ever develop in children who would, if I may so put it, educate themselves. These sentiments, though natural, require culture in order to develop themselves. This culture is the fruit of a civil education and of a solicitous care that early on impresses on the spirit of children the ideas of virtue and honor.

[12. *Man's reason, the natural analogue to*
animal instinct, requires education]

It pleases Rousseau to suppose that in the state of nature man would be stronger, because his strength would be proportionate to his desires and his desires to his needs, and that in the state of society he becomes feeble, because his desires increase beyond his power. I dare to say that this thought is more specious than solid. Either man in the state of nature would have only perception purely sensitive of heat, cold, pleasure, pain, and the like, without anything that could properly be called an idea, which is to say in Rousseau's language, without notions determined by relations;[66] or else in the state of nature he would be able to raise his sensation to the knowledge of objects and of their relations, thereby making some use of his reason. If in the state of nature man was limited to what was merely sensitive, without any settled idea of things, without having any use of his reason, it is quite true that his desires would be as limited as those of the beasts of the field. He would feel no other want than to satisfy his hunger, to defend himself from heat and cold, and the like. But however limited these desires and these wants may be, it is no less true that a man deprived of the use of his reason would be absolutely unable to gratify and supply them. For as we have already observed, man has not, like other animals, received from nature an instinct destined to one particular kind of work and furnished with organs or instruments solely adapted to particular operations. The sensation of want and the impression of sensible objects suffice both to trigger this instinct that nature has conferred as a guide to animals, and to make them punctually execute all the successive movements and operations by which she has provided for their preservation and defense. It is not this way with man. Nature has not limited him to one particular kind of work or to one particular order of operations that are, so to say, mechanical. The mere sensation of want or the mere impression of sensible objects do not suffice to determine his organs to the actions necessary for his defense and preservation. This sensation, this impression only give him, as it were, notice of his wants and rouse his knowledge and reason to think of some means of satisfying them. He must learn to know the objects that surround him, to discern their relative fitness or unfitness with respect to himself, to imagine ways of acquiring or avoiding them, and the manner of using them.

Reason is like a universal art, which for man takes the place of all the particular arts by enabling him to vary his industry in a manner best suited to the circumstances he finds himself in. Also, as Galen observes following Aristotle, nature has given him hands as a universal instrument adapted for making and using the particular instruments that are necessary to secure his ends.[67] I would, at this point, willingly ask a philosophical materialist what is this nature that has made a being whose species needs to perpetuate itself and yet whose preservation essentially depends on intellectual ideas. It is then certain that if in the state of nature man could be limited to having only purely sensible perceptions, far from being strong, he would be the most wretched of all beings and would perish through the absolute want of power to procure himself the least support.

From this it follows that man could never exist in the way that Rousseau describes him in his book on the inequality of man.[68]

Therefore, in order that man may be able to support himself in the state of nature, we must allow him some degree of knowledge and some use of reason. Accordingly, his reason would either remain in that coarse and imperfect state that was always the lot of people living without laws and without government, and we know that men, so far from acquiring power or strength in this state, are reduced to the most wretched necessity without the power of supplying even the most urgent wants of nature. Or else, which is contrary to all experience, reason would acquire in the state of nature as much lucidity, force, and extension as in a well-ordered society, but in this case man would have new desires and new wants, with less means for satisfying them. The order and development of man's inclinations correspond exactly to the order and development of his perception and knowledge. Does he have only sensations? Then all his desires are limited to the sphere of the sensible. Does he have ideas in the proper sense of notions determined by relations? Does he understand by means these relations the fitness or unfitness of objects? Then from these intellectual notions will immediately arise a new order of inclinations relative to the idea that reason gives us of perfection and happiness.

How little reason there is to Rousseau's notion that laws and society have reduced man to a state of childhood – as if man springing from the bosom of nature, as it were, was furnished with whatever would be necessary to preserve, defend, and maintain himself in his natural independence, to supply all his wants, and thus to live contented and happy. Nothing is less reasonable than such a thought.

For we have seen, first of all, that without the guidance of reason man is utterly incapable of making the least use of his own strength, to the extent that we may say that he has only so much strength as he has reason, because the application of his strength always presupposes a choice which cannot exist without some degree of knowledge and some use of reason. But reason requires culture for it to develop. It resembles the fire concealed in the flint, which only shows itself when struck by the steel. The culture of reason necessarily requires a communication of intelligence, which can only be had in society.

And secondly, even reason itself, enlightened as it may be, does not suffice to procure man all the assistance he may want. Rousseau might have been convinced of this by the real or symbolic adventures of Robinson Crusoe on his island. Notwithstanding the knowledge and experience he had acquired in society, notwithstanding the assistance he received from the wreck of his ship, still what labor he expended and what fatigue he suffered in order to procure himself a moderate subsistence. But all of his industriousness would not have been sufficient to save himself from certain death if the island had been less temperate or if it had been infested with wild beasts.

Reason was not given to a man so that he might supply his own partial wants. It was given to men so that they might learn to unite and in a mutual commerce of reciprocal duties and assistance find everything that would be necessary to live in a manner suitable to the dignity of their nature.

There is no necessity for us to travel as far as the countries of the Hurons or Hottentots to see a troop of men living together nearly in the state of nature. Every country of Europe offers us the image of it in the class of wandering beggars. This class forms as a separate body within the state. They live without care on the daily alms they receive from the rich, in the same manner as savages live on the fruits they gather, with this difference, however, that they find at the foundations of humanity characteristic of every civil society, more certain resources against want than savages generally find in the productions of nature. They also derive from society the advantage that the fear of punishment prevents them from giving way to those excesses that might otherwise disrupt the general order. Apart from these exceptions, they feel very little influence of the laws. No bond ties them to the country; they lack property, commerce, arts, and industry. They possess nothing. They have no rank, no place in the state, no civil interests, nor any share in the civil institutions. They aspire at nothing, their desires being fully satisfied if they can drink, eat, and do nothing. These men, flocked together purely by chance, represent rather well the state of nature, isolated from the greater body of citizens, and living in a total independence from one another. Here are men who have not been corrupted by social institutions; they educate themselves and follow without restraint the propensities of nature. These are the men, therefore, in whom we should find sound reason, pure manners, hardy souls, with noble and generous sentiments. But this is far from being the case. Most of them lead the greatest part of their lives in an utter ignorance of the duties of man and of the most common principles of religion and morality, without culture, without any of that knowledge that honors and perfects reason. Their only thought is to take advantage of people's compassion, and for this purpose they use every kind of cunning and fraud and sometimes the most criminal artifices when they think they will not be discovered. With a suppliant air, affecting a mild and hypocritical manner, they beg their alms, but if you refuse them, they soon utter the vilest invectives. The distribution of some pieces of money often occasions sharp quarrels among them, at which times they breathe forth all the festering bitterness of their soul. Indolence and laziness constitute the pleasures of their life, and they are said to abandon themselves in secret to debauchery and the most shameful lewdness. Such are the wretched who, detached from the bonds of society, fully enjoy their natural liberty. Such are not the poor who are taken into hospitals, where they are brought up in the fear of God, are accustomed to labor, and are taught the sentiments of a just subordination. We may hence conclude that natural independence is not so favorable to the perfection, as Rousseau thinks. For man's nature is such that he cannot make progress of any sort without the cooperation of others like him, a cooperation that necessarily entails a society, a society to which a certain order is indispensable, an order that can only subsist through laws, laws that can only be maintained through a government, which comprehends within its essence the correlative ideas of authority and subordination.

Yet one more reflection on an observation of Rousseau: "all animals have exactly the faculties necessary to preserve themselves. Man alone has superfluous faculties," and he pretends that "this superfluity [is] the instrument of his unhappiness." Whence he concludes that "if man were wise enough to count his superfluity for nothing, he would always have what is necessary." To this he adds that "any man who only wanted to live would live happily."[69]

Even if the observation is philosophical, the conclusion is hardly so. It is from nature, or rather from the author of nature, that man derives all his faculties. If he has some that are superfluous to his preservation, does it follow that they are in every respect superfluous? It would be absurd to think so. Animals only possess the faculties necessary for their preservation because the animal life they lead can have no other object. But the life of man should be reasonable and sociable. Man does not live merely with a view of existing; he lives to cultivate his reason, in order to enjoy the inestimable fruits of wisdom, and to fulfill the immensity of his duties to God, to himself, and to his own kind. If nature has given to man alone more faculties than are necessary for his preservation, it is a clear proof that she did not mean to limit him, like other animals, to the care of his preservation alone. It is in vain for us to count this superfluity for nothing. Man will never attain to happiness by aiming short of the goal that the author of nature has appointed. Sound reason will always tell us that man cannot attain to happiness except by making a good use, not by a chimerical curtailment, of those faculties that he has received from nature.

[13. *Whether children are capable of understanding moral categories*]

To Rousseau's two principles which we have already examined, namely (1) that the first movements of nature are always right and there is no original perversity in the heart of man and (2) that the dependence of man is disordered, we must add another, namely, (3) that at the age of ten or twelve years, or even more, reason is not sufficiently developed in children to render them capable of morality. These three principles are the foundation of his practical education until nearly the age of fifteen years. From these principles Rousseau concludes:

[1] One ought not to get involved with raising a child if

one does not know how to guide him where one wants by the laws of the possible and the impossible alone. . . . Do not give your pupil any kind of verbal lessons; he ought to receive them only from experience. Inflict no kind of punishment on him, for he does not know what it is to be at fault. Never make him beg pardon, for he could not know how to offend you.[70]

[2] It is necessary that he be dependent and not that he obey. . . . He is only subject to others by virtue of his needs. . . . No one, not even the father, has a right to command the child what is not for his good.[71] Keep the child in dependence only on things. . . . Never present to his undiscriminating will anything but physical obstacles or punishments which stem from the actions themselves and which he will recall on the proper occasion. . . . Experience or impotence alone ought to take the place of law for him.[72]

[3] I return to practice. I have already said that your child ought to get a thing not because he asks for it but because he needs it, and do a thing not out of obedience but only out of necessity. Thus the words *obey* and *command* will be proscribed from his lexicon, and even more so *duty* and *obligation*. But *strength, impotence,* and *constraint* should play a great role in it.[73]

[4] The weakness of the first age enchains children in so many ways that it is barbarous to add to this subjection a further subjection – that of our caprices – by taking from them a freedom so limited, which they are so little capable of abusing.[74] . . . Why do you want to deprive these little innocents of the enjoyment of a time so short which escapes them and of a good so precious which they do not know how to abuse?[75] Let us . . . leave to childhood the exercise of natural freedom that keeps at a distance, for a time at least, vices contracted in slavery.[76]

44

It is needless to observe how different this practice is from that recommended in the Holy Scriptures. Rousseau would not have children obey but only be dependent, because they have need for assistance. St. Paul would have children obey because it is right in the sight of God.[77] Rousseau forbids fathers giving their children any verbal instructions or ever speaking to them of duty or obligation. Moses, whose legislation Rousseau admires, commands fathers to instruct their children in the law of God from their earliest years.[78] Rousseau says that fathers should not chastise their children. Yet Eli is punished for not having chastised his children.[79] Rousseau would have us leave children the full enjoyment of their natural liberty. The wise man recommends that they should be accustomed to the yoke from their infancy.[80] Even if this method had not been warranted by the word of God, still the experience of many ages would be a sufficient guarantee of its solidity.

This is not to say that one cannot take advantage of physical obstacles to oppose the indiscreet volitions of a child and, as much as possible, to make them find in them the punishment of their faults as a natural consequence of their disorder. But the absolute exclusion of every prohibition and of every chastisement is an untenable paradox. To be praised and blamed are the natural consequences of good and bad actions in society. It would be proper for the child to feel these effects from all those who are connected with him. He would begin to feel through direct experience the consequences of a good or a bad reputation. Such a matter is not an indifferent concern; it is a plan to be sagely arranged.

Rousseau supposes that until the age of fifteen years children do not have enough reason to distinguish moral good from evil. Is it Rousseau who speaks this language, he who is persuaded that the sentiment of the just and the unjust is innate in the heart of man? Let us recall what he says on this subject.

> I shall never forget having seen one of these difficult cryers thus struck by his nurse. He immediately kept quiet. I believed he was intimidated. I said to myself, "This will be a servile soul from which one will get nothing except

severity." I was mistaken. The unfortunate was suffocating with anger; he had lost his breath; I saw him become violent. A moment after came sharp screams; all the signs of the resentment, fury, and despair of this age were in his accents. I feared he would expire in this agitation. If I had doubted that the sentiment of the just and the unjust were innate in the heart of man, this example alone would have convinced me. I am sure that a live ember fallen by chance on this child's hand would have made less of an impression than this blow, rather light but given in the manifest intention of offending him.[81]

What! An infant at the breast can discern in a slight blow an intention of offending him, and the sentiment of this offense wounds him more forcefully than would a hot firebrand. And yet one is to say that a child of ten, twelve, or even fifteen years of age is still at this point incapable of distinguishing actions in terms of their morality!

But let us pass over infants at the breast and consider children at the age of seven or eight years of age. Let us examine their conduct and see whether there does not appear some discernment of moral good and evil. Suppose two children quarrel; you need only ask those who witnessed the event, and they will know to tell you who was in the wrong and who in the right. The strictest inquiry will only serve to further convince you of the equity of their judgment.

Children know quite well when one rewards or punishes rightly or wrongly. On this point they never deceive themselves. But to distinguish actions as deserving reward or punishment is to be able to discern moral good from moral evil.

Horace, the poet of reason, does not hesitate to summon men to deeds of rectitude, which is visible even in children's play. "*At pueri ludentes, 'Rex eris', aiunt, 'si recte facies* (But boys at their game would cry out, 'You will be king, if you do the right thing')"[82] – Yes, children in their play confer royalty on those who do the best. They are cognizant that merit should correspond to preference. Is this what it means to be deprived of all ideas of morality?

Children distinguish the evil that was done inadvertently from that which was done by design. They excuse the one, but do not pardon the other. They therefore know to hold one culpable only for those deeds done with evil intention.

When a child would take for his own the book or playthings of one of his companions, all the rest declare him to be in the wrong. They have already this sentiment of equity that it is only just that everyone should enjoy what belongs to him or what has been appropriated to his use. Children of seven or eight years of age are capable of possessing all these ideas of morality, and their conduct continually furnishes the proof and examples.*

I would like as little to insist that a ten-year old be five-feet tall as that he possess judgment. Actually, what would reason do for him at that age? It is the bridle of strength, and the child does not need this bridle.[83]

---

* Rousseau himself says that children "will find a secret pleasure in catching you misbehaving. . . . One of children's first efforts . . . is to discover the weakness of those who govern. . . . Overburdened by the yoke imposed on them, they seek to shake it off, and the shortcomings they find in the masters furnish them with good means for that" [*Emile* 2.170 (B, 121)]. There is great truth in this remark, but then it proves in contradiction to the author that children are not devoid of all notions of morality. If they take a secret pleasure in discovering their master's faults, they then certainly know what a fault is, and can distinguish between moral good and evil. Here then Rousseau is confuted by himself. Nothing can be more ingenious than the subterfuge this writer has contrived to screen himself from whatever contradictions may be laid to his charge; this is to acknowledge that "his expressions" clash, but not "his ideas" [*Emile* 2.120 fn (B, 108)]. He says absolutely, in one place, that "[the child] does not know what it is to be at fault" [*Emile* 2.61 (B, 92)], but in another part of his work [*Emile* 2.170 (B, 121)] he says, children take a secret pleasure in detecting their masters in a fault. Is this contradiction merely in the expression, or does it not in some measure affect the ideas? [Gerdil's note.]

It would be absurd to require that a child of ten years old should be five feet high; it would be equally absurd to require that he should at that age have as ripe a judgment as a man of thirty. Judgment is a faculty that develops and forms itself little by little. We see this faculty first begin to appear in children from the age of seven or eight years, and at ten years old it has made perceptible progress. "Reason," says Rousseau, "is the bridle of strength." I would rather say that it should serve as a bridle to the first interior movements, which incline us to use our strength. A child of ten years of age has a lively sentiment of his nascent strength, a sentiment active and vigorous prompting him to be act, to be continually fidgeting, to take those objects that are near at hand, and to turn them about and work them in every manner. It is in this fashion that by a hidden impulse of nature the young bull shakes his proud head and strikes his impotent blows, testing the weapons that he does not yet possess. This nascent strength in animals is governed by a certain and unalterable instinct that guides them, but in man there is no immediate rule other than reason.[84] Why then should reason be entirely useless to a child of ten years old? This interior propensity that stirs and agitates him, which prompts him to continual action and keeps him always out of breath – does it not need some restraint? It is true that at this age reason is too weak to suffice by itself. It needs to be assisted and fortified by precepts, examples, and appropriate practices. "We are born weak . . . we need judgment . . . [and it is] given us by education."[85]

[14. *On the importance of the fear of God in the moral education of children*]

The most appropriate and efficacious method of leading children to what is good and distancing them from evil is to inspire them with the fear of God. It will be in vain for Rousseau to say that the idea of God is too sublime for children.[86] We are not speaking here of the speculative ideas that Simonides puzzled over, when he had asked of Hiero a day's time to explain to him what God was, the next day asked two, and afterwards four days, and concluded with saying that the more he reflected on the question proposed to him by Hiero the more obscure and difficult he found it.[87] A child knows that a house, a statue, a picture, or a piece of furniture did not make itself. He knows it, and let us point out to him whatever we choose, if he notices design and regularity in it, he will not fail to ask who made it. This disposition is natural to all children, and it may naturally open their minds to the knowledge of God. Let them be told that the world, which exhibits to their view so magnificent spectacle, did not make itself. In telling them this you tell them nothing new; they already knew that a house could not make itself. But who made the world? It is God, we shall answer. At the same time we will explain to them that God, who made the world, does not have a body like men, that we cannot see him with our eyes, that he knows everything and can do what he pleases. We shall further explain that he is good, that he created men to make them happy, that he is just, that he rewards the good and punishes the wicked. These truths are undoubtedly sublime, and we cannot wonder too much at the fact that they are nevertheless brought within the capacity of even the simplest souls. The reason for this fact is that the truths are necessary to the perfection and happiness of man. Hence we have the reason why they are found so conformable to the first reflective notions which develop in the mind of children and why they take hold with kind of homogeneity.

A child instructed in this manner, regardless of what Rousseau thinks, will be disposed to neither idolatry nor anthropomorphism. The greatest difficulty is to make him understand that God is not corporeal. The following is a method I have used successfully with some children. The child begins by asking: "God has no body? How can he have anything if he has no body?"

Teacher. Observe all the bodies you see. Isn't it true that all have some
length and some breadth?

Child. This is true

Teacher. Do you not see that they have a kind of figure, which is
round, square, etc.?]

Child. I see it.

Teacher. Do you not feel that they resist your hand when you touch and try to stir them?

Child. I feel it.

Teacher. Would you like to know in what manner God is not corporeal?

Child. Yes.

Teacher. You really have the will and the desire to know it.

Child. Yes.

Teacher. Assure me, then, that you have this will and this desire. I am still somewhat doubtful you have it.

Child. I assure you of it, believe me I have.

Teacher. You feel then this desire, this will?

Child. I do feel it.

Teacher. Strongly?

Child. Yes, strongly.

Teacher. Well, then, this *desire* which you so strongly feel in yourself, is it nothing or is it something?

Child. It is something.

Teacher. Come now, I tell you it is nothing.

Child. Nothing! If it was nothing, I should not feel it.

Teacher. Then this desire that you feel is something.

Child. Yes, without doubt.

Teacher. Tell me then is this desire as long and as broad as that table?

Child. O dear! It is neither long nor broad.

Teacher. Is it round or square?

Child. O dear!

Teacher. Is it yellow or green, as heavy as lead or as light as a feather?

Child. It is nothing of the sort.

Teacher. It is nothing, then.

Child. Pardon me, it certainly is something.

Teacher. It is then something that is neither long nor broad, neither yellow nor green, neither round nor square?

Child. Exactly.

Teacher. Your desire, then, is not a body like your hand, your hair, this mirror, this table, this fountain, nor like the air which may be felt when it is agitated.

Child. This is true.

Teacher. You conceive then that there are things that can be neither seen nor touched, and that nevertheless are something.

[15. *On the authority of fathers and the obedience of children*]
Rousseau limits the dependence of children to the need they have for their father, and he excludes every sentiment of obedience. This we have already seen. He adds in another place:

> Command him nothing, whatever in the world it might be, absolutely nothing. Do not even allow him to imagine that you might pretend to have any authority over him. Let him know only that he is weak and you are strong, that by his condition and yours he is necessarily at your mercy. Let him know it, learn it, feel it. Let his haughty head at an early date feel the harsh yoke which nature imposes on man, the heavy yoke of necessity under which every finite being must bend. Let him see this necessity in things, never in the caprice of men. Let the bridle that restrains him be force and not authority.[88]

It is very strange that one should want to teach children not to depend on their father or on those who substitute in his place except because of the inevitable necessity of submitting to a superior power, which they cannot resist. Rousseau would have the child know that he is at the mercy of the strongest and that he must learn to be dependent; moreover, this dependence is to make him cognizant of the heavy yoke of necessity which nature imposes and accustoms him to bear. It seems to me that such a state of dependence is very sad and that it closely resembles that subordination of a slave to a despot, who is able to crush him at any instant. Even though every finite being bends, however unwillingly, to the yoke of domineering necessity, this submission does not prevent the heart from often rising up and murmuring at the burden that oppresses it. The submission of a son to his father should not be of this sort; nor is it at this school that he should learn to bear up under the unavoidable yoke of necessity. Every subordination founded exclusively on the superiority of an irresistible power serves only to inspire sentiments of fear, aversion, and a desire to free oneself. A child educated in accordance with such principles will only suffer with horror every human authority no matter what kind. He will bear the yoke to the extent he is unable to avoid it, but his heart will shudder at this hard necessity, and he will seek out every means to liberate himself from it. I ask whether, with such a disposition, it is possible for a child to become a good citizen in any part of the world he might find himself? I know that according to Rousseau's principles every human authority ought to be abolished. [89] And it is perhaps the most original and novel idea that has been produced for many centuries. The discoveries of Newton, wonderful as they are, to some extent depended upon ancient theories, which contained their seeds. The abolition of all human authority, beginning with that of fathers over their children, is an idea for which Rousseau is indebted to no one. But while awaiting this great revolution in which all Europe will be divided into three or four hundred thousand cities[90] where natural liberty will be so well maintained that by putting a man in prison one only obliges him to be free, it would seem one runs a great risk by educating children in principles that are so little consistent with the government of all the monarchies and all the republics that have so far existed and which will probably exist for a long time to come.

Let us consult nature and see if she has not arranged gentler ties to establish that dependence which children ought to have upon those who gave them life. Rousseau himself shows us the way. Children are susceptible of a natural affection toward their fathers and their mothers.

The child ought to love his mother before knowing that he ought to. If the voice of blood is not strengthened by habit and care, it is extinguished in the first years, and the heart dies, so to speak, before being born. Here we are, from the first steps, outside of nature.[91]

A child, badly treated by his mother, does not entrust himself to the first person who comes his way and tries to attract him with caresses; he returns to his mother, tries to soften her by his embraces, and finds comfort only on her breast. Children are susceptible of a parallel sentiment of affection toward their fathers.

Children have no difficulty conceiving that they belong to those who gave them life. They regard themselves as masters of the balls they have made with their own hands. This dominion which they assume over what belongs to them disposes them to recognize an analogous power over themselves in those to whom they belong.

Children know that their father and mother love them and that they only use their authority over them for their own good. They are aware that they are not in a position to procure for themselves the common necessities of life, that their parents voluntarily undertake this care upon themselves, and that they know better than themselves what is suitable for them.

We commonly find all these ideas in children of ten years of age. They are therefore capable of recognizing in their father and mother four kinds of power. (1) There is a power founded on a superiority of strength, but this is perhaps what they think of least. (2) There is a power founded on the fact of having given them life and by which they are charged with guiding them. It is the power they approve of and consider very differently than that of a robber who would carry off a child and keep him in his cavern. Children do not know how to express themselves on this subject in artful terms. But if they are questioned, one will see by their answers that they know very well a robber does wrong in seizing children who are not his own, but that a father has just reason for commanding those who belong to him. (3) Another power follows on the knowledge of what is to their advantage, and it requires on their part a subordination that will turn out to their own benefit. (4) There is a power that is tempered by love and requires on the child's part a return of affection and acknowledgment. Now the dependence founded on the motives we have described is nothing other than obedience and filial submission.

To these motives let us join the fear of God, a motive capable of acting powerfully in directing children toward the good. Let them be told that God rewards children who obey and punishes the disobedient; their still-fresh souls will open themselves spontaneously at the impression of these salutary maxims. Their nascent reason finds nothing in them to oppose. Depravity has not yet armed them against the force of truth. They do not know that it is the privilege of thinking beings to believe nothing of what vulgar people believe. It would therefore be difficult to find any children whose hearts would be closed to those beautiful sentiments that the Holy Spirit has put into the mouth of the wise man for their instruction:

> Honor your father with all your heart, and forget not the sufferings of your mother. Remember that without them you would not have been at all, and do everything for them as they have done all for you. Listen, children, to the counsels of your father, and follow them that you may be saved. For God has made the father venerable to children, and has appointed over them the authority of the mother. He who fears the Lord will honor his father and mother, and will serve as his masters those who have given him life. Honor your father by actions, by words, by an unlimited patience, that he may bless you, and that his blessing may remain on you to the end. My son, comfort your father in his old age, and cause him no sorrow while he lives. How base is he who abandons his father, and how accursed of God is he who embitters the soul of his mother.[92]

This is not Rousseau's philosophy. But we must at least acknowledge that it is better suited for maintaining the peace, order, and harmony in families, for the formation of men, who from docile children become virtuous citizens, and by that means contribute to the happiness of humankind.

Can we say as much of Rousseau's principle that "no one, not even the father, has a right to command the child what is not for his good"?[93] The author of nature has charged fathers with raising their children, and in charging them with this responsibility, he has invested them with the authority necessary to carry out their duties. But has God, in imposing such a duty on fathers with respect to their children, imposed no duty at all on children with respect to their fathers? If it is just that the father should work for the sake of the child, is it not also just that the child should work for the sake of the father? Why therefore has not the father a right to command his son to do things, which though they may not be of any advantage to the son, may be profitable to the father?

The abuse that one makes of a right does not always justify the privation of the right. A man acts wrongly who squanders his substance at gambling. Shall we say that on this account he has no right to make use of his property? A father ought not to command things absolutely useless. But while he limits himself to the administration of his family, the son is obliged to obey, as long as he can obey without sinning.

In short, it cannot be repeated too often that Rousseau's doctrine is by no means adapted to maintaining peace in families. Teach this lesson to a child, and he will set himself in judgment over all of his father's commands. He will want to know if that which is commanded of him would be of some good for him, and if, taken by some fancy, he were to find that what is commanded of him were of no good to him, then he will decide, trusting the word of Rousseau, that his father has no right to command him. He will disobey, or he will obey with an ill will, murmuring and champing against his father's authority. Can a lesson so dangerous in its consequences be true in its principle? Fathers and mothers who live in the sweet familial union, which Rousseau with so much reason recommends and which he paints so truly and in such charming colors,[94] would, I believe, be quite aggrieved were their children taught that a father has no right to command his son to do any thing that will be of no advantage to him.

It is as a consequence of the same principle that Rousseau establishes the following maxim, which seems to require some correction: "The children remain bound to their father only as long as they need him to survive" (we shall see he should have added: 'and to guide their conduct'). "As soon as this need ceases to exist, the natural bond is dissolved."[95]

A well-respected doctor in the Catholic schools, esteemed by Grotius and Leibnitz, despised by the elegant crowd [*beaux esprits*] who know him only by name, sees this matter in quite a different light, but more consistently with the ends of nature, which is to say, with the designs of Providence. We find it where he deals with the stability of the conjugal bond.[96] I shall only report what immediately relates to my subject. He first observes that in those animals where the female alone is sufficient for nourishing the young, as in the case of quadrupeds that nature has supplied with milk, the male does not remain with the female but immediately quits her. By contrast, in those species where the cooperation of the male is necessary to rear the young, the male does not separate himself from the female until their nurslings are in a condition to do without their assistance. This we see in birds, which nature has not furnished with a reservoir of milk for feeding their young ones. The father and mother go alternately in search of food for them, while one of them always remains in the nest to defend them and guard them from the cold. Now in the human species, the education of children requires, more than in any other, the cooperation of the father and mother. For children need not only nourishment with regard to the body, but instruction with regard to the spirit.

It is also useful to observe that other animals receive from nature an instinct, a kind of art and industry that quickly and invariably directs them to the pursuit of that which is necessary for their preservation and defense. Man alone has received no parallel instinct because reason is meant to serve him as a rule in his conduct. Now reason cannot properly guide him unless it is itself enlightened by prudence.

This is why it is necessary that children remain a long time under the direction of their father and mother who, being instructed by experience, are in a position to share with them the insight they have acquired, in order to form their judgment and teach them as the occasion offers how to conduct themselves in life. This education is particularly necessary at the age in which the body is already grown strong and when the passions begin to have their play. At this age, reason is weak and the passions are violent; this is the time when young people most require restraint and correction. And this care falls particularly to the father, who has the greater maturity for instructing and that greater force for correcting.*[97]

It must be that these ideas are consistent with nature and sound reason, for we see that the better ordered states preserve their customs and, as a consequence, their laws and their power, to the extent that the authority of fathers and the respect for elders, which follows from it, are maintained. It is not necessary to describe the evils that premature liberty of young people is capable of causing.

---

* We add this passage from Montesquieu's *Spirit of Laws* Bk. 23, ch. 2: "Among animals this obligation [to nourish the young] is such that the mother can usually meet it. The obligation is much broader among men: their children partake of reason, but it comes to them by degrees; it is not enough to nourish them, they must also be guided; even when they can sustain their lives, they cannot govern themselves." [Gerdil's note; Cohler trans.]

[PART TWO
Reflections on Particular Educational Practices, and Most Especially on Matters of Curriculum]

[16. *On reasoning with children*]

Let us now return to Rousseau's practical education.[1]

> To reason with children was Locke's great maxim. It is the one most in vogue today. Its success, however, does not appear to me such as to establish its reputation; and, as for me, I see nothing more stupid than these children who have been reasoned with so much. . . . The masterpiece of a good education is to make a reasonable man, and they claim they raise a child by reason! This is to begin with the end, to want to make the product the instrument. If children understood reason, they would not need to be raised.[2]

Locke's maxim is not such a bad one.[3] If success does not always follow, it is because there are too few men (I mean among those who are charged with the education of children) who are capable of reasoning with them as they require. We should not so much lecture children as lead them by the hand. I will explain myself.

By observing the discourse and actions of children, one easily perceives that they begin to exercise the faculty of combining their ideas, of comparing the objects within their grasp, and of arranging them according to their own design. Such is the first effort of reason, which is nothing more than the faculty of arranging, *facultas ordinatrix*. If it happens that their combinations lack proper measure, this defect generally arises from their overlooking some intermediate idea, which their eagerness made them neglect, even though it is usually a simple idea that was easily within their capacities. This is the time to suggest the idea to them, and one will see them make the corrections by their own reasoning. This is the way, it seems to me, one can teach children to reason by reasoning with them. A child scrawling on some paper draws a man and a house: A man is as tall as a house? What could be easier than to make him perceive this error of proportion and teach him to envision objects in their just proportions in order to situate them properly?

The observation of Horace that children confer royalty on those who do the best[4] proves, as we have already observed, that children have the capacity for moral ideas, that they know that merit and preference, reward and punishment are consequences of moral good and evil, duty, authority and obedience. I do not say that these things should be explained to them by abstract definitions, through the method of divisions and subdivisions. But I do say that one must try to render these notions sensible by making them recognizable in particular actions, which bear their character and which will affect them vividly. A child complains to his teacher of some wrong he has suffered at the hand of one of his companions; he wants reparation for his wrong and his companion to be punished. This is a practical circumstance ripe with the opportunity to teach him by his own experience regarding the necessity for a superior authority, which keeps all things in order, prevents the wicked from hurting the good, and to which every one should submit. A thousand similar cases will furnish occasions equally favorable for developing other ideas of morality, and for making sensible to children, in the circumstance of their lives, the motives which ought attach them to virtue and distance them from vice.

Here is an essay, for the sake of example, on some moral ideas that may be suggested to children in practical cases, and which, since they are not at all beyond their capacity, can furnish the subject and the occasion for reasoning with them. By ideas I mean, with

Rousseau, notions determined by relations. Those who might find the following details too minute should consider that we intend to speak the language of children.

1. *If you love your dear mother, you must not displease her.* This notion is simple, yet it is a reasoning, an idea determined by a relation, a means apt for making a child conceive the connection between the sentiments of the soul and the actions which correspond to them.

2. *When you suffer you are glad to be consoled; you should therefore console others.* Here then is the seed of active compassion, a quality that would constitute the happiness of mankind, if it held sway in every heart.

3. *See that man clothed in rags; do you believe yourself better than he because you are better clothed? Don't you know that all men are brothers, and that this poor man, if he is wiser than you, is greater in the eyes of God than you are?* Regardless of the rank into which a child is born, we cannot too often remind him that he is a man. Is he born into misery? Teach him that he is a man, lest his soul be debased. Is he born into grandeur? Teach him that he is a man, lest his soul be puffed up with vanity. Make him aware that he should esteem himself by his quality as a man; let him know that there is no spirit more base than the one that places titles before nature.

4. *If fine trappings were put upon an ass, wouldn't it still be only an ass? It is the same with a child richly clothed; if he is not wise, his clothes do not render him more worthy of esteem.* This maxim is closely related to the previous one.

5. *Do you pretend to know better than others, you who are so young?* Do not let children take on a preemptory tone, and seek out occasions to convince them they are not in a position to judge matters. It is the presumption, even more than the tone, which needs to be corrected.

6. *Is it becoming for a ten years old lad to cry over a small hurt like a child of four? See whether men cry over such small things.* Teach him to overcome sentiments of pain by the sentiment of honor.

7. *Isn't it shameful to throw oneself greedily at one's food, and to eat with the voracity of the animals?* Comparisons that can impress the elevated idea of the dignity of man should not be neglected. It is a remedy that serves equally well against debasement and against haughtiness. It is the source of what the ancients called "decorum" and which I would call decency, if it were not all but reduced to vain exteriority.

8. *If you want your companions to love you, you must be obliging with them.*

9. *See how a person who is surly and quarrelsome is hated by everybody.*

10. *What have you gained by your impatience? You have only worsened your pain. Learn that patience softens pain.*

11. *Aren't you ashamed at wanting to do nothing? Look at this person and that one; they are esteemed because they apply themselves. An idler is scorned by all the world.*

12. *Laborers and artisans are obliged to work to get their bread. Do you imagine that God made the rich so that they might live in idleness? The rich and the poor are equal before God. It is his will that each should work in a manner suited to his station.*

These ideas of morality, I believe, are not above the capacity of children, and they can be successfully employed in particular cases in order to inspire them with a love of virtue and to deter them from vice. But, according to Rousseau, "the masterpiece of a good education is to make a reasonable man, and they claim they raise a child by reason! This is to begin with the end. . . ."⁵ Not at all. The state of reason where education begins is not the state of reason where it ends. Reason is a faculty susceptible of development and progress. When it begins to show itself (fix this period at whatever age you please), it is extremely weak, as much because the mind lacks ideas which are, as it were, the materials of reason, as because it is not exercised in combining them, in finding their relations, and in deducing from them other relations. In this state of imperfection reason has need of being helped and supported, so that it may raise itself by degrees sooner and more certainly to that degree of consistency and maturity that is the chief end of an education. There is neither contradiction nor mystery in this. The chief end of the teacher of penmanship is to teach his pupil to write well, and for this purpose he begins by making him trace out the letters. Will anyone say that he begins with the end? By no means. A child has a natural aptitude for forming letters, but his first attempts are shapeless and rude, and it is under an able teacher that he will eventually attain a sure and light hand. What should we say to a man who would think to disapprove of such a method and would pretend to show that it was beginning at the wrong end by saying in a serious voice, "the chief end of a penmanship teacher's lessons is to teach the pupil to write, and he begins by making him write"? – *Risum teneatis amici* (can you keep from laughing, my friends).[6]

[17. *Rousseau's dialogue misrepresents how to reason morally with a child*]

Rousseau says that,

> By speaking to [children] from an early age a language which they do not understand, one accustoms them to show off with words, to control all that is said to them, to believe themselves as wise as their masters, to become disputatious and rebellious. . . .[7]

This would not be the case with a child with whom Locke would have reasoned. Such unseemly behavior does not take its rise from the method that Rousseau disapproves of, but from the abuse of it by unskillful teachers, who are willing to appear learned at the expense of their pupils. To reason with a child does not consist in teaching him to chatter. Nothing is more pernicious than to want children to appear what they are not and, indeed, what they cannot be.

Rousseau continues this subject:

> This is the formula to which all the lessons in morality that are given, and can be given, to children can just about be reduced:

Teacher. You must not do that.

Child.   And why must I not do it?

Teacher. Because it is bad to do so.

Child.   Bad to do? What is bad to do?

Teacher. What you are forbidden to do.

Child.   What is bad about doing what I am forbidden to do?

Teacher. You are punished for having disobeyed.

Child.   But I will fix it so that nothing is known about it.

Teacher. You will be spied on.

Child.   I shall hide.

Teacher. You will be questioned.

Child.   I shall lie.

Teacher. You must not lie.

Child.   Why must I not lie?

Teacher. Because it is bad to do, etc.

> This is the inevitable circle. Get out of it, and the child
> does not understand you any longer. Is this not most use-
> ful instruction? I would be quite curious to know what
> could be put in the place of this dialogue. Locke himself
> would certainly have been very much at a loss. To know
> good and bad, to sense the reason for man's duties, is not
> a child's affair. [8]

Observe that he is here speaking of a child of ten years of age.

I believe that, without being Locke, we may offer some reflections on this model of a dialogue and even make substitutions for it
in some places.

Teacher. You must not do that.

I note, in the first place, that this first question is too general to
serve as the foundation of the model of a dialogue between a teacher
and a child. We have already seen that we should not reason with

children on abstract and general ideas of good and evil. We need to make them envision good and evil in particular actions and then reason upon those actions. Thus in order to give the model of a dialogue between a teacher and a child, it is necessary to suppose some determinate action which provokes the dialogue, and then allows us to make a particular application of the notion of good and evil and not put us in the position of needing to explain it by vague and general ideas. This is the reason why in Rousseau's dialogue the teacher finds nothing better to say. It should then have begun thus.

Teacher. You must not beat your companion.

Child.   Why shouldn't I?

Teacher. Because it is bad to do so.

Child.   Bad to do? What is it to do bad?

I note in the second place that the child would be more likely to ask: "Why is it bad to do so?" and not "What is it to do bad?" He would be more apt to ask the reason for calling his action bad, rather than for the general explanation of what doing wrong is. But be this as it may, when any particular action is in question, for instance, beating his companion, the teacher will not be at a loss for the following answer.

Teacher. Have you forgotten the complaint you made when someone struck you? Didn't you think he did wrong and that he merited punishment? Now you also do wrong when you beat others, and you deserve to be punished.

This metaphysics is not above the capacity of a ten-year-old child, and it seems well adapted to impress on his mind, by his own experience, this great fundamental maxim in morality: we should not do to others what we would not want them to do to us.

But in order to continue with Rousseau's dialogue, let us imagine another action that is in itself indifferent:

Teacher. You must not go into that room. Why? Because your father has forbidden you.

Child.   What wrong is there in doing what I am forbidden to do?

A child capable of asking such a question has more malice in him than Rousseau imagines. He has a wholly different idea of evil than is attributed to him in this dialogue, to the effect that the wrong consists in doing what he is forbidden. For if he had only this idea of wrong, he would not ask, "What wrong is there in doing what I am forbidden to do?" because were he to have no other idea of wrong than that it consists in doing what he is forbidden to do, it would be the same as if he has said, "Why is it wrong to do what is wrong?" – a question which even children would not think of asking. He would sooner say, "Why may I not do what is wrong," or "Why may I not do what I am forbidden to do?" But by saying, "What wrong is there in doing what I am forbidden to do?" it is evident that he has some notion of wrong or evil that does not depend on the forbidding and that he wants to know what relation that which is forbidden him has to this idea of evil.

Teacher. You will be punished if you disobey.

Before coming to this response, can the teacher find nothing better to say that will convince the child he ought not to disobey his father? It is your father who gave you life. You are indebted to him for what you are; you belong to him. It is his duty to guide you. God wants children to obey their fathers. He promises a long life to those who fulfill this obligation, and he severely punishes those who neglect it. Accordingly, he may say:

Teacher. Is it for the blind to lead those who see, or for those who see to lead blind?

Child. It is for those who see to lead the blind.

Teacher. Very well. You are the blind man, and it is your father who sees.

Child. How so?

Teacher. If you did not have your father, how would you get wheat and make bread? (For examples to convince children of their ignorance, the teacher should appeal to circumstances in which they find themselves.) You are blind with respect to all these necessary matters, and your father knows them all. Besides, he loves you, and does nothing except for your good. It is therefore his part to guide you, and you do wrong in disobeying him.

Let us return to our author's dialogue:

Child. But I will fix it so that nothing is known about it.

Teacher. You will be spied on.

Child. I shall hide.

Teacher. You will be questioned.

Rousseau acknowledges in the later books of *Emile* that the law of nature has sufficient sanction only because of the promise of rewards and punishments in a future life.[9] He condemns the false philosophy of those who in their morality believe they can dispense with the will of the Supreme Lawgiver. It is very strange that a father or a teacher should not use the motive of the fear of God in order to prevent children from doing wrong, especially when they think they can conceal it. It flies in the face of experience to pretend that children of ten years old are not susceptible of this fear. If one does not take care to teach it to them at a very early age, we may bid farewell to every hope of integrity throughout their lives.

Let us substitute a different response:

Teacher. Though you may hide yourself from the eyes of man, God will see you and punish you.

But let us keep close to the original dialogue:

Teacher. You will be questioned.

Child. I shall lie.

Teacher. You must not lie.

Child. Why must I not lie?

Teacher. Because it is bad to do, etc.

Would it not be better to say: Suppose someone was to give you a bag, saying there were in it some candied almonds, and when you eagerly open it in hopes of a gift, you find nothing but pebbles. Don't you think it wrong that they told you a lie? Do you see, then, whether it is wrong to lie? Or better: Aren't you full of shame when you are caught in a lie? Note how you feel it wrong to speak contrary to what you yourself think.

I have not attempted to give here a model of a dialogue. Locke could have done it. What I have said, however, is sufficient to show that it is not impossible and that without falling into vicious circles and without reaching beyond the capacity of children, we can make them discern good and evil in particular actions and also comprehend the moral reasons for their duties.

One of the best methods of reasoning with children is to make them envision in examples the good they ought to do and the evil they should avoid. Such was the method of Horace's virtuous father in the education of his son. Horace has himself given us a most instructive account of it in the fourth satire of his first book.[10] Coste says that it is a passage that cannot be read too often by those who are entrusted with the raising of children.[11] They should know it by heart and have it always present to mind.

[18. *On a child's capacity for handling ideas*]

As to the studies proper for children, Rousseau condemns out of hand all that has been to this day practiced by the most able teachers, ancient and modern. Fables, languages, history, geography, chronology, geometry – none of them, in his opinion, is proper for children under twelve or fifteen years of age. I acknowledge that there are many abuses in the methods of teaching all these things, particularly in private educations. And it is not without reason that our author bitterly laments the unhappy success of these frivolous methods that only tend to form "young doctors and old children"[12] or those "little prodigies who shine for an hour and are never heard of again."[13] This topic was already treated in a work printed some years ago in Italy. Permit me to append some passages from the treatise at the end of this work. [14]

Nevertheless, it is not right to proscribe absolutely the use of things, which can be good, on the pretext that their abuse is harmful.

Let us therefore see if in all these studies which Rousseau indiscriminately rejects there is not something that children can be taught.

In the first place, we agree with him in one principle which cannot be emphasized too much, namely, that children should not be accustomed to be content with words and to believe themselves capable because they can repeat things which they do not understand. One should not introduce them to sciences of which it is impossible to give them exact concepts. The first strokes that form the outline of a picture cannot be too accurate. If you fail in these first sketches, the most brilliant and rich colors will not conceal the lack of proportion; they will only make the deformity more apparent. Indeterminate notions serve only to confuse the minds of children. They teach them nothing, and they limit the possibility of learning anything afterwards, because the false ideas they receive will always thwart what true ideas we would have in their stead. The first impression always resists the second, and what takes shape is always a disfigured, composite impression.

The method of preserving children from so harmful a consequence is not to keep the intellectual faculties of children in a state of total inaction, as Rousseau prescribes, for this would only expose them to adopt the false notions of the objects which surround them. We cannot prevent curiosity in a child by refusing him instruction: the child will reason, but he will reason badly. Let us avoid extremes, and though we do not want to form pedants, let us apply ourselves to the instruction of children. Let us discover the range of their mind, strive to sustain their curiosity, and never be afraid of teaching them what is proportionate to their capacities. Let us take the prudent caution always to proceed slowly and to check to see if with each step forward we have made ourselves intelligible and if we have been effectively understood.

Rousseau responds that it is precisely at this point where one usually fails:

Apparent facility at learning is the cause of children's ruin. It is not seen that this very facility is the proof they learn nothing. Their brain, smooth and polished, returns, like a mirror, the objects presented to it. But nothing remains; nothing penetrates. The child retains the words; the ideas are reflected off of him. Those who hear him understand them; only he does not understand them.[15]

He adds:

Before the age of reason the child receives not ideas but images; and the difference between the two is that images are only absolute depictions of sensible objects while ideas are notions of objects determined by relations. . . . When one imagines, one does nothing but see; when one conceives, one is comparing.[16]

Let us agree with these remarks; they will serve as a rule for us to distinguish whether a child does or does not conceive, whether he has or does not have ideas. If I explain to a child the nature of a multiple number, and he repeats the definition I have explained, this is not sufficient to allow me to confirm that he has formed the idea. I ask him what numbers are six, eight, and twelve the multiples of, and he finds them one after the other. Not content with this proof, I ask him once more what are the sub-multiples of twenty-five, thirty-six, and forty-eight; he considers a little, and finds some, mistakes others, perceives his mistake, recollects himself, corrects his error, finds them, and is convinced that he has found them. I can have no reason therefore to doubt that this child has conceived what I have explained to him. He has notions determined by relations; he compares. By Rousseau's rule, then he conceives and has ideas. I offer him an image; he distinguishes the parts and forms them in new combinations. This is more than a smooth and polished mirror that can only reflect the light; it is rather a prism, which is penetrated by the light and does not reflect it, until it has modified it.

Rousseau was aware that one might object to him that children learn the elements of geometry. He answers that this is in his favor:

Far from knowing how to reason by themselves, little

geometers do not even know how to retain the reasonings of others. For follow them in their method, and you see immediately that they have retained only the exact impression of the figure and the terms of the demonstration. At the least new objection they can no longer follow. Turn the figure upside down; they can no longer follow. Their entire learning is in sensation; nothing has gone through to the understanding.[17]

We deal here with a fact, which is rather easy to verify in an age that is perhaps more taken with the spirit of the geometer than the philosopher. Let us follow the little geometers who study under good teachers, and I am certain we shall be in a position to convince ourselves that they do more than see the figures and retain the sounds. Some understand very well what is taught them, and what is more important, they acquire through these first impressions a habitude, a propensity, and a disposition of mind that put them in a position to subsequently make great progress. In all likelihood, there are few good geometers who did not begin their course of geometry at a very early age. Rousseau should have been silent on this topic. The true method of teaching mathematics has been known for a long time. Emile may be a great man, a greater man than "one of these men of our days: a Frenchman, an Englishman, a bourgeois, . . . a nothing,"[18] but unquestionably he will never be a greater geometer than Archimedes or Newton.

J. Terrasson, in his *Sethos*, says:

> Childhood has the particular advantage that we know perfectly only those sciences and arts whose early difficulties we overcome at that age. And to take an unfortunate example from my personal experience, I will confess that though I have tried at different times of my life to acquire the kind of knowledge so highly esteemed among the Greeks, in a manner satisfactory to myself, I only know how to read and write, because they are the only arts whose difficulties I overcame in my childhood.[19]

This modest admission of a wise man should serve as a counterpoise to the somewhat rash assertions of our philosopher. This part of his system is very well adapted to encourage the negligence of fathers with regard to the instruction of their children. What can be more suitable to a negligent father than to hear from the mouth of a philosopher that the best thing to be done with children is to do nothing? He will hardly fail to adopt a maxim so agreeable to his predominant inclination, and he will believe himself a philosopher precisely because he is indolent.*

[19. *On teaching fables*]

Let us turn now to some details regarding the studies that are appropriate for children: "Emile," says Rousseau, "will never learn anything by heart, not even fables, not even those of La Fontaine."[20] To say that it is absolutely improper for children to learn anything by heart is too sweeping a claim; and if we can teach them some good thing, why should we neglect this means of strengthening their memory through its exercise and of filling their minds with good things?

> How can people be so blinded as to call fables the morality of children? They do not think about how the apologue, in giving enjoyment to children, deceives them; about how, seduced by the lie, they let the truth escape; about how what is done to make the instruction agreeable to them prevents them from profiting from it. Fables can instruct men, but the naked truth has to be told to children. When one starts covering the truth with a veil, they no longer make the effort to lift it.[21]

Plato, the philosopher so much esteemed by Rousseau for his thoughts on education, recommends that nurses teach their children Aesop's fables.[22] They are not deceived by being amused with these

---

* "Keep his soul idle for long as possible" [*Emile* 2.69 (B, 94)]. And here again is another maxim analogous to it, and not less singular: "You will never get to the point of producing wise men if you do not in the first place produce rascals" [*Emile* 2.164 (B, 119)]. [Gerdil's note.]

innocent fictions. A child of eight or ten years of age, who hears the fable of the wolf and the lamb for the first time, is not deceived by it. He knows very well that the wolf and the lamb never spoke. The veil, which covers truth in this apologue, does not need to be removed. It is transparent; it allows the truth to appear in a totality, and it gives it features that are more affecting. Dryly tell a child that the strong should not oppress the weak: so unadorned a truth will make a minimal impression on his mind, and still less on his heart. Abstract and general maxims are of no use to him. Such discourse does not affect him; he does not listen to it. But bring the wolf and the lamb on the stage, and he is immediately roused. He does not ask for anything better than to listen to you. He is attentive to you throughout, always with emotion, sometimes with transport. You see him moved at the fate of the lamb; he wants to snatch it from the ravenous jaws of the rapacious animal. Such is the effect that this fable will generally produce in children.

Even if it would only present to them "an image [that] can stand alone in the mind [without an idea],"[23] it would still be an innocent amusement, and it is no small matter to find amusement for children from which we have nothing to fear. But there is more. This image conveys ideas and sentiments. The child is really touched with the innocence of the lamb, with his mildness, with the candor of his answers, and he pities his weakness. Through his concern for the lamb, he learns to love those qualities that make him amiable. By contrast, in detesting the ferocious beast who devours the lamb, he conceives horror and aversion for his arrogance, his brutality, his injustice, and all the other qualities that render the wolf so odious. There is no child who is not struck with the contrast that this fable presents between the mildness of the lamb and the brutality of the wolf. The mind of the child therefore receives more than a simple image. He perceives the relations between the different qualities of the wolf and the lamb; he distinguishes and compares them. He receives, therefore, ideas, and these ideas are accompanied by an active sentiment which interests him in favor of innocence and inspires him with a horror of cruelty, and makes him detest the unjust power that abuses force by oppressing the innocent. Unadorned truth would not have such power.

Talk plainly to a child of the beauty of virtue and the ugliness of vice, and his imagination will not be moved, it will receive nothing, and nothing will pass on to the understanding. If you would have the child understand, personify virtue and vice. Put them into action. Show them to him clothed in their proper characters in the behavior of the wolf and the lamb. You will not need to tell the child that virtue is loveable and brutality is hateful; he will see it, he will feel it, and he will judge the difference between these qualities by the different impressions they make on him.

Let Aesop's fables follow the nurse's stories, advises the judicious Quintilian, who united sound judgment with consummate experience. They should first learn to tell them with a lively voice in a pure but familiar style; afterwards allow them to exercise themselves by putting them in writing.[24]

The good Rollin, worthy imitator of Quintilian, though perhaps with less genius and less philosophy, does not openly declare himself on the usefulness of fables. He outlines in a few words the character of the principal fabulists:

> The fables of Aesop are bare of every ornament and embellishment, but they are full of sense, and within the capacity of little children for whose use they were written. Those of Phaedrus are more elevated in tone and more elaborated, but they have a simplicity and elegance, greatly resembling the Atticism of the simple style; that is to say, whatever was most refined and delicate among the Greeks. La Fontaine, who well understood that the French language was not capable of that simplicity and elegance, enlivened his fables with a naïve and original style, unique to himself, and which no one has yet been able to imitate. It is not easy to understand why Seneca in fact says that in his time the Romans had not yet tried their hand at this kind of composition. Were the fables of Phaedrus unknown to him?[25]

We may then say with Rollin that the fables of Aesop are within the capacity of children. One might only wish that some fine writer would try to put them into French in the style that Quintilian wished for them to be rendered into Latin, namely in a style that is pure, but simple and familiar. In such a work, one must scrupulously adhere to the most essential aspect of language, which is beyond doubt, the propriety of terms. Every figurative or ambiguous expression should be avoided. Each thing should be called by its own proper name, and each word should be given the precise meaning that is appropriate to it. I know that a figurative style is used by good writers to give more energy, more grace, and more vivacity to their discourse. But I also know that in ordinary usage it is often employed out of necessity when we must make ourselves understood but really do not know how to say what we want. When we are at a loss for a proper term to express our thoughts, we borrow a figure, which by a kind of analogy serves to reveal to others the idea that we do not know how to express. This vague, confused, and indeterminate usage which we often make of a single term to express different ideas, or of different terms to express the same idea, is perhaps one of the causes of the imperceptible alteration of language. A collection of fables that could serve as a model of the plain narrative style and in which the propriety of terms would be exactly observed would in a great measure remedy this problem. Children would learn from this work the value of words and would as a consequence know how to make proper use of them. Such a work could only come from a good pen, and many would profit from it.

The fables of Phaedrus are much more elevated than those we attribute to Aesop, and are for that reason less suited to children. After all, it was not for them that he wrote. He meant for his work to please people of taste by adding elegance of style to the matter, which he had taken from Aesop. This is apparent from his prologues and from the responses he makes to his critics, where he defends himself against the charge of being a mere transcriber and attributes to himself the honor of having perfected the genre that Aesop had only sketched. The frequent use of the poetical style eclipses in so many of his fables the propriety of terms, which is however the most necessary part for children who are learning a language. Phaedrus is not in Latin what Aesop is in Greek. His fables are not for children, according to Quintilian's criteria.

It is perhaps because of this consideration that Seneca thinks that the Romans were not yet proficient in this genre of composition. The passage in Seneca is as follows. "I do not have the audacity to encourage you to take up, with your customary stylistic grace, the fables and apologues of Aesop, a work not yet attempted by the Romans." He had been praising Polybius, the favorite of Claudius, for having translated Homer and Virgil, that is to say, Homer into Latin and Virgil into Greek. He seems to wish (for this book of Seneca is a monument of the basest flattery) that Polybius would also apply himself to the fables of Aesop, by translating them into Latin. Pincianus would have us read "*convertas*" instead of "*connectas*,"[26] but by retaining the last mentioned word, we may say that Seneca exhorts Polybius to add the fables to Homer and Virgil, which he had already translated. Seneca wanted something in the style of Aesop, and Phaedrus was not at all in the style of Aesop. Perhaps, however, Seneca did not count Phaedrus as a Roman, since he was born in Thrace. We know Phaedrus had been forgotten for a long time. Perhaps he would have been better known had he chosen to be more simple and had he been content to be the Aesop of the Latins. He did not realize that though he put himself beyond the sphere of children by virtue of his style he was brought back within it because of his subject matter, with the result that he was read by neither the young nor the old. Those who want philosophy in Latin verse take up Horace and lay aside Phaedrus.

Phaedrus only elevated his style; La Fontaine knew to elevate his subject. His fables are not mere fables, but characters and animated pictures, representing the theater of human life. He not only paints the virtues, vices, passions, and all of the moral qualities in the determining and salient features that characterize them, but he also excels in depicting the characters which result from the various combinations and the modifications they receive as a result of the customs and practices of society. By showing men how they feign to appear, he reveals how they really are. He knows how to combine to an extraordinary degree two qualities that seem hardly compatible, namely, subtlety [*finesse*] and simplicity [*naïvité*]: it is his capacity for uniting the subtlety of allusion with the truth of expression. We must admit that all this is well adapted to excite the admiration of people of taste, and it is nonetheless suitable for the instruction and amusement of the younger ages. It is true that La Fontaine frequently makes use of expressions that are now obsolete; it is a great disadvantage to children raised in foreign lands. Though in France, the ordinary style of conversation can serve them as a corrective and rule for common usage.

Notwithstanding all this, I am persuaded that children can profit from reading many of La Fontaine's fables. They will not understand the whole, but they will understand something, and this little will contribute to their pleasure and instruction. Rousseau attempts to prove the contrary by the analysis he makes of the fable of the Crow and the Fox, which he regards as La Fontaine's masterpiece. I shall proceed to make a few observations on his analysis.

In the first place I say that the subject is not beyond their scope. Children are fond of praise; we can therefore teach them what flattery is. They are also quite pleased to have a little money either to keep or to buy toys or candied almonds. We can also help them understand that there are rich people silly enough to want to be flattered, and, instead of sharing their wealth with those who are needy and deserving, which would be to their great honor, they lavish handfuls on those who are base enough to flatter them. There are always clever people who know how to turn the foolishness of the rich to their advantage and who, after getting their money, make fun of them in the market-place. The craft of these flatterers is, however, a vile and shameful business, which makes them despised by all honest people. There is nothing in all this that cannot be made sensible to children by providing sufficient particulars.

But let us take up Rousseau's analysis.[27]

The Crow and the Fox.
A Fable.

Master Crow, on a tree perched.

Master! What does this word signify in itself? What does it signify in the front of a proper name? What meaning has it on this occasion?[28]

Master is a word with several meanings. Before a proper name it is a title given to artisans, as Master John the Cobbler. It is something less than *Monsieur*, which is added to a surname and given to persons of higher stature. Master Crow and Master Fox, in this fable, signify that they are people of modest condition. A child knows all this and distinguishes very well between Master Robert the gardener, *Monsieur* the Judge and *Monsieur* the Officer.

What is a Crow?[29]

It is an animal that is not too uncommon. If a child has never seen one, show him one. It is necessary for children learn to recognize the different things that exist. It is a very important part of their education.

Held in his beak a cheese.

What cheese? Was it a Swiss cheese, a Brie, or a Dutch? If the child has not seen crows, what do you gain by speaking to him about them?[30]

Should we wait until a child has seen a whale before we talk with him about it?

If he has seen them, how will he conceive of their holding a cheese in their beak? Let us always make images according to nature.[31]

Excellent advice. But this is not outside the bounds of nature. All cheeses are not made so large as those of Gruiéres or Lodi. There are some made so small that a crow might very well hold one in its beak.

Master Fox by the odor atticed.

Another master! but to this one the title really belongs: he is a past-master in the tricks of his trade. One has to say what a fox is and distinguish its true nature from the conventional character it has in fables.[32]

Here is another opportunity for instructing your pupil in the facts of natural history. It is not lost time. A child is in the world; it is good that he recognize the beings that surround him.

"Atticed by the odor of a cheese!" This cheese held by crow perched on a tree must have quite an odor to be smelled by the fox in a copse or in his hole! Is this the way you give your pupil practice in that spirit of judicious criticism which does not allow itself to be impressed except by real likelihoods and knows how to discern truth from lie in others' narrations?[33]

Rousseau is not ignorant of the indisputable proofs which natural history provides of the subtle sense of smell that many animals possess. There are so many very curious facts on this subject that might be conveyed to Emile. Knowledge of this sort, altogether instructive and entertaining in itself, will serve to give Emile practice in the most important and judicious critical spirit of not regarding our own senses as the measure of the reality or activity of objects. Common people judge the propagation of a quality such as heat or odor by the impression it makes on them. They believe there is neither heat nor odor when they cease to perceive the heat and the odor. This is a common error, which seems to have guided the pen of our author on this occasion. At the distance of ten paces he does not smell a cheese, therefore its odor does not extend farther. He allows himself to be misled by this evidence, and surely this is not on the basis of good grounds. Although to speak truly, the effect of critical judgment would be to not allow oneself to be misled at all. To allow oneself to be misled on the basis of solid grounds – is it not the same thing as to deceive oneself with reason?

> *Made to him a speech of this kind.*

A speech! Foxes speak, then? They speak, then, the same language as crows? Wise preceptor, be careful. Weigh your response well before making it. It is more important than you think.[34]

A child of ten years of age knows that a crow croaks and does not speak; that a fox yelps and does not speak. He knows that all this language is a fiction in order to make the fox represent a cunning flatterer and the crow a silly fool.

> *Well, good day, Monsieur Crow!*

Monsieur! A title that the child sees used derisively even before he knows that it is a title of honor. Those who say "Monsieur du Crow" will have a lot of explaining to do before they explain that *du*.[35]

What child does not know that *Monsieur* is a title of honor? He gives it to the friends of the household and not to the servants. A child educated in France knows that *de* or *du* is granted to persons of rank. *Monsieur Crow* is a bourgeois name; *Monsieur du Crow* signifies nobility. One remarks to him that the fox, anxious to flatter the crow, affects to treat him with greater respect by calling him *Monsieur du Crow*, instead of simply saying Master Crow.

> *How charming you are! How handsome you seem to me!*

Padding, useless redundancy. The child, seeing the same things repeated in other terms, learns slovenly speech.

Rousseau is fastidious and imposes a rather strict law in his conversations with Emile!

> If you say that the redundancy is part of the author's art and belongs to the plan of the fox who wants to appear to multiply the praises with words, this excuse will be good for me but not for my pupil.[36]

When a child turns to caresses to obtain a favor, see if he does not know to vary his expressions and his praises. Tell him that this is a well-known piece of cunning, that is the part played by the fox in order to get into the good graces of the crow.

Without lying, if your song

Without lying! One lies sometimes, then? Where will the child be if you teach him that the fox says "without lying" only because he is lying?[37]

No need to fear this. There is no harm in the child's knowing at an early age that there are wicked people in the world. Tell him there are people of bad faith, who lie and deceive and who, the better to cover their intentions, assume the appearances of integrity. Tell him that these scoundrels are found out sooner or later, that they are detested by the whole world, that they are shunned as the pests of society, that nobody will have any dealings with them, and that they become the horror and abomination of mankind. This lesson will not be wasted.

Corresponds to your plumage,

Corresponds! What does this word signify? Teach the child to compare qualities so different as voice and plumage. You will see how he will understand you![38]

To correspond here signifies to agree with. The ideas of agreement, of fitness and of symmetry, very naturally enter into the minds of children. They see examples of them in the works of nature and of art; and since they are imitators they endeavor to copy them in their play. Nothing is easier than to make a child understand whether there is symmetry in the arrangement of some furniture or in the construction of a pasteboard house, which he has made, whether, for instance, one window corresponds to another; and the reason why. As to the plumage and the voice, it is not a matter of comparing these two qualities with respect to one another in order to find a correspondence between colors and sounds. The affair is much more simple. Make a child observe that his goldfinch has a beautiful plumage and also a beautiful voice, but that, to the contrary, the peacock has a beautiful plumage, but a disagreeable voice. The child will immediately comprehend, that in the goldfinch the voice agrees with the plumage insofar as his voice delights the ear and his plumage charms the eye, and that this agreement is not at all found in the peacock, whose plumage pleases the eye, but whose voice is disagreeable to the ear. By comparing these qualities, not one with the other, but inasmuch as they agree in giving pleasure, the child will find no difficulty in conceiving how the voice may be comparable to the beauty of the plumage.

> *You would be the Phoenix of the landlords of these woods.*

The Phoenix! What is a phoenix? Here we are cast suddenly into antiquity's lies, almost into mythology.[39]

What harm would there be in describing this mythical bird?

> *At these words the Crow cannot contain his joy.*

One must have already experienced very lively passions to have a feeling for this proverbial expression.[40]

I dare to say that it can only be fully felt in childhood, at that age in which the soul has frequently no sentiment of itself other than that of the joy which penetrates it, which inundates it, a joy pure and unmixed, which is not troubled by the unhappy remembrance of the past nor by gloomy worries over the future, a joy which springs from the inmost soul, which is like the first blossoming of a being that begins to know itself and to enjoy the novelty of its existence. Such is not the tumultuous pleasure of excited passions. It is not the joy of a riper age, of the age when the more attached we are to existence the less we enjoy the pleasure of existing, when joy becomes like a stranger to the soul; rushing through it only at intervals and always against the background of boredom and disgust. Can we then know the meaning of this proverbial expression without recollecting what happened in childhood?

And to show his fine voice

> Do not forget that to understand this verse and the whole fable, the child ought to know what the crow's fine voice is.[41]

The child needs to know that a crow croaks disagreeably, but also that, since in the fable he plays the character of a fool, he ridiculously imagines he has a fine voice and a will to parade it.

He opens his big beak, lets fall his prey.

> This verse is admirable. The harmony alone produces an image. I see a big ugly beak opened; I hear the cheese falling through the branches. But this sort of beauty is lost on children.[42]

I have seen children responsive to this image before they understood that it was only an image constructed for a story. Do you not seem to see, we might say to a child, the crow open his large beak and the cheese, which he drops, falls through the branches? Have no doubt about effect of this picture on a lively imagination. Point out to him that he is listening to a story, but that, nevertheless, it is as if he saw the things happen before his eyes. Then tell him what an image is, and he will understand you.

The Fox grabs it and says: My good monsieur,

> Here, then, goodness is already transformed into stupidity. Assuredly, no time is lost in instructing children.[43]

It is not necessary to become so subtle. We may point out to the child that the fox, after seizing the cheese, mocks the crow. What is more suitable as a precaution against flattery and against the folly of those who lap it up? What is more proper for making a child aware of how laughable the character of the crow is and how odious that of the fox?

> *Learn that every flatterer lives at the expense*
> *of the one who listens to him.*

General maxim. We can no longer follow.[44]

We can indeed follow, because this general maxim is applied to a particular case.

> *The Crow, ashamed and embarrassed*

Another pleonasm; but this one is inexcusable.[45]

So be it. But what great harm is there in a pleonasm?

> *Swore, but a little late, that he would not be caught that way again*

> *Swore!* Who is the fool of a teacher who dares to explain to the child what an oath is?[46]

This must certainly be explained to him, if he is to learn his catechism. I am aware that Rousseau will allow no catechism, but it is a paradox contrary to religion and to sound philosophy.* What we have

---

* "I do not know which our catechisms lead to most – impiety or fanaticism – but I certainly know that they necessarily lead to one or the other" [*Emile* 4.76 (B, 378)]. And, in another place, he says, "all the answers in the catechism are misconceived. It is the pupil who teaches the teacher. In the mouths of children these answers are really lies, since the children expound what they do not understand and affirm what they are not in a position to believe. Even among the most intelligent men, show me those who do not lie in saying their catechism" [ibid.]. A man born blind can by no means conceive what he hears said relative to light and colors. The manner and effect of vision are to him incomprehensible riddles. Yet he does not entertain the least doubt that by means of their sight men can perceive objects at a considerable distance; that the interposition of a glass is sufficient to make them appear sometimes

already said regarding the moral ideas of which children are capable is more than sufficient to demonstrate its falsity.

Fables are of immediate use to children and may be of still greater advantage at a future time. They are like so many aphorisms or emblems of human life. Each moral is the result of a long series of observations through which we learn the ways men act under various circumstances and what consequences follow from them. I do not want to say here that for young people fables can substitute for experience. I only say that they will serve to make experience more useful to them by starting them to reflect on the various occurrences of life. In order to profit from experience, one must know how to bring particular cases back to a law or to a common principle, so as to discover its connection and dependence. This is chiefly how general rules serve in the sciences and the arts. How many people pass their whole lives and see the daily occurrences, without ever thinking to connect events that follow one another, in order to discover their causes and consequences? Such people seem to have experience, but they do not have it. They have seen much, but have observed nothing. It is the faculty of reflecting and combining that constitutes the principal difference between man and man. This excellent faculty requires assistance. All men have more or less the need for an advisor to provoke them to reflect. This is how the study of fables may be of great use to young people. When they begin to venture into the world, they usually see the outside of the things that happen. A youth will witness a hundred events, which will be for him particular or isolated cases, for he will see among them no principle, connection,

larger, sometimes smaller; that a looking-glass represents man in his proper form, and imitates all his actions and motions; and that a painter, by disposing his colors on canvas, causes all the objects in nature to appear in relief on a plane surface. These are things which a blind man hears every day mentioned, which he by no means conceives, and which he yet believes. Nothing then can be more absurd than the metaphysical principle of unbelievers that we cannot believe or affirm anything we cannot conceive. I attempted to clarify this in my book *Introduzione allo studio della Religione (Introduction to the Study of Religion)*. [Gerdil's note] or dependence. He finds it beyond his capacity to draw some general induction that can serve as a rule in his conduct. A great deal of time will pass before he begins to know how to make use of his experience. But because fables allude to the various situations of human life, it may happen that an event, which of itself would not have made a proper impression on the mind of a youth, may call to mind for him the fable that relates to it. The moral of this fable, which until then had only been for him a vague and indeterminate maxim, will at this point present itself concretely in the application to the particular case that he encounters. He will learn in practice, so to say, the moral that he previously had only understood in theory. It will serve him as a rule to discern what spirits move men to action in given circumstances, what things he needs to be watchful for, and how he ought to conduct himself. It will be the first link of the chain, to which will be joined all the other similar cases.*

[20. *On the study of languages, and especially Latin*]

With respect to the ancient languages, I find it rather useless to make children study them before the age of eleven or twelve years, particularly in private educations.[47] At this age a child will learn as much

---

* Rousseau acknowledges fables have this use, but then he would have the reading of them deferred to the time when men are liable to commit errors, that is to say, to the time when fables will afford little of either amusement or advantage [*Emile* 4.140 (B, 247)]. Little children are amused by the spectacle of fables, and those who are mature prefer the moral. But youth, at the age when the passions begin to bear sway, are not amused by this kind of spectacle and the moral bores them. We should arm youth against the impetuosity of their passions, if we want to prevent their precipitating themselves into errors, which frequently cannot afterwards be remedied. The ancients said, "*Principiis obsta . . .*" This is an axiom, the truth of which experience will always confirm. [Gerdil's note.] [See for example, Ovid, *Remedia Amoris*, vv. 91–92: "*Principiis obsta: sero medicina paratur / cum mala per longas convaluere moras*" (Put off at the beginning, the cure is readied too late, since the disease has become rooted).]

in a year as he would have imperfectly learned earlier in four or five years, and then only with trouble and disgust.

I agree that if the study of languages were only the study of words – that is to say, of figures or the sounds which express them – it could be suitable to children. But in changing the signs, languages also modify the ideas which these signs represent.[48]

It is true that the different arrangement of signs in different languages often gives a different twist, a different imprint to thoughts that are quite similar to one another. But the arrangement or use of signs is one thing; and the primitive, basic establishment of the signs is another. For example, that the endings of the declensions or conjugations be one way rather than another, this will have no influence on our thoughts. They are arbitrary signs necessary to agree upon in order to form a language and to speak it. But it is not in these that the language consists, but in the phrase, in the arrangement of these signs, which in expressing the thought, modify it and give it an imprint it would not have had in any other arrangement. This is the reason that in every language there is but one way of properly expressing a thought. I shall readily acknowledge that the phraseology of a foreign language is beyond the capacity of a child if he has not learned it by familiar usage.

But the basic formation of signs and their reduction into certain classes based on their different endings are facts established by convention, and their study is only a matter of words. This study is extremely necessary, but at the same time extremely distasteful to those of a maturer age, and consequently more fitting for consuming the tedium of childhood, which has nothing better to do and cannot be better employed. This exercise of the memory will enable a child at the age of twelve or thirteen years to begin reading good authors where he will learn the phraseology of the language.

Besides the exercise of the memory, grammar furnishes several notions within the capacity of children and which may be regarded as the first steps into logic, especially apt for rendering ideas with accuracy and precision. In this manner, they can learn to distinguish the names that signify things from those that signify the qualities of things, as well as names that signify real objects from those that signify abstracted beings formed by the intellect. They can be brought to understand what is the subject and the attribute of the proposition and how they are connected by the substantive verb; how the other verbs add an idea of action to the idea of affirmation; what is the object of a verb, and a hundred things of the same nature. These notions, readily grasped by children when they are properly explained to them, serve equally to form both reason and language.

> It is to hide this ineptitude of theirs that they are by preference trained in the dead languages, of which there are no more judges to whom one can have recourse. The familiar usage of these languages having been lost, one is satisfied with imitating what is found in written books. And that is what is called speaking them.[49]

Rousseau says that he would rather deal in paradoxes than prejudices, yet he adopts a prejudice founded on the authority of some celebrated writers who would not have us write in Latin today. The reason they give is that if Virgil or Cicero could read the works of our best Latinists, they would undoubtedly smile at them and find in them many strange phrases. Of this I have not the least doubt, but I doubt whether the consequence deduced from it is sound. These are my reasons. Though Latin is a dead language, men of letters still make sufficient progress in it to have a real feel for the beauties of Cicero and Virgil. I do not say that they are in a position to penetrate the genius of the language or to understand it as perfectly as did the court of Augustus. But certainly the character, the taste, and the subtlety [*finesse*] of the language need not be unknown to those who are capable of feeling and appreciating the most beautiful passages of the Prince of Poets and the Prince of Orators. Quintilian said that he who tastes the beauties of Cicero knows he has made some progress in the Latin language.[50] Now it is a fact that today there are people whose Latin permits them to taste the style of Cicero and distinguish it from the style of writers of a debased Latin.

It is another fact that they who have acquired this perfect knowledge of Latin cannot help admiring the style of Paulus Manutius, for example, or Fracastoro[51] and find it so much like that of Cicero and Virgil that they can hardly perceive any difference.

There are, then, at this time, two methods of writing Latin: one in a style that at first is hard to recognize as Latin, and the other in a style that the greatest connoisseurs can hardly distinguish from that of the best Latin. Now there must surely be some merit in knowing how to imitate the style of the ancients so well that the most able experts can be deceived.

But of what use, one might ask, is this imitation of style, which is only apparent and always leaves room for questioning the exactitude of its conformity? I admit that this doubt has some foundation, and I am persuaded that to learn the Latin language we should not take the modern Latinists as our model but only the original ancients. However I think that in order to preserve a taste for the Latinity, there should always be some masters who make it their particular study and possess it to a superior degree. Now no one can possess a language well if he does not practice writing it, and no person would want to practice it, if by such practice, instead of acquiring esteem, he earned only contempt. This is not to say that everyone who wants to master Latin, in order to be able to taste the good authors, need aspire to write it with as much purity as Bembo or Sadoleto.[52] Yet it is necessary at the least that they be instructed and directed by teachers of consummate ability, who make them feel in their reading of the authors the character and genius of the language, and who through their instruction make up for lack of the exercise, which perhaps is not suitable for everyone. But if everyone in a country were content with learning only so much Latin as would enable them to understand the good authors, we would arrive at the point where no one could any longer perceive the beauties of the language, and no one could tell the difference between the commentaries of Caesar and the chronicles of Sigebert de Gembloux.[53]

Moreover it is important to preserve a taste for good Latin. The testimony of eighteen centuries sufficiently proves that Caesar, Cicero, Virgil and Horace, Titus Livy, and Sallust are good models. I do not say that we should slavishly copy them and do only what they have already done. This would be labor lost, since we could not excel them. But with regard to whatever subject we would deal with or whatever novelty, whether with respect to the matter or the plan, we would produce, we cannot learn better from anyone than them how to think and to write soundly, how to proportion the style to the subject, to put each thing in its place, to develop our ideas and dispose them with precision and grace, and to beautify nature with those embellishments that do not depart from nature . The ancients have not exhausted all the forms, all the possible species of the true and the beautiful, but they have, as it were, fixed the limits. They are limits which leave a vast field for the new and original works of great genuis, but which cannot be exceeded without falling into error. In an academy for sculpture, when the finest pieces of Grecian antiquity are placed before the eyes of the young artists, they are not enjoined to make only what they see, but to make everything in the taste of what is before them. It is the same for works of the mind. Dante, Boccaccio, Petrarch, Ariosto, Della Casa,[54] Galileo, etc. have enriched the Italian literature with such noble works only because they nourished themselves by reading the ancients. They have become perfect models only because they had been perfect imitators. It would have been vain for them to have found the richest material in the fecundity of their genius, in the revolutions of their countries, in the customs of their times, or in the new discoveries of philosophy – they could not have composed such noble works – had they not learned from the ancients the art of putting these things into a work. The neglect of antiquity in the seventeenth century was followed in Italy with an almost total extinction of every kind of literature. In the beginning of the eighteenth the ancients were again consulted and the taste revived. It is the age of Augustus and the ages when ancient Greece flourished that have formed age of Louis XIV. Racine, Molière, Despreaux, Bossuet, and Fénelon[55] attest to it.

In other times men have endeavored to free themselves from the yoke of imitation. They have disdained to travel along the path too much beaten by the ancients. These spirited geniuses [*beaux esprits*] would open new routes; they would have only themselves as guides, but yet serve as guides to others. What has been the result? Have they really created anything new, whether for good or for evil? Haven't they fallen back into affectation, antitheses, and word play, into overly refined thoughts, into stiff, forced expressions, in a word, into all the defects that other ages experienced when caprice was substituted for imitation. It is necessary to stress that the human spirit is limited in its digressions, as well as in its progress. The writer who is most jealous of thinking exclusively in his own way will find that, without knowing it, he has followed those who have had the same fancy before him. In vain has the graceful, the smiling Fontenelle[56] spangled his encomiums with the most charming flowers. They cannot soften the harshness of those dazzling points that distract the mind at every instant. He surprises us at the first reading, but fatigues at the second. He seems more eager to display himself than expose the subject he is treating. The supreme talent in writing is to make us forget the author in favor of the work. The writer must find the secret of interesting the reader in the object that he presents to him; he must continually engage his attention, without ever diverting it in order to gain admiration for himself. It is nevertheless true that a precious style will find its admirers at a time when literary reputation will depend less on those of real knowledge than upon a crowd of curious people who read only to amuse themselves and for that reason are supposed ignorant of greater things. But men accustomed to the solid beauties of the ancients will be hesitant to renounce them in order to run after the false glare of an errant imagination.

The study of antiquity, therefore, should be regarded as one of the strongest barriers that can be opposed to the degeneration of taste. It will serve as a protection for mediocre writers, and will enable great geniuses to make themselves models for posterity. It is important for a nation to preserve the taste for good Latin. This cannot be done unless the language is studied at an early age, and care is taken to encourage by the public esteem those who devote them-selves to it and who apply themselves to writing in Latin with as much purity and elegance as those moderns who have in this way ac-quired the greatest reputation.

But one might still object that there is a host of moderns, con-sidered to have written fine Latin verses, who have never succeeded in writing a good French verse. Is this not a sure sign that these Latin verses, which are so highly esteemed, only appear fine because we are not capable of judging of them? After all, these same writers do not succeed in a language where we could appreciate their merit.

Is it true that it is so easy to compose good Latin verses? Do we find many writers equal to Fracastoro, Sannazzaro, or Vida? The cel-ebrated Muret prevailed on Scaliger[57] to publish under the name of an ancient some verses of his own writing, but it must be admitted that few people are capable of writing verses like those of Muret.

The lack of success of some French versifiers in their own lan-guage is no proof that they might not succeed in Latin. It is said that Ménage and Régnier Des Marais[58] wrote only mediocre French verse, though they had success in Italian, a living language, which does not lack for good judges. Could it be that the French language is perhaps less poetical than the Italian or the Latin?

The principal author of the objection seems to furnish us with an answer in one of his discourses:

> We have almost insensibly banned ourselves from all the objects, which other nations have dared to describe. There is nothing that Dante, taking the example of the ancients, has not expressed. He has accustomed the Italians to say everything. But in what manner can we at this time imitate the author of the *Georgics*, who names all the instruments of husbandry? We scarcely know them, etc.[59]

Voltaire complains of the narrow limits to which the French lan-guage is confined when it comes to poetry. It is no wonder that au-thors would have succeeded in Latin in some genres when they would have miscarried had they attempted to write in French.

It seems in general that languages that have a certain harmonic variety in their movement and construction facilitate the unfolding of thoughts by a kind of mechanical connection. A man ruminates on a discourse in Latin. He has vague and confused thoughts, which are not yet determinate enough to give place to either the choice of proper expressions or their arrangement in a period. There occurs to his mind the beginning of a phrase, which might be quite apt, but there is great difficulty in finding a sequel to it, because he lacks the precise ideas that need to be expressed. In this embarrassment, the language itself will assist the writer if he has a superb mastery of it. The obscure thought that he turns about in his head presents to him some terms. These terms find themselves connected by various authors a thousand different ways in order to form the different constructions of which the language is susceptible. In recollecting these different constructions, a man is sometimes fortunate enough to find those that suit him. In other words, he discovers those phrases that capture the thought he sought, expressed in the most proper manner, or else he comes upon a thought that, naturally connecting itself to that which the writer already has in his head, supplies him with the means to advance his thought.

We can add here an even more general reflection. In whatever language one knows, whether dead or living, it is often easier to assume an elevated than a familiar style. The reason is that the elevated style is a style of formality, reserved for extraordinary occasions. The ear, not being accustomed to it, is less likely to catch the irregularities that slip into it. One expects a language beyond what is common, and so a happy error will sometimes pass for a beauty. But this is not the case with the familiar style. The ears are much too practiced not to take offense at the least inaccuracy. A phrase not in common use is immediately perceived, and it is bad precisely because it is not in common use. An irregular expression will scarcely be noticed in a tragedy. The people, by nature a judge of the language of man, will hardly dare to judge of the language of the gods. The sublime style admits of bold strokes, which equally serve to produce beauties and to conceal faults. Those who are learned in the professions have found failures of exactitude in the language of Bossuet, Pascal, and other writers of the first order. But perhaps it is less the ear than grammar that is offended by these defects. This will not be the case with the speech we should put into the mouth of the townsman or the maidservant in a comedy. They must speak the language of the people. Nothing can escape. Expression unwarranted by common usage will be simply repugnant. This is the reason why a person obliged to write in a living foreign language often has more difficulty expressing himself on the simpler subjects than on those that require a more elevated style. For the same reason, it would perhaps be less difficult for a modern to imitate Cicero, particularly in his philosophical works, than to write well in the style of Plautus or Terence. Italy is fortunate in having professors whose eloquence shines forth from their university chairs, but who would not find it so easy to converse familiarly in Latin.

I add that the authors of the objection [to the study of Latin] never tire of repeating that we ought not to exclude any genre of writing, that nothing is more pernicious than to want to limit the development of the arts, that we cannot encourage too much whatever delights us. So be it. I am certain that every man who is capable of enjoying Virgil can take pleasure in reading the *Anti-Lucretius.*[60] Why then want to dry up the source of so innocent a pleasure?

Rousseau adds:

> Minds are formed by languages; the thoughts take on the color of idioms. Only reason is common; in each language the mind has its particular form. This is the difference which might very well be a part of the cause or the effect of national characters; and what appears to confirm this conjecture is that in all the nations of the world language follows the vicissitudes of morals and is preserved or degenerates as they are.[61]

This remark is philosophical. Seneca made it before Rousseau;[62] it is the subject of one of his finest letters. It gives us another strong reason for initiating youth into the study of the ancient languages. Let us limit ourselves to Latin. "Minds are formed by languages; the thoughts take on the color of idioms." If this is true, what a happy color must the mind of a young man take on from reading the ancients! What clarity, what precision from Caesar's commentaries, but at the same time, what nobility in the sentiments, what elevation in the thoughts. Caesar's great soul is here exposed to view. He speaks of the greatest affairs with the greatest simplicity. It seems that it is no burden for him to conduct enterprises on which the destiny of the universe depends.

What can be of greater consequence than to enable a young man at an early age to receive, by reading the works of the greatest writers, impressions perfectly suited for elevating the soul, by making him experience and, as it were, taste the nobility of sentiments to which it is susceptible?

We add another of Rousseau's reflections:

> Restrict, therefore, the child's vocabulary as much as possible. It is a very great disadvantage for him to have more words than ideas, for him to know how to say more things than he can think. I believe one of the reasons why peasants generally have clearer minds than city people is that their lexicon is less extensive. They have few ideas, but they are very good at the comparison of ideas.[63]

It is true that the children of villagers have a more solid sense than the children of good family who are educated in the city. I once made some inquiries into the reason for this. It did not occur to me to think it could depend on the greater or lesser extent of one's vocabulary. Here is what I concluded. It seemed to me that the children of the villagers were brought up more seriously than their counterparts. As soon as they are capable of thinking and acting, they are obliged to live a laborious and regular life; they are put to a succession of jobs which, though they require no elevated thought, have a certain connection that subjects the mind to a regular series of combinations. The child must drive the flock to pasture, bring in the firewood, and as far as he is able, assist his father and mother in the work of the household. In all that he is set about, in all he sees others do, he easily discerns the proposed end, and the appropriateness of the means used to attain it. This methodical course of operations is well adapted to make him methodical in his thoughts. It is truly a narrow circle of ideas; but then everything in it is orderly. This is not the case with children of a higher class. At the age when the young villagers are taught to work seriously, one is concerned only to amuse the more privileged children. In order to amuse them, one must distract them. One needs to present them a crowd of objects, one following after the other without connection, which they entertain as something outside themselves so that they become accustomed to play rather than to reflection. The little villagers are sometimes under the necessity of exerting themselves and forcing their minds to find the way to supply some real need, to removing some inconvenience, or to finish the job that is imposed on them. This is never the case with the others. They play, they smash and break things, they dissipate themselves, and that is all.

Eventually one must interrupt their amusements with some studies and religious exercises. One does them great service. It is the sowing of seeds that remain covered at the beginning, but which soon enough germinate and produce fruit in due season. Yet children do not at all see the relevance of the studies that are required of them. They do not see, for instance, any relation that grammar has to the magistracy for which they are destined. They do not conceive any better the duties attached to the offices in which their parents are invested, even though they see them carried out before their eyes. Not knowing the reason for anything they themselves do or for what they see done by others, they cannot justify to themselves the particular work asked of them. The disproportion that there is between the end for which they are educated and the actual state of their knowledge hardly permits them to see any order to the sequence of their activities. Consequently this order, which they do not at all know, can little serve to give continuity to their ideas. This is the reason, as regard solidity, the little villagers up to a certain age surpass the child of the city and why the childhood of the latter must be prolonged.

But beyond a certain age, the situation reverses itself for a certain number. I say for a certain number, for there are those who, for want of genius or through some essential deficiency in their education, never leave behind that early spirit of frivolity but only supply it with other objects. This accounts for those agreeable men who are nothing among a wise people but are everything among a corrupt people. In vain would one seek in these fickle heads for any traces of judgment or solidity. It is a state of childhood prolonged to old age. But there are others in whom reason, wisely cultivated, is strengthened little by little through the knowledge they acquire in the course of their education. The range of their vocabulary, that is to say, the multitude and variety of their ideas, enable them to perceive a greater number of relations between objects, to determine them with greater precision, and consequently to combine them with more judgment. What is the good sense of peasants and even the acuity that can show in the pursuit of their small interests when compared to the extensiveness and preciseness of thought, which is generally characteristic of persons who have cultivated their minds by solid studies and who have exercised themselves in the employment of civil life? It would be to compare the rough technique of the simple laborer to the intelligence of a skilled machinist. It is not at all through the scarcity of ideas that one succeeds in perfecting reason. It comes through the order we bring to these ideas.

[21. *On the study of history*]

Rousseau also eliminates the study of history from the child's curriculum. In his usual way of reasoning, he argues that since children do not understand everything in history, they understand nothing of it. He admits that "if the study of languages were only the study of words – that is to say, of figures or the sounds which express them – it could be suitable for children."[64] Now the catalogue of the names of kings, emperors, pontiffs, chiefs of nations, and monarchies that have succeeded each other or existed at the same time is only a simple collection of words. This study is, therefore, proper for children. But he answers:

> what is the use of inscribing in their heads a catalogue of signs which represent nothing for them? In learning the things will they not learn the signs? Why put them to the useless effort of learning the signs twice?[65]

It is because it is easier to inscribe a catalogue of signs in the head of a child than in the head of man more advanced in age. It is because this catalogue of signs, which is impressed in one's early years, will scarcely ever be effaced. If a child were to have learned and retained the sequence of the names of kings, emperors, and so forth, would it not be easy for him later when he reads original authors to fix each event in its proper place, to arrange the facts in their natural order, and to apprehend in the bat of an eye the contemporary revolutions of different countries, in order to better understand what they refer to and how they are connected? "The words of history are [not] history," says our author.[66] I agree. But it is a preparatory step enabling him to undertake the study of history with greater success afterwards. It is not lost time.

> One imagines that history is within their reach because it is only a collection of facts. But what is meant by this word *facts?* Can anyone believe that the relations which determine historical facts are so easy to grasp that ideas are effortlessly formed from the facts in children's minds?[67]

These determining relations are not all of the same nature. Some are more and others less easy to comprehend. It would be vain to expect a child to follow the dark subterfuges of the political artifice of Tiberius or Cromwell. He would understand none of it. But history furnishes an infinity of impressive events, quite simple in their causes and their effects, and consequently very instructive to children. In order to support his own thesis, Rousseau relates the comic adventure of a child who in his presence recites with a great grace the well-known anecdote of Alexander and his physician Philip. This child especially admired Alexander's courage. But where did he see this courage?

> Solely in having swallowed at a single gulp a bad-tasting potion, without hesitation, without the least sign of repugnance. The poor child, who had been made to take medicine not two weeks before, and who had taken it only after a mighty effort, still had its aftertaste in his mouth. Death and poisoning stood in his mind only for disagreeable sensations; and he did not conceive, for his part, of any other poison than senna.[68]

It proves that children do not understand what they seem to comprehend the best. I do not doubt the facts of the story as Rousseau tells it. But was it the child's fault that he did not grasp what undoubtedly had been very badly explained to him? Is it really so very difficult to make a child comprehend death or poisoning? Was it impossible to explain to him Alexander's perplexity, by giving him a richly detailed account of the circumstances (for with children we should not be stingy with details) – Alexander, who perceiving himself to be sick on the eve of battle, was desirous of either being speedily cured or dying, rather than fall into the hands of the Persians. Could one not have laid before the child the trouble which Parmenion's letter must have caused for Alexander? Could he not have been brought to understand that the step he took in swallowing the potion was the effect partly of his impatience at the predicament in which he found himself and partly of the trust he put in a physician, whose fidelity and attachment he had experienced over many years.

I could cite some remarkable and well-authenticated facts, which would prove that children have a greater aptitude for history than Rousseau supposes. They are capable of penetrating up to a certain point the relations that determine historical facts, of understanding the connection of causes and effects, of recognizing the resemblance and opposition among characters, and of seeing those events in which character either bears up or gives way.

Without going so far, isn't it enough that all the events of history that form pictures are within their capacity? Were these events to do nothing more than amuse them, could they have too much of this kind of amusement? But they do more. They are the beginning of learning that prepares the way for a deeper study. They are subjects on which one may begin to usefully exercise the faculty of combining their ideas, that is to say, the faculty of reasoning, and it would be rare if they did not draw from it some solid instruction in manners. Nothing can be of greater utility in this regard than to show them virtue and vice in action; nothing can be more apt for making them see the beauty of virtue and the deformity of vice.

But it is essential that we should not be mistaken in our method. No short summaries. As we see them in the *Encyclopedia*,[69] brief digests are good for reviving the ideas we already possess, but they do not at all serve those who need to acquire them. Summaries, therefore, are not made for children.

Others say that one should begin by studying the history of one's own country, because it is that which is of most importance for us to know. It is true that it is the history we should know best, but it does not follow that we should begin with it. The history of every country presents to our view, at every page, wars and treaties of peace, of alliance, of commerce with the neighboring states. It teaches you what you have done among foreigners and what foreigners have done among you. To judge the strength, the wealth, the power of a state, one must compare it with other states.

The revolutions of one country have often been brought about by changes that have happened in other countries. History is not the picture of an absolute and isolated thing. Like the world, it is a sequence of changes relative to other changes. You cannot then properly understand what has happened in your own country without acquiring a sufficient knowledge of the revolutions in foreign countries that have influenced it. Relate the history of every country to that of your own nation. That this should be the principal object of your study is good. But put yourself in a position to understand it before you begin to study it.

Still others have urged an innovation to the effect that we reverse the order of time, by starting with modern history and proceeding back to ancient history. The reason they give is that modern history is the more interesting to us. This is a good reason, but proves the contrary. Modern history is more interesting to us than the ancient, because it has greater influence on the present course of affairs. Therefore, in order to be in a position to profit from it, we must know the nature of current affairs. It is this that young people do not know, for lack of experience.

Setting aside all subdivisions, I would divide history into four principal epochs. The first would comprehend all the ancient history up to the fall of the Western empire caused by the inundation of the barbarian peoples. The laws, manners, and customs that these people brought with them into the different countries they occupied in some way interrupted the influence that the events of ancient history would have had on those of later times. Their arrival was the epoch of the establishment of a new system, which changed the face of Europe.

The second epoch would be from the inundation of the northern nations to the time that the people of Europe attempted to overrun Asia, that is to say, to the time of the crusades. The establishment and revolutions of the people of the North in different countries they conquered merit more attention than is generally thought. It is in their customs and in their opinions we must search for the origin of certain practices and prejudices, which prevail even now among the most civilized nations. The present system of affairs would in many respects be an enigma to a philosopher who did not take stock of that source. The original government of those people was an informal aristocracy in which the military without discipline possessed in common the authority to make the laws and reserved to themselves in particular the power to disobey them. They believed that they were subject to their chief only so long as they wished and that they might treat their subjects as they pleased. It was the feudal spirit prior to the institution of fiefs, lords without restraints, chiefs without authority, and people without liberty.

The third epoch would extend from the crusades, that is, from the eleventh century to the discovery of America. The culmination of evils caused by the informal aristocracy mentioned above excited some sparks of a more wholesome polity, which thanks to the crusades was established in some countries of Europe. This is the origin of several institutions that still exist today. Moreover the eleventh century appears to be the epoch in which a few royal families and several states subsisting today seem to have achieved their stability.

The fourth epoch would begin with the discovery of America and proceed to the present. In this period commerce, having become a principal object of statecraft, causes a new revolution in the system of Europe. It changes the fortune of states and varies their respective interests. In this age, the search for equilibrium seems to have produced a perpetual motion in the balance of the political system.

Ancient history can be seen from two points of view: either with respect to the collection of facts or in relation to the treatises of the great writers, which it has transmitted to us. As a simple collection of facts, it is of only mild interest to us, because the communication of the influence that the ancient events would have had over those that followed had been interrupted, as we have already observed, by the incursion and establishment of the northern peoples. In this respect it is a picture more interesting for the purposes of erudition than statecraft. It is a spectacle of curiosity very attractive to youth.

From the second point of view, however, ancient history is of much greater importance. It is a course of civil morality and polity. The facts that it presents to us amount to moral experience systematically ordered by philosophical historians, that is to say, brought to certain general principles which give them a kind of connection and unity. I would say that an ancient history, such as Rollin's,[70] is useful to beginners as an introduction to modern history. For those who have studied modern history, the study of the ancient history in the originals can be most useful in order to understand the proper connection among the facts, to know the men, and to discover the original motives that occasion the events. In mentioning Rollin's ancient history, I do not mean his Roman history, which is an admirable work in many respects, but whose tedious prolixity, so often empty of events, would likely discourage young people.

To those who cast a universal doubt over the whole of ancient history due to the great length of time that has passed and who look upon it as "a tissue of fables,"[71] to use Rousseau's expression, we dare to say that they reason on this subject very much as common people usually reason on the discoveries of astronomy. If you say to many people that the mountains on the moon are higher than those on the earth, they will smile and ask you in an ironical tone whether you have been there. They do not imagine that we can possibly know what there is on the moon, when we are ignorant of an infinity of things right here under our eyes. These honest folks do not realize that it is not the spatial proximity or the distance of objects that either brings them within or draw them out of our understanding. It depends solely on the sufficiency or insufficiency of the means we have for recognizing and judging them. I do not know what is now happening in the household of my neighbor, who lives under the same roof with me, yet I know what occurred nearly two thousand years ago in Cicero's home. His mother, for instance, who was a good housekeeper, took the precaution of sealing the bottles as they were emptied and putting them among the others, for fear that the servants should take it into their heads to open some of them and say they had already been empty. We find this anecdote in Cicero's letters.[72] The public affairs in Athens and Rome were decided in the assembly of the people. No secret could be kept. The contemporary historians were well informed on what they wrote. By contrast today, public affairs are deliberated in councils, of which ordinarily nothing is made public. In many respects, therefore, it is possible to be better informed on the political interests of the ancient republics than on the present state of the affairs of Europe.

But there is another history that we cannot neglect to make known to children. Surprisingly Rousseau did not recognize its excellence and usefulness. It is Sacred History, the only book that supplies lessons equally proportioned to the wisest and the most simple.

The wise find an illumination of wisdom superior to every philosophy; the simple find solid instructions that give them the intelligence they need to conduct their lives. It is the divine book that teaches us to understand the language of heavens that makes known the glory of the Creator. The majesty of the Supreme Being, his power, his divinity are announced by the grandeur of his works. The universe brought from out of nothing, the earth covered by the waters of the flood, the sea parted, the sun stopped in its course – they seem to show the hand of the most powerful suspended over all of nature. It is a terrible and beneficent hand which hurls thunderbolts and distributes the light, which humbles man before his Creator at the astonishing spectacle of his marvelous works, and which raises him up to himself by the sentiments of trust and love that his providence inspires. On the other hand, what reading can be more wonderful to a philosopher or more fascinating and instructive to children than the entire sequence of the history of the people of God? What an abundance and variety of events! What a mixture of grandeur and simplicity in the lives of the patriarchs! Never was man more truthfully depicted. The movements of simple nature are developed in their own right; they are represented by the features that characterize them as they really are, without alteration, without constraint, without disguise. The divine Homer, the profane writer who has best succeeded in this genre, does not come near to this quality of candor. The richness of his poetry elevates all that he depicts and inevitably tints it with the fire of his enthusiasm, giving it a strange hue that is not there in the thing itself. In the hands of the Sacred Historian, it is nature that speaks and acts; in Homer it is the poet who depicts nature. All of the objections that Rousseau levels against the study of history fail in this case. His objections come down to the single difficulty in knowing the relations that determine historical facts. These relations in sacred history are of the utmost simplicity. Children easily comprehend them. Moreover, they learn to love God and to fear him. They learn to recognize and distinguish the deep-seated, primitive dispositions of the human heart. What a source of wisdom and piety!

[22. *On the study of geography*]

Geography is essentially connected with history. Rousseau, therefore, does not fail to ban it from his plan of education. There would be merit to what he has to say on this subject were he not to exaggerate so much.

> In any study whatsoever, unless one has the ideas of the things represented, the representative signs are nothing. However, one always limits the child to these signs without ever being able to make him understand any of the things which they represent. Thinking he is being taught a description of the earth, he learns only to know some maps. He is taught the names of cities, of countries, of rivers which he does not conceive of as existing anywhere else but on the paper where he is showed them. . . . I set down as a fact that after two years of globe and cosmography there is not a single child of ten who, following the rules he has been given, knows how to get from Paris to Saint-Denis. I set down as a fact that there is not one who, on the basis of a map of his father's garden, is able to follow its winding paths without getting lost. These are the doctors who know on the spur of the moment where Peking, Ispahan, Mexico, and all the countries of the earth are.[73]

Rousseau says that youth (and he speaks of children ten years old) do not conceive that the countries, the towns, and the rivers, whose names he is taught, exist anywhere other than on the paper where they are pointed out to him. This appears to me extraordinary, and I confess I do not understand it at all.

The view of a globe or of a map of the world is not sufficient to give a child an accurate idea of earth's sphere, nor does he conceive what relation the map before his eyes has to the earth under his feet – this I readily agree. But it does not follow that it is of no use to teach him to understand the map. For the child who has a correct map of the earth impressed upon his mind the time will come when he will know how the world map corresponds to the terrestrial globe.

At that moment and without further study, he will know how to locate on the surface of the earth those countries, towns, and rivers, which his imagination will represent to him drawn on the map, and from the positions they occupy there he will know what their true positions are on the globe.

Rousseau asserts that after two years studying the globe and cosmography there is not a single child ten years of age who by the rules given to him would be able to find his way from Paris to Saint-Denis. This is something that I do not doubt at all. But, as if he had proved everything he wanted, he concludes ironically that these "are the doctors who know on the spur of the moment where Peking, Ispahan, Mexico, and all the countries of the earth are."

I do not see what relation a walk from Paris to Saint-Denis can have in common with a course of study on the globe or cosmography. I believe one would hardly consult the degrees of latitude or longitude for so short a journey, nor would one steer oneself there using the same principles employed in a voyage to China or Mexico. It would be more a matter of topography than cosmography. The most able cosmographer might find himself unsure on his way to Saint-Denis. Two roads joining at an acute angle might be enough to puzzle him. In such a case, would he pull out his instruments or consult the tables in order to know whether he should take the right or the left fork? A child may in fact have acquired some useful knowledge in geography without knowing how to find his way from one town to another.

I am, however, far from thinking that a formal course in geography is within the range of children's capabilities. In the first place, it is necessary to distinguish scientific geography, such as is that of Varen,[74] perfected by Newton, from historical geography, which consists in recognizing on the map the places which one speaks of in history. The first, which comprehends cosmography, supposes a great knowledge of geometry. The abridgments of it, which are prefixed to many books, are for the most part little more than useless decorations. One loses a good deal of time in studying them, and then when one later opens books that treat the subject more seriously, one understands nothing of it. One has to start over at the beginning in order to know something of it. This is not the case with historical geography; its agreeableness and utility cannot be disputed. Children take pleasure finding on the map the places they have heard mentioned in history. They enjoy following Alexander and Hannibal in their expeditions. The sequence of places and the succession of events mutually reinforce one another through the identity of impression they make upon the mind. History will make geography more interesting, and geography will bring greater clarity to history. In order to make children learn the places on the map this method succeeds more surely and more easily than the application of the study method generally practiced. A long list of strange names cannot interest them, whereas they examine them with pleasure to the extent that it is history that brings them before their eyes.

But before we make use of regional maps in relation to history, we should take the preliminary step of giving children a succinct idea of the map of the world, so that they are able to compare the map that they have before them and recognize in relation to the other parts of the universe the position and the extent of the land they will be covering. Nothing is easier than to make this preliminary study agreeable to a child. The child, for instance, knows that his father has traveled in France, Spain, and England. With what eagerness will he listen to the story of his adventures in different cities! What pleasure will it give him to be shown these cities on the map! If he loves coffee, sugar, or what have you, we show him the places they come from.

Maps should not be over-crowded with names, nor should they be too bare. If they are too full, it causes confusion; if too empty, they are of no use. By simplifying too much we leave off many points of comparison, which facilitate the study of geography rather than impede it. A city placed by itself on a uniform background, as it were, presents the mind with an isolated point, from which one conceives nothing. A city standing in relation to other cities causes ideas. All our knowledge is founded on comparisons. The mountain chains, the principal rivers, and the borders should be clearly signified. It is a disadvantage to a child, who has before him a map of France, if he must struggle to distinguish Spain from seas surrounding it on either side.

[23. *On the study of geometry*]

Let us turn for a moment to the reform that Rousseau proposes to the study of geometry.

> I have said that geometry is not within the reach of children. But it is our fault. We are not aware that their method is not ours, and that what become for us the art of reasoning, for them ought to be only the art of seeing. Instead of giving them our method, we would do better to take theirs. . . . Make exact figures, combine them, place them on one another, examine their relations. You will find the whole of elementary geometry in moving from observation to observation, without there being any question of definitions or problems or any form of demonstration other than simple superimposition. As for me, I do not intend to teach geometry to Emile; it is he who will teach it to me; I will seek the relations, and he will find them, for I will seek them in such a way as to make him find them. For example, instead of using a compass to draw a circle, I shall draw it with a point at the end of a string turning on a pivot. After that, when I want to compare the radii among themselves, Emile will ridicule me and make me understand that the same string, always taut, cannot have drawn unequal distances.[75]

Nothing can be of greater service than to make exact figures, to combine them, to place the one upon the other, and to examine the relation they bear to each other in such a manner as to enable Emile to discover them himself. But Rousseau is certainly wrong to suppress the definitions, propositions, and demonstrations that naturally follow. I say he is wrong; for certainly it must be wrong to find fault with a method which in the past has produced, and even today continues to produce, such great geometers and in such great numbers. The worth of a method is known by its effects.

These two methods, far from being opposites, mutually illuminate one another. The sort of observations Rousseau recommends serve to make the definitions better understood, and the definitions, for their part, serve to direct the observations. De la Chapelle[76] is especially committed to the conjunction of the two methods of art and mechanical observation in his geometry; Wolff[77] as well as others have not neglected it. A highly esteemed man, who had been a disciple of Rondelli,[78] told me that this able professor at Bologna always made use of real and amusing examples to explain his demonstrations. If he needed to divide a circle, he managed that it be a cake that needed to be portioned into shares. This was apparently the method that was employed to instruct the young geometer of Turin, who according to Rousseau had learned to judge of the relative characteristics of surfaces from waffles with equal perimeters.[79]

We should not abandon the scientific method, but the method of observation that Rousseau recommends can be usefully combined with it. It is only good sense to see the utility of clarifying through practice what we demonstrate in theory and to show a child by amusing and instructive operations the usefulness of the truths he is taught and what advantages may be derived from them.

As to the particular methods of learning the synthetic elementary geometry, they may be reduced to three principal types. The first is that of Euclid. With this name I refer to all the elementary treatises where nearly the same order has been followed and where nothing has been changed other than to transpose, suppress, or add some propositions, or to simplify some demonstrations. The second type is that of Arnauld.[80] It consists chiefly in the progression from the simple to the compound, from lines to angles, from angles to surfaces, and so forth. Such are the elements of Varignon, Sauveur, Malezieu or the duke of Burgundy, Lacaille,[81] and others. The third method is that of Clairaut.[82] It consists in developing the propositions of geometry largely in the order that they are occasioned by the need and the natural progress of our knowledge. It is an imitation of invention. Each of these methods has its advantage. The first is praised for the rigor of its demonstrations. The second is esteemed for the order and universality of its theorems, from which an infinity of propositions may be deduced as so many corollaries. By this we are taught to reduce to one same principle everything that can be determined by that principle, and we learn to comprehend within the same point of view a greater number of objects. The method contributes to the enlargement of the mind and makes us think with greater precision. The third appears best adapted to rouse or to nourish a spirit of invention.

It is for the geometers to decide which method in practice is preferable in all respects. It is said that the English are particularly attached to Euclid, and this is a prejudice with advantages. The rigor of demonstration seems to be an essential merit and perhaps the distinctive character of geometry. One cannot, therefore, too scrupulously adhere to it. It is true that we cannot help noting a kind of disorder in Euclid; but some geometers have in part remedied the problem by the transposition of some theorems, without essentially altering the order of any particular book. But if Euclid has neglected the systematic order of the abstract notions of lines, angles, and surfaces, he has not neglected the natural order or connection of the truths. All the propositions are in an essential relation to those that precede and those that follow them. The mind, led from consequence to consequence, develops a commendable habit of accuracy and precision. The different examples of constructions, where one employs equally lines, triangles, angles, etc., show a young student how in order to arrive at the discovery of truths of which he is ignorant he must take advantage as need be of all the materials that his mind furnishes to him. In fact, we are certain that the elements of Euclid contain all that is necessary to know in order to follow as far as the mathematicians have advanced through synthesis. A young man who has a solid grasp of the first three or four books of Euclid does not know much geometry, but he at least knows well what he knows, and he will not have to retrace his steps if he should desire to advance farther. I once asked the celebrated Eustace Manfredi[83] what book he would recommend for the first elements of geometry. "One should not depart from Tacquet,"[84] he replied. The methods of Arnauld, Varignon, and the others are also recommended by very able masters. The method of Sauveur, which is the same type that served

Prince Eugene,[85] is extolled in the *Encyclopedia* and recommended to military officers. Above all, one should consult the genius of the student who is being taught mathematics and the purposes for which he is being instructed.

[24. *Francis Bacon's observations on studying and reading*]

I cannot conclude this article86 any better than with Francis Bacon's wise observations on the subject of study and reading. I shall take the liberty of adding a few remarks relative to their use in the education of youth.[87]

Three advantages may be derived from study and reading: the pleasures of knowing, facility at speaking well, and capability in business affairs. But there are excesses to avoid. We relish the pleasures of contemplation most in retirement, but it is an abuse if we devote ourselves to it at the expense of our duties to the state. To dedicate to reading time that one should give to business is a beautiful indolence, if you will, but it is still indolence.[88]

Studia, et lectiones librorum, aut meditationum voluptati, aut orationis ornamento, aut negotiorum subsidio inserviunt. Usus eorum quatenus ad voluptatem, in secessu et otio imprimis percipitur. . . . Temporis nimium in lectione, et studiis terere, speciosa quaedam socordia est.

Let me offer a reflection here. There are few men who are so busy so as not to have some moments of solitude, whether voluntary or forced, even if only in the hours set apart for necessary rest. At such times, nothing can be of greater benefit than to find in reading and reflection a relaxation that is useful for restoring the mind with new energy. No weight is so oppressive as that of a fatigued spirit buried under itself. There are many people who strive to avoid themselves. Such people avoid themselves even more than the world avoids them, because they cannot even endure themselves, for they have failed to develop a habit of reading and thinking. We must therefore strive to inspire young people with a taste for reading. It is a charming speculation to pretend to lead children through the whole course of their studies by always amusing them. The most necessary studies require hard work and self-denial. We may partially mitigate the coercive quality of study, but we cannot entirely remove it, and still hope to make solid progress. And therefore it is not by means of these kinds of studies that we will inspire children with a love for reading. But we will succeed with reading that is amusing and instructive, so long as we take care not to propose it as part of their studies, – for the very word will ruin everything, – but rather as a reward for applying themselves to their studies. Selections from history, strange accounts of travelers, dialogues, a series of prints, medals, natural curiosities of various kinds, and so forth, – these can all serve this purpose.

But in order to draw from these different pieces the profit that one might hope for, it is necessary to introduce a certain order and to fashion it so that all this extra work, under the direction of an experienced teacher, bears upon and enriches the general purpose of education. Without this attention, we should expect that too great a variety of badly arranged objects and ideas will only produce confusion in the head of a young man. It will accustom him to indulge in a formless accumulation of superficial knowledge without regard to choice or method, rather like Gothic ornamentation that only embellishes by disfiguring. It is to embellish the mind at the expense of precision and solidity, the acquisition of which is the most valuable fruit of study and learning. A head is better off empty than badly filled; now it is badly filled when it contains either bad things or good things amassed without order.

In addition, these sorts of exercises, which do not have the appearance of studies, are also effective in rousing the curiosity of children who never fail asking a thousand questions about the objects that they encounter. In those precious moments one well-timed word will be more effective than a long lesson. The child thinks you mean only to satisfy his curiosity, unaware that he is learning to reason with you regarding the object you have put before him. He learns to compare the objects, to form combinations, and to connect them to principles in order to deduce the consequences.

Study and reading serve, in the second place, says Bacon, to enhance our talent for speech. One exercises this talent in formal discourse as well as in familiar conversation. Affectation is its abuse, and one needs to take great care to avoid it.[89]	Quatenus ad orationis ornamenta, in sermone tam familiari quam solemni locum habet. ... iisdem ad ornatum mollius abuti, affectatio mera est, quae se ipsam prodit.

A fine speaker always presents himself successfully. It is a talent that inevitably brings out the merit of what he has to say, and sometimes substitutes for it. One cannot be too careful to avoid the prodigies of excessively dazzling discourse. Genuine talent only succeeds when it is natural. Nothing exposes one to ridicule more than the affectation to want to appear a fine speaker. It is in vain that you show off the most elegant phrases and the best-chosen expressions; your artifice betrays you. The listener sees that the effort you have taken to assemble these parts of the speech does not come naturally from the heart. You offend the integrity [*amour propre*] of your listeners when you betray your desire to overwhelm them. Far from gaining their confidence, you prejudice them against you. The better way is to strive to speak clearly and judiciously. It is not the way to win the admiration of fools, but it is the way to please sensible men and to displease nobody. This talent, which is not beyond those of more limited geniuses, depends in great part on the early stages of education. If you want a child to learn to speak with justness and precision, accustom him to conceive clearly what he is to say and then to say it naturally, without effort and without affectation. Reading will give his language precision, and experience in the world will add agreeableness to it. A young man should not try to appear witty in what he says. Let him conceive well what he wants to say, and then say it simply. If he has wit [*l'esprit*], it will appear without having to force it, and it will appear in the course of things [*à propos*]. If he does not have it, it will be vain to force it. If wit fails to come of its own, the efforts he makes to display it only serve to reveal his lack of ability. Books that sparkle with wit are therefore unfit for young people. Fontenelle and other authors who have written in that style should be put into their hands only with great caution. Bossuet, Fénelon, Fleury,[90] and Rollin are authors who speak naturally and who speak well. But let me return to Bacon.

With regard to worldly affairs, reading and study furnish aid in undertaking them and conducting them with greater judgment and maturity. Those who have only experience may succeed in the execution and in the details, but their knowledge is useless when it come to a broader view of issues and in the conduct of great affairs. We must not, however, always want to decide by appeal to the rules of art; this is pedantic and does not succeed. Study assists nature; experience perfects study. The precepts of art are too general, unless they are determined by experience.[91]

Quatenus vero negotiorum subsidium, huc spectat, ut accuratiore judicio res et suscipiantur et disponantur. Etenim homines rerum gerundarum gnari, ad negotia exequenda idonei fortasse sunt, et in specialibus judicio non malo utuntur. Verum consilia de summis rerum, eorumque inventio et administratio recta felicius a litteratis promanat. . . . De rebus autem ex regulis artis judicare, scholam omnino sapit nec bene succedit. Naturam litterae perficiunt, ab experientia autem ipsae perficiuntur. . . . Litterae generalia nimis praecipiunt, nisi ab experientia determinentur.

General maxims are undoubtedly good; but if they were all that were needed, we would quickly acquire prudence. It is essential to know how to apply general maxims appropriately to particular cases. It seems to me that general maxims may be compared to the compass. It serves to direct the pilot, but if he should believe that he can do nothing but hold rigidly to the course indicated by the compass, he would often founder upon rocks and sandbanks. The main point is to know precisely when to alter our course without losing sight of the point we are aiming at.

Let us add that there are two kinds of advantage to be derived from study, and it is extremely important to carefully distinguish them. The first is simply to embellish the mind with the knowledge we acquire. The second is to form our manner of thinking by the exercise of our intellectual faculties and thus amplify the force and range of the intellect. Some parts of knowledge are absolutely necessary; others are sometimes useful and always valuable. But once one has acquired the knowledge that is necessary for the conduct of one's career, then it is no longer a matter of more or less knowledge that determines merit or capability; instead it is a manner of thinking, a superiority of views, and an aptitude for making proper use of the knowledge acquired – these are the qualities that render one man incontestably superior to another. How many geometers are there today who have more knowledge of mathematics than did Galileo? But are they for this reason greater geometers than Galileo? Folard had more knowledge of military arts than Turenne;[92] but although he would pass as a good officer, there is some doubt that he would have been as great a general as Turenne. A wise instructor must, therefore, concentrate his attention more on the manner of thinking and less on the amount of knowledge. He is less concerned to embellish the mind than to properly exercise the mind's faculties. This approach is altogether contrary to normal practice.

Cunning people, adds Bacon, have little use for literature (perhaps, according to La Rochefoucauld's observation, because cunning is generally a mark of a little mind). Simple souls are amazed at it. But prudent individuals know how to put it to use. Arts and sciences do not themselves point out their usefulness to society. This belongs to a superior prudence that is acquired by observation.[93]

Callidi litteras contemnunt; simplices admirantur; prudentes opera earum, quantum par est, utuntur. Neque enim litterae verum sui usum satis edocent; sed ea res prudentia quaedam est, extra eas et supra eas sita, observatione tantum comparata.

One ought not to read with an intention of finding fault, neither should one take everything for granted, nor should one study the lesson of the day in order to retail it in conversation. Instead, with a view to instruction, one should weigh what one reads and make use of one's judgment in reading.[94]

Libros non legas animo contradicendi, et disputationum praeliis concertandi, neque rursus omnia pro concessis accipiendi, aut in verba auctoris jurandi; neque denique in sermonibus te venditandi; sed ut addiscas, ponderes, et judicio tuo aliquatenus utaris.

It is sufficient to read only bits and pieces of some books. Other books need to be read from beginning to end, but not with too much attention. And there are some, though not many, which one cannot read or study too much.[95]

Libri quidam per partes tantum inspiciendi; alii perlegendi quidem, sed non multum temporis in iis evolvendis insumendum; alii autem pauci diligentur evolvendi, et adhibita attentione singulari.

Reading instructs; disputing gives a quickness and ease; writing and taking notes[96] assist the memory.[97]

Lectio copiosum reddit et bene instructum; disputationes et colloquia promptum et facilem; scriptio autem et notarum collectio perlecta in animo imprimit et altius figit.

History gives one lessons in prudence; reading the poets supplies inventive thoughts; mathematics makes the mind more subtle and exact; natural philosophy makes it more profound; morality gives it greater gravity; rhetoric and dialectic make it more ready at discussion.[98]

Historiarum lectio prudentes efficit; poetarum ingeniosos; artes mathematicae subtilitatem donant; naturalis philosophia judicium profundum parit; moralis gravitatem quemdam morum conciliat; dialectica et rhetorica pugnacem reddunt, et ad contentionem alacrem.

Bacon claims that the mind has scarcely any defect that cannot be remedied by the appropriate study, just as there are certain gymnastic exercises that remedy particular infirmities and indispositions of the body.[99]

Perhaps one is dealing with a flighty, unsteady, inattentive mind. Mathematics will help to fix it. In the other sciences one can sometimes flatter oneself that he comprehends what he only understands halfway. One contents oneself with superficial notions that demand little attention, and so one believes oneself to have done everything. On the other hand, in a demonstration of geometry, one grasps nothing if one does not understand everything. The mind needs to fix itself on all the parts of a demonstration in order to connect them and hold them together from within a single point of view.[100]

Bacon recommends the method and the formal opinions of jurists for those who lack versatility and a facility for passing from one thing to another or for drawing upon different sources either for evidence or for the clarification that is required by the subject one is dealing with.[101]

Quin et vix occurrit in intellectu impedimentum aliquod insitum, aut naturale, quod non studio quopiam idoneo emendari et edolari possit: quemadmodum morbi corporis, exercitiis quibusdam propriis levari possunt.

Eodem modo si cui sit ingenium vagum et volucre, mathematicis incumbat; in demonstrationibus enim mathematicis, si mens vel minimum aberret, de novo incipiendum est.

Si quis ad transcursus ingenii segnis sit, nec alia in aliorum probationem et illustrationem accersere, et arrigere dextre noverit, jureconsultorum casus evolvat.

Is the mind lacking the penetration necessary for knowing the differences among objects? Bacon recommends the subtle analyses of the schoolmen.[102]	Si cuipiam ingenium sit minus aptum ad rerum differentias, et distinctiones eruendas, ad Scholasticos se conferat: illi enim cumini sectores sunt.

Although the suggestion will be somewhat off-putting to our present age, one can make up for a deficiency in reasoning through *The Art of Thinking*[c103] and some other solid treatises on logic and criticism. Among the large number of writers, with which the age abounds, we see rather often a fine speaker and a weak reasoner. The neglect of logic has had a greater effect than is generally thought. Had Rousseau not forgotten his logic, he would not have said that the end of education is to form a reasonable man but that to want to begin reasoning with children is to begin at the end. A celebrated writer who has criticized the *Pensées* of Pascal cites two examples to prove that "two contraries may be false."[104] The first pair of propositions is: "An ox flies to the South with wings," and "An ox flies to the North without wings." These two propositions are not contraries. If they are false it is in fact, because oxen fly neither to the South nor to the North, with or without wings. One only needs to change the subject matter and both propositions may be true, as in "A vessel goes toward the South with sails," and "A vessel goes toward the North without sails." This example shows that the writer in question did not have a precise understanding of what contraries are and of why contrary propositions may both be false. Logic gives the basis for the rules, rooted in evident principles, that explain why two contrary propositions, by virtue of the relation that constitutes their contrariety, can never be both true but may be both false. Familiarity with these rules is not useless in the conduct of our reasoning. It seems that a man is in a position to reason with greater power, when he has reflected on the ideas that clarify and certify the exactness of reasoning.

One cannot deny that many of the schoolmen have excessively disfigured logic, whether by the barbarous language they affected, or by the vain subtleties with which they overloaded it. We acknowledge the abuse. But what comes of it? What results is what almost always happens in disputes and partisan affairs: one only escapes the one extreme in order to precipitate oneself into the other. It became a mark of merit to have nothing in common with the schoolmen. The proscription was even extended to the rules and the art of reasoning. The good Abbé Pluche claimed to prove that the human mind had no need of rules in order to be taught to reason. Yet by his own example he proved that by neglecting rules we do not always reason justly.[105] (1) It is a constant fact that in all operations where the human mind risks going wrong, it needs to be guided by rules, which are nothing more than the result of the observations that have been made on the way to most securely attaining the proposed end. This can be made evident by an infinity of examples. (2) The art of reasoning merits being known for its own sake, independently of the advantages to be derived from it. In this part of logic we determine the number of possible combinations of the terms and propositions of an argument that lead to valid inferences. The rules that result furnish a valuable instance of a sequence of rigorously geometrical demonstrations in a subject matter that falls outside the province of geometry itself. (3) By practicing these rules the mind acquires the fortunate habit of arranging the terms and propositions of an argument in such a manner as to reason justly on any subject whatever. It is habit that remains with us long after we have forgotten the rules. We can illustrate the point by recalling how the rules of grammar aid us with regard to exact and correct speech. (4) By means of this same practice the mind acquires a greater facility not only for recognizing defective reasoning but also for immediately identifying the fallacy in the argument. (5) The greatest writers of antiquity, Cicero among others, set a great value on these rules. (6) The great writers of the previous age, who are justly regarded the restorers of philosophy, thinkers such as Galileo, Bacon, Grotius, Descartes, Gassendi, Leibnitz, Newton, Bossuet, and Nicole, were all formed from their earliest youth by long practice in the art of reasoning, of the sort commonly taught in the Schools. Their more profound study allowed them to recognize immediately the abuses that were made of logic and insured that they would adopt from it only what was solid.

I do not know but that the habit acquired through their long practice in the rules of logic contributed in great part to that degree of strength and clarity that we so much admire in their writings and that we seldom find in the writings of those who in their researches and reasonings abandon themselves exclusively to the impulse of nature.

[25. *The intellectual temperament of Rousseau's student*]

It remains to make some observations on the qualities or dispositions that Rousseau desires in his student. They concern the character of the mind, the climate, the temperament, and the birth or social status of his student.

> If I could choose, I would take only a common mind, such as I assume my pupil to be. Only ordinary men need to be raised. . . . The others raise themselves in spite of what one does.[106]

One ought to be grateful to Rousseau for the generosity he has shown in choosing a pupil. Given the cares that one wants well taken in order to shape a man, for him to prefer a common mind over a rare genius can only be the effect of a nobility of soul that has no other purpose than the public good. But in the justification of this preference, Rousseau seems to have sacrificed truth to the desire of saying fine things. "Only ordinary men need to be raised. . . . The others raise themselves in spite of what one does." Has he forgotten the fundamental proposition of his treatise: "we are born weak . . . we need judgment. Everything we do not have at our birth and which we need when we are grown is given us by education"?[107] Will this judgment pronounced on all of human kind admit of any exception? Does it not include great geniuses? Are there not some geniuses who come to nothing for want of education? Are there not others given over to great perversity, for want of a good education? It is necessary to educate both mediocre spirits and great geniuses, to teach the first to do good and the latter not to do evil.

We could have wished also there had been more justice in the rule he lays down for discernment of intellectual temperaments.

From giddy children come vulgar men. I know of no observation more universal and more certain than this one. Nothing is more difficult in respect of childhood than to distinguish real stupidity from that merely apparent and deceptive stupidity which is the presage of strong souls. It seems strange at first that the two extremes should have such similar signs. Nevertheless, it is properly so; for at an age when man as yet has nothing that is truly an idea, the entire difference between one who has genius and one who does not is that the latter accepts only false ideas, and the former, finding only such, accepts none. Thus the genius resembles the stupid child in that the latter is capable of nothing while nothing is suitable for the former.[108]

Is it really true that a child born with a genius, but which is concealed throughout childhood under an apparent stupidity, receives no false ideas? Is this proved by experience? And is it really demonstrated that the stupid child receives only false ideas? Even if it were true, how would similar exterior manifestations result from the two cases? Does a head destitute of ideas resemble one filled with false ideas? Whatever fund of genius or of stupidity there may be in two children, our author agrees that neither will yet have any true ideas. Where does he find a basis for the criterion that permits all the false ideas to enter into the head of the one child and that rejects all of them from the head of the other? Doesn't one need discernment in order to reject false ideas? And doesn't this discernment suppose true ideas?

Be this as it may, Rousseau continues:

Cato the Younger during his childhood seemed an imbecile at home. He was taciturn and stubborn – this is all he was judged to be. It was only in Sulla's antechamber that his uncle learned to know him. . . .[109]

Rousseau's wide brush does not know the art of nuances. According to him, there is no medium between the dullness, which produces a mediocre man, and that seeming stupidity that announces a strong soul. He rapidly passes from one extreme to another, and always exaggerates his portraits. Nature, however, advances by degrees. That amiable vivacity that one observes in most children is not all of the same character. There is a kind of vivacity that is only dullness; and Rousseau is correct when he says that from it we can only expect mediocre men. But there is also a vivacity that announces spiritedness and genius. How many great artists have there been whose talents were revealed in the amusements of their childhood? This is how the first impulses of a fortunate disposition would tend to develop themselves. The vivacity of dullness manifests itself in children who confuse everything and distinguish nothing. Their head is like the battlefield for a host of ideas, which collide against one another but are never connected to one another. These irregular sallies are to the mind what ungainly movements are to the body. Such irregularities are endearing in childhood, because children add a grace to all that they do, but at a more advanced age they are offensive. But there is another kind of vivacity, which one can regard as the dawning of genius. It is a mobility of imagination, which easily applies itself to different objects, is quick in understanding them, and combines them with accuracy. One can see in the application of a point in a fable to a fact in history, or of a fact in history to a current event, in just comparisons, and in consequences properly deduced the perspicuity for recognizing resemblance in things that are different and difference in things that are similar. In a word, the traits of precision and penetration are the characters by which one can distinguish vivacity of genius from the vivacity of dullness.

As to the seeming stupidity that foretells the strong soul, it seems it must belong to those children who are born with a single type of genius or talent, who have only an instinct, so to say, and a disposition for one sort of thing. If the sort of objects that alone could affect them does not present itself to them during their childhood, nothing moves them, nothing awakens their attention. One would be tempted to confuse this indifference, this insensibility with stupidity.

With respect to these two characters, the vivacity of spiritedness and the seeming dullness, which equally foretell great men, it seems that the first must produce a more universal genius, and the second a more concentrated soul. Caesar was admired in his childhood on account of the vivacity of his spiritedness; nonetheless he was a great man. His fertile, luminous, dominating genius is superior to the dark soul of Cato of Utica. The great soul of Alexander, from whom Rousseau cannot withhold his admiration, was not at all foretold by a seeming stupidity. Is it necessary to cite other examples? Need we mention Pascal, Pope, and so many others who were bright from their childhood? Are they to be counted among the ordinary men?

[26. On the native climate of the ideal student]

As to the climate, Rousseau would have his pupil born in a temperate country.

> Locale is not unimportant in the culture of men. They are all that they can be only in temperate climates. The disadvantage of extreme climates is obvious. A man is not planted like a tree in a country to remain there forever; and he who leaves one extreme to get to the other is forced to travel a road double the length of that traveled by him who leaves from the middle point for the same destination. Let the inhabitant of a temperate country visit the two extremes one after the other. His advantage is still evident, for although he is affected as much as the one who goes from one extreme to the other, he is nevertheless only half as far from his natural constitution. A Frenchman can live in Guinea and in Lapland; but a Negro will not live likewise in Torne, nor a Samoyed in Benin. It appears, moreover, that the organization of the brain is less perfect in the two extremes. Neither the Negroes nor the Laplanders have the sense of the Europeans. If, then, I want my pupil to be able to be an inhabitant of the earth, I will get him in a temperate zone – in France, for example – rather than elsewhere.[110]

If Rousseau means only to save his pupil half the distance when he intends to travel either toward the pole or the equator, he should take Emile from a middle latitude. If his intention is to enable him to better endure the transition from one extremity to another, the advantage is still on the side of the middle climate. Still even in a temperate zone, he should be careful not to take him from a region where the air is either too thin or too thick; the disadvantage would be evident in the abrupt passage from one to the other. However, if his object in the choice of a climate is to find a student who will become everything that a man can be, and who has a brain organized in a manner most conducive to his having good sense [*bon sens*],[111] then what he proposes regarding the temperature of the climate deserves some reflection.

In the first place, he needs to allow for a wide range in temperatures. Hannibal, Massinissa, Ghengis Khan, Gustavus Adolphus, and Peter the Great are sufficient evidence that from the burning sands of Numidia to the frozen seas of the North, in Africa, in Tartary and in Scandinavia, men can become all that men can be.

That the climate has influence over temperament and a certain constitution of the soul is generally acknowledged by everyone. One notices a visible difference in this regard between a Spaniard and an Englishman. But the climate does not at all affect the faculty for combining ideas. Reason is absolutely the same in the Spaniard and in the Englishman. It is through this faculty that men are all that they can be. It is through their reason that a Spaniard may succeed as well as an Englishman, and an Englishman as well as a Spaniard, no matter what kind of activity it is. Rousseau makes two assumptions: that Negroes and Laplanders do not have the good sense of Europeans, and that this deficiency of sense is owing to a defect in the organization of the brain. It is true that Negroes and Laplanders do not have the sense of Europeans, and in like manner the Indians of Quito and all Peru do not have the sense of the Spaniards. These Indians have universally and from time immemorial been submerged in a senseless brutishness. In spite of this, all those who are educated from their earliest years do very well and become as reasonable as other men. This is a fact well documented, as we have seen, through the eyewitness of philosophers and observers. These same witnesses praise the vivacity and natural penetration of the inhabitants of Lima. Abbé Prevost mentions somewhere in his *History of Voyages* the case of a young Negro Prince who was in England some time ago and was universally admired.[112] The climate of Arabia approaches very near one of the extremes; yet it has given birth to some extraordinary men. But let me grant that the Negroes and Laplanders do not have the good sense of Europeans. Still, one can always ask: Is it from lack of culture? Is it from deficient organization of the brain? Of these two causes the first is most certainly true. For the education of the Negroes and Laplanders is assuredly very different from that which one receives in Europe. Notwithstanding this, Rousseau attributes it solely to the second cause. Without hesitation he advances two propositions, for which it will be impossible to find the least proof; namely, that the deficiency of sense in the Negroes and Laplanders arises from a defect in the organization of the brain, and that this defect in the organization is due to the climate. The common example of the Indians of Peru, who naturally seem to have much less sense than the Negroes, and who are transformed by education into men as reasonable as the Europeans, seems to prove the contrary. The ancient Romans, judging of the natural character of the Britons by the state of barbarism in which they found them, believed them incapable of what they called "culture of humanity." The Romans were mistaken. It is possible that Rousseau is likewise mistaken. Our forefathers conferred on the Swiss and Germans the honor of thinking them incapable of succeeding in any works of taste. If one would have asked them for the reason, they would undoubtedly have attributed it to the climate. Yet today Haller, Gessner, and Klopstock[113] enjoy the admiration of the most refined nations.

Rousseau wants his student to be born in a country from the temperate zone. The reason he gives is that the organization of the brain is more perfect, and that it is only in temperate climates that men are all that they can be. On the other hand, he prefers for his student to have only a common mind, for, as he says, he only wants to educate an ordinary man. Is he consistent with himself here? Doesn't he hope to make out of a common mind all that a man can be? And if this is not what he hopes for, if it is not what he wants, why then choose only from a climate where men are all what they can be?

The end, object, and chief work of education is to make a man reasonable. Rousseau says it expressly. Now is there any country, in the torrid climates or in the frozen climates, where men cannot become reasonable and where, consequently, the perfection of education is not attainable? If Rousseau's method is only good for temperate climates, it is much too restricted. Christianity is of a totally different nature; it makes men reasonable in all countries.

I do not know whether Rousseau counts among the temperate countries those that are inhabited by the savages of North America. He cannot, however, deny them an eminent degree of reason. A good government is, as everyone would agree, the masterpiece of reason. Now Rousseau teaches us that the savages we are speaking of enjoy this inestimable advantage, which, according to him, is absent in all the temperate countries of Europe. In his *On Social Contract* he announces the remarkable discovery that "the savages of North America are all well governed."[114]

What he says in another place regarding the marks of a good government, however, might prove embarrassing.

> [I]f it is asked what signs can show us whether a given people is well or poorly governed, . . . the question, being one of fact, could be resolved. It is not resolved, however, because each person wishes to do so in his own way. . . . As for me, I am always astonished that people fail to recognize such a simple sign, or that they have the bad faith not to agree to it. What is the aim of political association? It is the preservation and prosperity of its members. And what is the surest sign that they are safe and prosperous? It is their number and their population. Do not, therefore, go elsewhere to seek this much disputed sign.[115]

But if the number and population are the single mark by which one can judge the prosperity of a good government, I do not know how one can say that the savages of North America are so well governed. How ironic for Rousseau that it turns out that the unique mark of a good government is to be found in a despotic empire, such as China, and one would hardly expect to find it among the savages.

[27. *On the ideal student's physical constitution*]

As to the constitution, Rousseau wants a robust and well-formed child.

> I would not take on a sickly and ill-constituted child, were he to live until eighty. I want no pupil always useless to himself and others, involved uniquely with preserving himself, whose body does damage to the education of his soul. What would I be doing in vainly lavishing my care on him other than doubling society's loss and taking two men from it instead of one? Let another in my stead take charge of this invalid. I consent to it and approve his charity. But that is not my talent. I am not able to teach living to one who thinks of nothing but how to keep himself from dying.[116]

I doubt that this passage will do honor to Rousseau's humanity. He reproaches certain philosophers for loving the Tartars in order to be dispensed from having to love their neighbors.[117] Might not these philosophers, if any exist, reproach him with greater justification for the severity he shows toward sickly and feeble children? Doesn't he say that he approves the charity of those who care for these infirm children? But then he recommends this charity in a tone that weakens the desire to practice it. "What would I be doing in vainly lavishing my care on [the sickly child] other than doubling society's loss and taking two men from it instead of one?" What a repulsive way to speak of humanity! Is it an injury to society to take charge of a sickly child, to devote oneself to his care, to watch over his health, to cultivate his reason, his understanding, and his talents?

Does Rousseau wish to see renewed in our day the horrible spectacle of the Spartan harshness toward these innocent creatures? But on this point Sparta violated the most sacred duties of humanity only because she had first misjudged the true end of government. Men are made in order to live in peace, not in order to wage war. War should only be a means of obtaining peace. Rousseau acknowledges that the end of political association is the security and prosperity of its members. Sparta took for its end what should have been only the means; there was no end other than war in her political association. Is it surprising that so essential an error regarding the object and the end of society should have resulted in laws contrary to the order of society? However awful the policy of the Spartans might have been, they reasoned coherently from their false principle. But for Rousseau, who establishes as the end of political association the security and prosperity of its members, to want to consider the care of infirm children as a loss to society – one cannot read such a thing without dismay. If this idea is logically connected with any thing in his system, it must be with the inability of a sickly child to live the life of a savage, for one needs to be a savage and all but a cannibal in order to please Rousseau. The truth is, however, that a sickly child may become the mainstay and the pride of his country. He may be a man of good sense, charitable, learned, capable of giving good counsel, and affording good example. Need one appeal to history to prove a thing that is so well known?

The indulgence and severity of our philosopher are incomprehensible. According to him, it is barbarous to in any way restrain the natural liberty of childhood. He pardons a child who lacks respect for his father; "but if on any occasion whatsoever a child were unnatural enough to lack respect for his mother . . . one should hasten to strangle this wretch as a monster unworthy of seeing the light of day."[118] Let us not carry things too far. Reason is not so indulgent, nor so severe. If a child is given to capricious impulses, one needs to curb them, even though it may cost him a few tears. If a child is so unfortunate as to lack respect for his mother, one should chastise him severely and neglect nothing in order to correct his bad tendency, but it is not necessary to strangle him. We should always suspect a virtue that does not seek the support of religion. Despite the parade of its firmness, its constancy, its heroism, this philosophical virtue will always be untrue to itself at some point. Such a philosopher loves the Turks in order to dispense himself from loving Christians. He wants to strangle children or to educate them so as to make them savages.[*]

* Nothing can be more extraordinary than the instruction Rousseau gives his pupil. He presumes first of all that Emile will never quarrel with any man. "But if someone picks a quarrel with him, how will he behave?" Rousseau responds with the following. "Neither the honor nor the life of citizens must be at the mercy of a bully, of a drunk, or of a brave scoundrel, and none can no more secure oneself from such an accident than from the fall of a tile. To meet and put up with a slap or being given the lie has civil effects which no wisdom can anticipate, and for which no tribunal can avenge the injured party. The insufficiency of the laws, therefore, gives him back his independence in this. He is then the only magistrate, the only judge between the offender and himself. He is the only interpreter and minster of the natural law. He owes himself justice and is the only one who can render it, and there is no government on earth so mad as to punish him for having done himself justice in such a case. I do not say that he ought to fight a duel. That is a folly. I say that he owes himself justice, and that he is the only dispenser of it. If I were sovereign, I guarantee that, without so many vain edicts against duels, there would never be either slap or giving of the lie in my states, and that this would be accomplished by a very simple means in which the tribunals would not mix. However that may be, Emile knows the justice he owes to himself in such a case and the example he owes to the security of men of honor. The firmest of men is not in a position to prevent someone from insulting him, but he is in a position to prevent anyone's boasting for long of having insulted him" [*Emile* 4.147 fn (B, 250–51)]. How could any knowledgeable person interpret this passage in any other sense than that Rousseau encourages private assassination, rather than the folly of a duel. Emile is insulted. No tribunal can vindicate him. The insufficiency of the laws in this case restores him to his natural independence. Behold, he becomes sole magistrate and sole judge between

[28. *On the social status of Rousseau's student*]

With regard to the social status of his pupil, Rousseau would rather have him rich than poor.

> The poor man does not need to be educated. His station gives him a compulsory education. He could have no other. On the contrary, the education the rich man receives from his station is that which suits him least, from both his own point of view and that of society. . . . Let us, then, choose a rich man. We will at least be sure we have made one more man, while a poor person can become a man by himself. For the same reason I will not be distressed if Emile is of noble birth. He will, in any event, be one victim snatched from prejudice.[119]

The poor, in some respects, have less need of education than the rich, for in their uniform and simple way of life, which requires the use of their bodily strength more than their mental faculties, they are less exposed to error. But in other respects, they have greater need for education than the rich, for they have fewer opportunities of being instructed in the truths that should regulate their conduct. The judgment, which we are deprived of at birth, but which we need as we mature, is given by education. This is Rousseau's maxim, and it holds for the poor and the rich alike. The poor are men, and they

> the offender and himself. He owes himself justice, and from himself alone it is to be expected. He is not to duel, yet the offender is not to boast for long of having insulted him. Is this the school of a philosopher, of a wise man, of a virtuous man? Should not this single passage open the eyes of those who so blindly abandon themselves to the extravagent notions of unbelievers? Emile cannot prevent himself from being insulted, but he can prevent a man from boasting long of having insulted him. What a disproportion between the offense and the punishment! And what about submission to public authority? Is this is the constancy, the moderation, and the patience of the wise man? Are they only empty words? O Socrates, O Epictetus, how your morality confounds those sophists who dare to praise virtue by preaching crime! [Gerdil's note.]

therefore need to learn to become reasonable, to be good sons, good husbands, good fathers, good friends, and to love, as they ought to do, their family, their country, and their religion. Many advantages redound to the state that properly educates its lower classes. It would prevent the total ignorance of the duties of humanity, the idleness, debauchery, and brutality. It would soften that roughness of soul that characterizes the common people and is the cause of so many evils. So long as the soul is tranquil, this roughness shows only in rustic manners. But at the instigation of some emotion even minimally violent, what passion of hatred, jealousy, self-interest, and revenge is roused. Immediately on taking fright, the rusticity degenerates into ferocity. This is the origin of those frequent and dreadful quarrels, which begin with a trifle, but end with blood.

One need only consider the present institutions of most of the peoples of Europe in order to imagine introducing the complex of rites and ceremonies that have produced such salutary effects in China. Montesquieu says that the legislators of China extend the rules of civility as broadly as possible with the principal object of making their people live in tranquility. They intend for all men to have great respect for each other and that each one should, at all times, be sensible that he owes much to others, and that there is no citizen who does not, in some respect, depend on another citizen.[120] Such is the spirit of the Chinese customs.

Now Christianity can operate more effectively than a simple formulary of courtesy that only regulates the exterior manners. The foundations, the complete substance of civility are comprehended in these words which St. Paul addressed to all the faithful of every social class: "Be of mutual service to one another. Rejoice with those that rejoice, and lament with those that weep. Insofar as it depends upon you, live in peace with all men regardless of social distinction. Bear with each other's failings and treat one another as brothers. Take revenge on no man. Do not do evil in return for evil."[121] The minister of religion is authorized to preach these salutary maxims in the name of God himself – to recommend them, not only as duties of society, adapted for rendering life more sweet, but as the sacred practices of religion, without which there is no salvation. This would be the subject of a most useful sermon. If the pastor's preaching is evangelical and if it is backed up by his personal example, it will bear fruit. It is a well-known, celebrated fact that in Catholic countries the face of a parish or village can be radically altered merely by the presence of a good parish priest. When I say a good parish priest, I mean a man who is both zealous and learned, for this is required of anyone who is to guide the ignorant. Prudence amounts to nothing where there is no understanding of the circumstances.

In order to make education more effective, care must be taken to convert the children's habits. Toward this end it would be sufficient if the school teacher, charged with teaching the children of the village to read, write, and calculate, would add to these useful exercises, one still more useful. That is, he should make them put into practice the lessons that the Apostle Paul addresses to all Christians regardless of their social status. He should accustom them to treat each other like brothers, to regard one another with reciprocal kindness, and to be of mutual service to one another in their little needs. There should be praise and reward for the one who tempers his anger when he has been wronged. Even greater praise and reward should be given to the one who responds to an injury with kindness. On the other hand, the offender's greatest punishment should be the neglect and contempt his behavior would earn him. Here there would be no mask of worldly politeness, which corrupt men often put on in order to conceal the contempt they have for each other. The practices would aim at awakening and nourishing sentiments of a sincere affection among the children. For the hearts of children open more readily to affection than to any other sentiment. The practical acts motivated by this affection, as they are converted into manners and habits, will increase the effectiveness of the pastor's instructions. Children of villagers are susceptible of the same sentiments as others. Nature is the same throughout, and in the distribution of her gifts she does not discriminate between gilded mansions and the poor man's shanty. A good education will always be capable of connecting in the heads of children the idea of honor with that of virtue, and the idea of shame with that of vice. One can teach them and inwardly convince them that cultivating the earth and all other honest occupations make honorable those who exercise them, and that only vice and idleness degrade men and make them contemptible. What a wellspring of good for a society if such an institution were uniformly established throughout a state! There is only one difficulty. Where is one to find capable educators and an academy that can imbue them with the spirit of this kind of formation? Considered in itself, this difficulty seems enormous. But when it is considered in relation to available resources, it is not so great as it seems.

Be all this as it may, Rousseau's desire to have a rich pupil springs from a laudable motive, which is to snatch one victim from prejudice.

> One of the miseries of rich people is to be deceived in everything. If they judge men poorly, need one be surprised? It is riches which corrupt them, and by a just return they are the first to feel the defect of the only instrument known to them.[122]

Rousseau's efforts would have been useful had he detailed the causes and effects of the corruption of riches and the abuses they have introduced into education. D'Alembert touched on this subject in his essay on the relationship between men of letters and the great persons of society.[123] We can imagine how compellingly Rousseau would have described the prejudices into which many rich men are educated. These prejudices are the ordinary sources of illusion in which they pass the better part of their lives. It is a world in which appearances substitute for reality, formalities often prevail over substantial matters, extravagant pomp accompanies matters of no consequence. Frequently much that is serious is treated frivolously, while frivolous matters are taken up with great seriousness. Rousseau would not have reformed the world, for the world is old, as they say, and incorrigible. But he would, perhaps, have undeceived some rich people, and the world would be that much the better.

[29. *The insufficiency of philosophy for forming a national ethos*]

With regard to the institution of public education, Rousseau pretends that

> Public instruction no longer exists and can no longer exist, because where there is no longer fatherland, there can no longer be citizens. These two words, *fatherland* and *citizen*, should be effaced from modern languages. I know well the reason why this is so, but I do not want to tell it. It has nothing to do with my subject.[124]

Why then didn't Rousseau first of all give his own example of the reform that he wished to introduce into the modern languages? In other words, how does he reconcile the title of "citizen," which appears at the head of his book,[125] with what he proposes in this passage?

He adds: "I do not envisage as a public education those laughable establishments called *colleges*."[126]

Rousseau is too little measured in his formulations. The epithet "laughable" is not at all apt for praiseworthy institutions from which we have derived much benefit. But, as with all human establishments, they are susceptible to a new degree of perfection. He could have offered some useful observations on this subject. He could have discussed the uniformity of instruction, its advantages, and the means of establishing it. During the long course of ages following the incursion of the barbarians (in order not to speak about some modern princes[127]), I know only of Charlemagne who understood well its importance.[128]

I shall say nothing of this public education, upon which: "the unlearned and learned alike indiscriminately write."[129] I shall content myself with emphasizing a point that has impressed me for a long time now in various writings on this subject. It is common to distinguish the department of letters to form the mind, that of philosophy to form the citizen, and that of religion to form the Christian. If we pretend that philosophy alone can form the citizen, I believe we have deceived ourselves.

First, philosophy is above the capacity of the multitude. To talk philosophy to farmers and artisans is to speak to them in an unknown language. People of worldly affairs are too busy to occupy themselves entirely with philosophy. Nevertheless these people form the large majority of citizens. It is, therefore, necessary to have some other principle besides philosophy to form the greater number of the citizens, and this principle, since it must be universal, will, in general, have to form all the citizens.

Secondly, philosophy is very easily corrupted in those who only skim its surface. This is an observation of Chancellor Bacon.[130] Sound philosophy is, therefore, limited to a small number. If it must serve the state, it will occur more effectively through the benefices that three or four great philosophers are able to pass on, than by this apparent, superficial diffusion of philosophy that gradually increases and spreads itself through every order of society. Of what use is it to a state to have twenty thousand idle citizens with a superficial knowledge in astronomy? The knowledge of these people will never serve either to regulate the calendar or to perfect the theories that could be of interest to society. The state profits from the labors of a certain number of the true astronomers; the rest is just about pure loss. Between astronomy and philosophy, however, there is the difference that a superficial knowledge in astronomy does no harm, but, on the contrary, serves to embellish the mind and to encourage a taste for good things, whereas, if philosophy does no good, it never fails to do harm.

Thirdly, philosophy offers no motives sufficient to make one practice with constancy the duties that it recommends. Bayle tried to prove that the beauty of virtue has of itself sufficient allure to induce men to attach themselves faithfully to her.[131] This is an illusion. The beauty of virtue can touch the human heart. The theater is proof of it. There exists no villain who loves wickedness by instinct, while there are many men who love virtue by inclination. Every man who could as easily achieve his end through legitimate as through criminal means will naturally prefer the first over the second. But if it happens that the attraction of virtue and the complacency it excites in the soul is balanced by some prospect of particular interest or by a strong passion, then we have an altogether different situation. A connoisseur is enraptured at the sight of a fine picture; he contemplates it with admiration, he is enchanted with it. Now will he sell his property to buy the picture? It will be a matter of calculation. But the choice of virtue ought never to be the effect of this sort of calculation. Will we then say that the general interest is a motive sufficient to attach men to virtue? Another illusion. It is true that on the whole the particular interest is bound up with the general interest. Notwithstanding this connection, however, are there not people who pursue their own particular interests at the cost of the general interest? Another matter for calculation. Consult the human heart. It will tell you that virtue is beautiful in itself, but that it does supply the want of all other things. Virtue, then, needs support, a counterweight to the pleasures that are put in the scale against it. This support, this counterpoise is found only in religion.

Fourthly, philosophy is not particularly suitable for establishing that uniformity of the patriotic spirit, which needs to animate and bind together the different members of the state so as to form a single body. This uniformity of the spirit results from a kind of unanimity in the customs and manners, founded on the unity of maxims. For it is the maxims that roughly decide the conduct of men. Forced situations, unforeseen accidents, or strong passions can sometimes cause one to deviate from them; but they are only transitory, violent deviations. As soon as the storm is over, a man returns to his maxims, for everyone is jealous of his own self-government, and he governs himself only so long as he is governed by his maxims. Therefore, in order to establish a uniformity of the patriotic spirit, it is necessary to establish a unity of maxims. Now this is something that religion can do, because religion tends to union; it is something that philosophy cannot do, because philosophy tends to disunion. Religion tends to union, because it is founded on an authority that captivates the spirit and reconciles it to the submission that it owes to the oracles of revelation. Philosophy, on the contrary, is only a complex of different systems, the work of different minds, which perpetually contradict each other, either in their principles or their conse-quences.[132] In reality, there is nothing in which philosophers agree but in the mere term philosophy. For the rest, there are as many sys-tems as there are heads.

Hobbes confounds right with force:[133] a terrible idea in the judg-ment of Montesquieu,[134] and resolutely rejected by Rousseau.[135] Some derive the origin of political right from paternal authority,[136] others from express or tacit conventions. Rousseau requires, besides, that the suffrages should be unanimous.[137] The author of *On the Mind*[138] recognizes no probity relative to the totality of humankind; he acknowledges no intrinsic moral difference between virtue and vice. Montesquieu establishes this difference upon relationships of justice and equity anterior to all positive law.[139] On the other hand, he pretends that virtue is not necessary in monarchies.[140] Voltaire says quite ingenuously at some place that it would be too great a mis-fortune if he were to be right in this opinion.[141] And Rousseau openly condemns it.[142] However, Montesquieu insists that virtue is required for republics.[143] The author of the *Recherches sur l'origine du despotisme oriental* says, to the contrary, that virtue has been injurious to certain ancient republics.[144] Montesquieu attributes much to the climate;[145] Helvetius will have nothing attributed to it.[146] Bayle pretends that society might subsist without religion.[147] "After having abused all re-ligions, he dishonors the Christian religion by daring to assert that true Christians are not capable of forming a state which could sub-sist." This paradox is refuted by Montesquieu as we have just re-ported in his own words.[148] The author of the *Code de la nature*[149] dares to say that no one has up to this point understood the true prin-ciples of legislation or morality, and maintains the community of property as the basis of both. Many are of opinion that the life which children receive from their father and mother does not impose upon them any duty in their regard. Rousseau would have it that there is no question of obedience among men.[150] One philosopher excuses suicide; another justifies dueling; a third represents luxury as the source of prosperity in a state; a fourth restricts it to the great monar-chies.[151] D'Alembert seems absolutely to condemn it.[152] Some even maintain that vices are necessary to a state and that they contribute to its flourishing.[153] One protests against the indissolubility of the marriage bond, while another justifies the temporary union of free persons.[154] If this anarchy of opinions were spread among the multitude of citizens, would it contribute to establishing the unity of the patriotic spirit?

But in blaming the abuse of philosophy, I am far from condemning philosophy itself. A true philosopher, that is to say, a wise man, can do much good for society; but it will be by directing those who work, not by making philosophers of those whose duty it is only to execute. My thesis is that the patriotic spirit cannot be introduced by the garrulity of philosophy, dispersed among persons of every social condition, in which the true and the false, the good and the bad, the probable and the paradoxical, and, in a word, everything is perpetually mixed, confounded, discussed, analyzed, contradicted, approved of, and where philosophical jargon at each instant dissipates the spirit and order of sound philosophy. Full of admiration for those wise men who, having a proper regard for religion and the laws, extend by their fortunate discoveries the sphere of human knowledge, I mean only to limit myself to emphasizing the ill consequences of that kind of philosophy which, according to the wise observation of the President Hénault,[155] has been the cause of much evil, due to the abuse that has been made of it, "insofar as one sometimes justifiably suspects it of not being favorable to religion when it enters into a poorly disposed head." This is the sort of philosophy that Bacon has characterized with his customary force:

> Certainly there be [those] that delight in giddiness, and count it a bondage to fix a belief; affecting free will in thinking as well as in acting. And though the sect of philosophers of that kind be gone, yet there remain certain discoursing wits, which are of the same veins, though there be not so much blood in them as was in those of the ancients.[156]

On the other hand, who does not know that legislation itself is the great achievement of philosophy? The most celebrated legislators of antiquity were philosophers. But when once philosophy or wisdom has drawn up the laws, they need to be sacred, for the philosopher as well as for the common people. Lycurgus drew his laws from the depths of philosophy, but Lycurgus, the philosopher, would not have permitted the Athenian babblers to dispute in Sparta against the laws of Sparta.

[Conclusion]

The above digression is not so far removed from my subject as it might appear. Rousseau declaims vigorously against philosophy and philosophers. If the comparison were not too low, I would say he resembles a mountebank, who discredits all of his colleagues in order to attribute to himself alone the possession of the universal remedy.

> Readers, always remember that he who speaks to you is neither a scholar nor a philosopher, but a simple man, a friend of the truth, without party, without system; a solitary who, living little among men, has less occasion to contract their prejudices and more time to reflect on what strikes him when he has commerce with them. My reasonings are founded less on principles than on facts.[1]

Rousseau is then no philosopher. He forms no systems. He is not the author of the precepts contained in his book. It is nature herself that makes herself known and exposes her views, her power, and her needs. The social man is not the man of nature; social institutions deprave and degrade him. Rousseau does nothing but liberate man of those alien connections in order to show him as he really is. Can we refuse to hear the cries of nature that speak through his book? Can we deny her the assistance she requires? And many people have been persuaded of this by Rousseau's dazzling eloquence. They do not see that the natural man he shows them is the most fictional being that ever existed in the imagination of any philosopher. No one today has ever seen a man wholly free from all social institutions, and no one can say how he would be. All that he delivers on the subject is abstraction, imagination, pure reverie. Yet, by means of these artificial disguises, what deadly impressions will not his book make on the minds of those who are so little protected against its seduction? A contempt for all revealed religion and for Christianity in particular,* and I would even say a neglect of the Divinity, a hatred for

---

  * Vernes's letters clearly show us what we should think of Rousseau's Christianity and of his sentiments on revelation. The way in which he speaks in his *Emile* [4.332 fn (B, 299)] of a law of Deuteronomy, and in his *On Social Contract* [Bk.1 , ch.2] of king Adam and emperor Noah is inconsistent with the respect he pretends to show in other parts of his works for "the majesty of the Sacred Scriptures" [*Emile* 4.355 (B, 307)]. He even dares to accuse Christianity of rendering its duties impracticable by carrying them to excess. [Jacob Vernes, *Lettres sur le Christianisme de Mr. J.-J. Rousseau* (Amsterdam: Neaulme, 1764)] Rousseau is mistaken in this accusation. Christianity carries nothing to excess; it is he who entertains himself by taking to excess everything he takes up. We give this example: "He who eats in idleness what he did not earn himself steals it. A man whom the state pays an income for doing nothing hardly differs in my eyes from a brigand who lives at the expense of passers-by. . . . Rich or poor, powerful or weak, every idle citizen is a rascal" [*Emile* 3.126 (B, 195)]. Christianity condemns idleness in all men; but though idleness is a great sin, does it thereby follow that he who, without doing any thing himself, lives on the wealth passed on to him by his ancestors, who lawfully acquired it, steals what he eats? The idle citizen is without doubt very much to be blamed for his idleness; but he is not a thief, a rascal, or a highwayman. It is this sort of claim that may be called carrying things to excess and making a good cause bad.

I do not accuse Rousseau of trying to encourage the neglect of the Divinity; but it seems that some of his principles are capable of leading that way. In his opinion, children, even at the age of fifteen years, are not capable of being instructed in the knowledge of God. What! How can we in the heart of Christianity permit children to arrive at the age of fifteen or eighteen years without acquainting them with their first principle and their final end, without teaching them that they have a soul to save? "I foresee how many readers will be surprised at seeing me trace the whole first age of my pupil without speaking to him of religion. At fifteen he did not know whether he had a soul. And perhaps at eighteen it is not yet time for him to learn it . . ." [*Emile* 4.171 (B, 257)]. But

all established governments, revolt against all legitimate authority, a mind of unbridled independence and liberty, obedience suppressed from the dictionary of children; a false indulgence that will not curb the impulses of child's natural liberty, a false reserve that will not reason with them, that will not cultivate their minds by studies suited to their age – such are the fruits of the new plan of education.

Rousseau has intermingled among these ideas some useful and illuminating truths, but in his book they only serve to better conceal

suppose he should die before that age? Rousseau here shelters himself under invincible ignorance [*Emile* 4.176 (B, 258)]. We must confess that a misplaced invincible ignorance favors the neglect of the Divinity. His Savoyard Vicar, whose profession of faith he presents as the best and most useful piece that has been published during the present century, is made to say, that "it is very strange that any other [than natural religion] is needed. . . . The greatest ideas of the divinity come to us from reason alone" [*Emile* 4.318 (B, 295)]. Every Christian will perceive the absurdity of this pretence, which tends to disfigure the idea of the Divinity with all the caprices of human philosophy. This same Vicar, in another place, says, ". . . I bless God for his gifts. But I do not pray to Him. What would I ask of Him? That He change the course of things for me, that He perform miracles in my favor?" [*Emile* 4.313 (B, 293).] One should fear that he who believes he has nothing to ask of God may soon tire of praising him for his gifts. From the neglect of prayer to the neglect of the Creator is a slippery step.

With regard to the contempt for all human authority, beyond the passage we have cited elsewhere on spirit of the laws of all nations, we shall cite the following passage: "Those specious names, justice and order, will always serve as instruments of violence and as arms of iniquity. From this it follows that the distinguished orders who claim they are useful to others are actually useful only to themselves at the expense of their subordinates" [*Emile* 4.99 (B, 236)]. I do not know what impression Rousseau's book would have on savages, but it is evident that it tends to unsettle the foundations of Christianity and of every civil state governed by laws and social institutions. It does not wrong this book, therefore, to say that it is apt to form bad Christians and bad citizens. Does this render any service to humanity? [Gerdil's note] the deadly poison that it contains and to cause it to be swallowed the more eagerly. Is Rousseau the only mortal to whom nature has unveiled herself? Between him and all the philosophers who have preceded him, the question is not whether he has been able to discover any particular truth, any secret fold of the human heart, or any remote consequence or detail that might have escaped the view of others. If Rousseau has hit the mark, if he alone has seen everything, then the others have seen nothing. Socrates, Plato, Xenophon, Cicero, Seneca, Quintilian, Plutarch, Bacon, Locke, Bossuet, Fleury, Fénelon, Nicole, and Rollin – these illustrious men knew nothing of the nature of man and were all mistaken in their researches on the way to guide and to educate youth. Rousseau opens a new road. Men will no longer be depraved by arbitrary institutions. They will no longer be debased by the obtrusive threats of religion. They will no longer be fatigued by studies so remote from nature. A robust body, a vigorous mind, an aptitude to do everything, health and happiness will be the inestimable fruits of this novel method of education. What chimeras! What visions!

Fathers and mothers, do not be seduced by the deceitful attractions of brilliant novelty. Be wary of subjecting your children to the perilous experiment of a method that is not yet warranted by any success. Keep always before your eyes the sacred maxims of our forefathers, maxims so venerable by virtue of their authority and antiquity. Be especially careful not to neglect religion in the education of your children. You vainly flatter yourself if you try to conduct them by any other path. If they are dear to you, if you expect from them honor and consolation, their happiness and yours must come from religion. Take care that mistaken vanity does not induce you to sacrifice these innocent victims to a deadly desire for singularity and that the unhappiness into which you will have cast them does not one day constitute your shame and despair.

Endnotes

PREFACE

[1] Rousseau gives an account of Abbé de Saint Pierre (Charles-Irénée Castel) (1658–1743), and his relationship to him in his *Confessions* Bk. 9. He was an influential French intellectual, known for his utopian reformist ideas, perhaps most especially for his proposals for international peace, in his *Le Project de paix perpétuelle* (*The Project for Setting Everlasting Peace in Europe*) (1713).

[2] In the original four-volume edition of *Emile* the first volume comprised the Preface and Books 1 and 2.

PART ONE

[1] The person who had asked Gerdil to review first volume of *Emile* is unknown.

[2] *Lettre de M. D'Alembert à M. J. J. Rousseau sur l'article 'Genève' tiré du septième volume de* l'Encyclopédie.

[3] *Emile* 1.45 (B, 45).

[4] *Emile* Preface. 6–8 (B, 34–35).

[5] *Emile* 1.2 (B, 37).

[6] *Emile* 1.29 (B, 41–42).

[7] *Emile* 1.32 (B, 42).

[8] *On Social Contract* Bk. 2, ch. 8.

[9] *Emile* 1.71 (B, 50).

[10] *Emile* 1.5 (B, 38).

[11] *Emile* 1.6–7 (B, 38). The doctrine of three teachers – nature, things, men – provides an architectonic structure to the *Emile*. The education of Book 1 is limited to the "lessons" of nature which are governed by the

subjective criteria of pleasure and pain; this first phase covers the first two years of life. In Books 2 and 3 Emile's education, from the age of 2 until 16, is augmented by his encounter with things and their utility. Books 4 and 5 develop the final phase of Emile's education, up through his mid-twenties, which ends with his marriage and the birth of a child; during this period he enters into the social world of men under the governance of a rational idea of happiness. His three "teachers" correspond to the three sources of civil society among the various social contract theorists.

[12] *Emile* 1.12 (B, 39).

[13] Cicero, for instance, whose works Gerdil admired and knew well, gives this tripartite division a central role his *On Duties* (*De Officiis*); see esp., Bk.1, ch. 3.

[14] By "nature" Rousseau here signifies those dispositions in us by which we are drawn to or repelled from objects as they are measured by the standards of pleasure/pain, useful/useless (relative to the individual self), and judged in conformity to reason's idea of happiness and perfection, unconstrained by custom and opinion. Rousseau believes that there is nothing in nature that would be inclined to set one tendency at odds with another. Contrariety in the human heart is therefore an artifact of bad education. Gerdil objects to the optimism regarding nature. The subsequent paragraph of *Emile* makes it evident that the un-alienated self is the subject of nature. We can put one of the central issues between Rousseau and Gerdil in the following way: Is contrariety in the human heart an artifact of avoidable bad education (Rousseau), or is it an inevitable, innate factor in the human condition (Gerdil)?

[15] *Timaeus* 69.

[16] Cicero, *Tusculan Disputations* (*Tusculanarum Disputationum*) Bk. 2, ch. 4; Bk. 3, ch. 3–6; also *On Duties* (*De Officiis*) Bk. 2, ch. 2.

[17] *Emile* 2.63 (B, 92).

[18] *Emile* 1.13, 15 (B, 39–40).

[19] Don George Juan and Don Antonio De Ulloa, *A Voyage to South America Describing at Large the Spanish Cities, Towns, Provinces, etc. on That Extensive Continent: Undertaken by Command of the King of Spain*, 2 vol., 5th ed , translated from the original Spanish by John Adams (London: Stockdale, 1807; reprinted, Boston: Longwood, 1978). The original Spanish: *Relación histórica del viage a la América méridional . . .* (Madrid:

Marìn, 1748). Gerdil likely knew the French translation, *Voyage histoirque de l'Amérique méridonale . . .* (Paris: Jombert, 1752).

[20] *Voyage*, Bk. 6, ch. 6; vol. 1, pp. 403–7.

[21] Rousseau's conjectural portrait of natural man is developed throughout the First Part.

[22] *Voyage*, p. 402.

[23] *Voyage*, pp. 417–20.

[24] *Voyage*, p. 419. The passage which Gerdil quotes in French, and which I have translated, does not exactly parallel the 1807 English translation.

[25] *Emile* 1.15 (B, 39).

[26] See Cicero, *On Duties* (*De Officiis*) Bk. 3, ch. 9.49; Plutarch's *Parallel Lives. Aristides.*

[27] See Cicero, *On Duties* (*De Officiis*) Bk. 3, ch. 12.86; Plutarch's *Parallel Lives. Pyrrhus*, ch. 20–21.

[28] *Emile* 1.15 (B, 40).

[29] Corsetti seems correct (in his endnote 32, pp. 114–15) in identifying this distasteful "system of philosophy" with the materialistic hedonism of the French philosopher, Claude-Adrien Helvetius (1715–1771), expressed in his chief work *De l'esprit* (*On the Mind*) (1758), in which he argues that physical sensibility lies at the constitutive origins of all human ideas, conduct, and institutions. For example, in *De l'esprit, or Essay on the Mind and Its Several Faculties*, translated from the French (New York: Burt Franklin, 1970; reprint of the 1810 edition), he writes in Essay 1, ch. 1, p. 7, "that all the operations of the Mind consist in the power we have of perceiving the resemblance and difference, the agreement or disagreement, of various objects among themselves. And this power, being the Physical Sensibility itself, every thing is reducible to feeling." And in Essay 3, ch. 4, p. 213, we find: "I easily discover the source of human virtues. I see that men, without a sensibility of pain and natural pleasure, without desires, without passions, and equally indifferent with respect to every thing, would not have known a personal interest: that without a personal interest they would not have united in society, would not have entered into conventions among themselves, and would not have had a general interest; consequently there would have been no action, either just or unjust; and *that thus natural sensibility and personal interest have been the authors of all justice.*" [Italics added.] It is interesting to note that his posthumously published treatise *De*

l'homme (*A Treatise on Man; His Intellectual Faculties and His Education*) (1773) argues against Rousseau's *Emile*; see esp. Section 5.

30 D'Alembert, *Essai sur la société des gens de lettres et des Grands, sur la réputation, sur les mécènes, et sur les récompenses littéraires* (Corsetti, Unitor, p. 115).

31 The story here is that Cardinal Richelieu (1585–1642), a most influential French minister during Louis XIII's monarchy, thought he had some claim as co-creator of Pierre Corneille's (1606–1684) poetic masterpiece, *El Cid*. It was a claim that the poet rejected even though it would likely have been to his worldly advantage.

32 In his *Discours en vers sur L"homme, Septième discours, sur la vraie nature*, Voltaire wrote: "Certain législateur, don la plume séconde / Fit tant de vains projects pour le bien de ce monde, / Et qu depuis trente ans écrit pour des ingrats, / Vient de créer un mot qui manque à augelas: / Ce mot est *bienfaisance. . . .*" And in his note to the text, identifying this legislator, he wrote: "L'abbé de Saint-Pierre. C'est qui a mis le mot de *bienfaisance* à la mode, à force de le répéter. On l'appelle législateur, parce qu'il n'a écrit que pour rèformer le gouvernment. Il c'est rendu un peu ridicule en France par l'excés de ses bonnes intentions." In *Mélange*, Bibliothèque de la Pléiade, Préface par Emmanuel Berlé, texte établi et annoté par Jacques van den Heuvel (Dijon: Gallimard, 1965), text, pp. 238–39 and note, p. 1378.

33 *On the Orator* (*De oratore*) Bk. 1, ch. 8. 30–34.

34 See *On Duties* (*De officiis*) Bk. 1, ch. 2. 5–6 for Cicero's insistence on the irreducibility of intrinsic goodness (*honestum*) to personal interest (*commodum*). In Book 1 of his *De finibus bonorum et malorum* he presents the Epicurean attempt to establish human happiness upon pleasure; he then argues against it in Bk. 2. See esp. Bk. 2, ch. 14 for Cicero's insistence that *honestum* is worthy of choice for its own sake: "Honestum igitur id intellegimus quod tale est ut detracta omni utilitate sine ullis praemis fructibusque per se ipsum possit iure laudari."

35 *On the Laws* (*De legibus*) Bk. 1, ch.14 –16.

36 Emile only begins to learn virtue and to appreciate being estimable in the eyes of others in Bk 4, when he enters into society; see also *On Social Contract* Bk. 1, ch. 8.

37 "The oldest of all societies and the only natural one is that of the family," *On Social Contract* Bk. 1, ch.2; translated by Julia Conaway Bondanella,

in *Rousseau's Political Writings*, Norton Critical Edition, edited by Alan Ritter and Julian Conaway Bondanella (New York and London: Norton, 1988), p. 86.

38 *Emile* 2.31 (B, 84).

39 *Emile* 2.34 (B, 85).

40 For example, *On Social Contract* Bk. 1, ch. 6.

41 Jacques-Benigne Bossuet, *Politics drawn from the Very Words of Holy Scripture*, Cambridge Texts in the History of Political Thought, translated and edited by Patrick Riley (Cambridge, New York, Port Chester, Melbourne, Sidney: Cambridge University Press, 1990), from Bk.1, art. 3, prop. 5 (pp. 16–18). *Politique tirée des propres paroles de l'Escriture sainte* was orignially published posthumously in 1709.

42 *Emile* 2.34 (B, 85).

43 *Emile* 1.35 (B, 43).

44 Turenne, Henri de La Tour d'Auvergne (1611–1675) was a brilliant military leader during the reigns of Louis XIII and XIV. Aguesseau, Henri-François d' (1668–1751), a jurist, was several times chancellor of France between 1717–1750.

45 *Emile* 1.32 (B, 42).

46 *Emile* 1.101 (B, 55).

47 It is interesting to note that Gerdil's first publication was a treatise on the immortality of the soul: *L'immortalité de l'âme démontrée contre M. Locke par les mêmes principes, par lesquels ce philosophe démontre l'existence et l'immatérialité de Dieu . . .* (Torino: 1747).

48 *Phaedo* esp. 107c–d, 113d–114c.

49 *Emile* 5.334 (B, 446).

50 *Emile* 2.25 (B, 82).

51 Paul of Tarsus; see Ph 1:12–26.

52 *Emile* 1.96–104 (B, 54–55).

53 *Emile* 2.35 (B, 85).

54 1Pt. 2: 13–14.

55 *On Social Contract* Bk.1, ch. 6; trans. Norton ed., p. 93.

56 *On Social Contract* Bk.1, ch.7; Norton ed., p. 95.

57 See the digest of *On Social Contract* in *Emile* Bk. 5 (B, 460–70).

58 Herodotus, *Persian Wars* Bk. 1, 96–101.

59 Daniel Defoe, *Robinson Crusoe.*

60 *Timaeus* 21e–22c.

61 *Emile* 2.34 (B, 85).

62 *Emile* 2.34 (B, 85).

63 Antoine-Yves Goguet, with Alexander-Conrad Fugère, *De l'origine des loix, des arts et des sciences, et de leurs progès chez les anciens peuples*, 3 vol. (Paris: Chez Desaint et Saillant, 1758), see vol. 1, p. 3; Eng. translation: *The Origin of Laws, Arts, and Sciences, and Their Progress among the Most Ancient Nations*, 3 vol. trans by Robert Henry, D. Dunn, and Alexander Spearman (Edinburgh: A. Donaldson and J. Reid, 1761; reprinted New York: AMS Press, 1975).

64 Thomas Hobbes, *Leviathan* Part 1, ch. 13.

65 *Emile* 1.5 (B, 38).

66 For the rudiments of Rousseau's theory of ideation see *Emile* 2.118–19; 3.155–58,(B, 107–8, 203).

67 Galen, *On the Usefulness of the Parts of the Body. De usu partium*, translated from the Greek with an Introduction and Commentary by Margaret Tallmadge May (Ithaca, N.Y.: Cornell University Press, 1968), I, 6 (p. 71); Aristotle, *On parts of animals*, 678a20–21.

68 *Discourse on the Origin and Foundations of Inequality among Men*, esp. First Part.

69 *Emile* 2.22 (B, 81–82).

70 *Emile* 2.60–1 (B, 92).

71 *Emile* 2.33 (B, 85).

72 *Emile* 2.36 (B, 85).

73 *Emile* 2.50 (B, 89).

74 *Emile* 2.49–50 (B, 88–89).

75 *Emile* 2.11 (B, 79).

76 *Emile* 2.49 (B, 89).

77 Eph 6.1; Col 3.20.

78 Dt 4: 1–14; 6: 4–9.

79 1 Sam 2.

80 Sirach 30.

81 *Emile* 1.152 (B, 65–66).

82 Horace, *Epistles* I.1. vv. 49–69, poses the question whether citizens

should prefer money to virtue. In favor of the latter he recalls the call to nobility reflected in a young boys' game, in which the boys would urge their comrades on with the promise of kingship to the lad whose manliness and courage led him to the top of the heap, as it were. "*Recte*" signifies both upward, straight to the top, as in the boys' game, and also uprightly or rightly in the moral sense.

83   *Emile* 2.54 (B, 90).

84   Compare Galen, *On the Usefulness of the Parts of the Body* Bk. 1, sec. 3.

85   *Emile* 1.5 (B, 38).

86   *Emile* 4. 175–8 (B, 258–59).

87   Cicero, *On the Nature of the Gods* (*De natura deorum*) Bk. 1, ch. 22.

88   *Emile* 2.57 (B, 91). Rousseau's antipathy to authority is unmistakably evident in the last sentence, where he distinguishes power from authority, allowing the use of the first and denying the use of the second in the rearing of children.

89   Rousseau's polemic against authority as the enemy of youth's necessary autonomy is pervasive. See, for example, *Emile* 2.30 (B, 84); 2.57 (B, 91); 2.161 (B, 118); 2, 170 (B, 121); 2.313 (B, 160); 2.318 (B, 162); 3.15 (B, 168); 3.54 (B, 176); 3.177 (B, 207); 4.161–63 (B, 254–55); 4.181 (B, 260); 4.365 (B, 313); 4.373 (B, 316); 4.405 (B, 325); 4.408 (B, 326–27); 4.74–6 (B, 377–78).

90   See *On Social Contract* Bk. 3, ch.13.

91   *Emile* 1.55 (B, 46–47).

92   Sirach 3:1–17 and 7:27–28.

93   *Emile* 1.33 (B, 85).

94   *Emile* 1.52 (B, 46); also see Rousseau's characterization of family life throughout Bk. 5, esp. in remarks on the education of Sophie, in the example of family life in Sophie's home, and in his depiction of Sophie and Emile's marriage.

95   *On Social Contract* Bk. 1, ch. 2; Norton ed., p. 86.

96   Thomas Aquinas, *Summa theologiae* 2-2, q. 154, a. 2.

97   Our translation is from Montesquieu, *Spirit of the Laws*, Cambridge Texts in the History of Political Thought, translated by Anne M. Cohler, Basia Carolyn Miller, Harold Samuel Stone (Cambridge, New York, Port Chester, Melbourne, Sidney: Cambridge University Press, 1989), p. 428. *L'Esprit des lois* was first published in 1748.

PART TWO

1 At this point in his reflections, Gerdil has completed a consideration of the five Rousseauian principles he enumerated in Preface and now turns to the more particular practices of educating youth.

2 *Emile* 2.51 (B, 89).

3 See John Locke, *Some Thoughts concerning Education* (1693), esp. sec. 80–2, where he says such things as the following: "I would have the father seldom interpose his authority and command in these cases [of minor childish misbehavior] or in any other but such as have a tendency to vicious habits. I think there are better ways of prevailing with them: and a gentle persuasion in reasoning . . . will most times do much better." "But when I talk of *reasoning* I do not intend any other but such as is suited to a child's capacity and apprehension. No one can think a boy of three or seven years old should be argued with as a grown man." "When I say therefore that they must be *treated as rational creatures* I mean that you should make them sensible by the mildness of your carriage and the composure even in your correction of them that what you do is reasonable in you and useful and necessary for them and that it is not out of *caprichio* [= caprice], passion, or fancy that you command or forbid them anything." "Virtues and vices can be by no words so plainly set before their understandings as the actions of other men will show them, when you direct their observation and bid them view this good or bad quality in their practice. And the beauty or uncomeliness of many things in good and ill breeding will be better learned and make deeper impressions on them in the *examples* of others than from any rule or instructions can be given about them." From *Some Thoughts concerning Education and Of the Conduct of the Understanding*, edited, with Introduction by Ruth W. Grant and Nathan Tarcov (Indianapolis and Cambridge: Hackett, 1996), pp. 57–59.

4 See endnote 82 above.

5 *Emile* 2.51 (B, 89).

6 ". . . spectatum admissi risum teneatis, amici? (. . . were you admitted to see [such a freak], would you be able to keep from laughing, my friends?)," Horace, *Ars Poetica*, v. 5; in Q. Horati Flacci, *Opera*, Oxford Classical Texts (Oxford: Clarendon, 1901).

7 *Emile* 2.51 (B, 89).

⁸ *Emile* 2.52 (B, 90).

⁹ See esp. *Emile* 4.308–9 (B, 291–92).

¹⁰ Horace, *Satires* I. 4. 105–31 "The best of all fathers trained me / To avoid all sort of mistakes, by forming the habit / Of pointing them out one by one, with examples. His advice / To me about living frugally, thriftily, happy / With what he himself had provided, used to go like this: / 'Don't you see what a mess Albius' son's life is, and how hard-pressed / Baius is? Let that be a lesson to you not to squander / The money you get from your father.' To deter me from having / A sordid affair, he'd say, 'Now, Horace, don't be / like Scetanus.' To keep me from adultery, when / I could form a decent liaison, he'd argue: 'Trebonius / Was caught in the act and acquired a bad reputation. / Philosophers may give you reasons about what is best / To pursue and best to avoid. For me, it's enough / If I keep within the bounds of tradition handed down / By my parents to me, and as long as you need a protector, / Keep your life and your name safe and sound. When time makes you strong / In body and spirit, you'll swim without needing the cork.' / So, with his words he formed me. . . . And because of my father's influence I am now free / Of the vices that prove ruinous, and only at fault / In certain minor matters you may well forgive." Translation by Smith Palmer Bovie, in *The Satires and Epistles of Horace: A Modern English Translation.* (Chicago and London: University of Chicago Press, 1959), pp. 56–57.

¹¹ Pierre Coste (1668–1747), widely respected for his understanding of contemporary literary movements, was know for his editorial and scholarly work, but especially for his translations of Locke and Newton. Corsetti (fn. 120, p. 137) thinks Gerdil refers to Coste's comments on Horace, *Oeuvres d'Horace, traduite en françois par le p. Tarteron de la Compagnie de Jésus. Quatrième édition revue e corrigiée. Avec des remarques critiques sur la traduction par Pierre Coste* (Amsterdam: de Coup, 1710).

¹² *Emile* 2.54 (B, 90).

¹³ *On Social Contract* Bk. 2, ch. 8.

¹⁴ Arrighi (p. 83, fn 2) thinks Gerdil is referring to *Vita civile e dell'educazione del principe* by Paolo Mattia Doria (1662–1746). Be this as it may, it is curious that Gerdil seems never to have appended the promised citations from this work.

¹⁵ *Emile* 2.117 (B, 107).

¹⁶ *Emile* 2.118 (B, 107).

[17] *Emile* 2.119 (B, 107–8).

[18] *Emile* 1.18 (B, 40).

[19] Jean Terrasson, *Sethos, histoire ou, vie tirée monumens anecdotes de l'ancienne Egypte* (Paris: Guérin,1731); English trans.: *The Life of Sethos, Taken from Private Memoirs of the Ancient Egyptians*, translated by Thomas Lediard (London: J. Walthoe, 1732).

[20] *Emile* 2.137 (B, 112).

[21] *Emile* 2.137 (B, 112–13).

[22] Socrates in the *Phaedo* 61b expresses a high regard for Aesop. In *Republic* 337b–c, he recommends nursery stories that have a proper moral. Rousseau acknowledges that the *Republic* is "the most beautiful educational treatise ever written" (*Emile* 1.21; B, 40).

[23] *Emile* 2.118 (B, 107).

[24] Quintilian, *Instruction of the Orator* (*Institutio oratoria*) Bk. 1, ch.9: "Let boys learn, then, to relate orally the fables of Aesop, which follow next after nursery stories, in plain language, not rising at all above mediocrity, and afterwards to express the same simplicity in writing." English translation from *On the Early Education of the Citizen-Orator. Institutio oratoria Book I and Book 2, Chapters One through Ten*, translated by John Selby Watson, edited with Introduction and Notes by James J. Murphy (Indianapolis, New York, Kansas City: Bobbs-Merrill, 1965), p. 69.

[25] Charles Rollin (1661–1741), *De la manière d'enseigner et d'étudier les belles-lettres*, four volumes, first published in Paris, 1726–1732. For a collection of 135 fables of Phaedrus see: Phèdre, *Fables*, texte établi et traduit par Alice Brenot Paris: Société D'Édition "Les Belles Lettres," 1969.

[26] Fernando Nuñez de Guzman (also known as Pincianus) (c. 1480–1558), *Annotationes in Senecae philosophi opera* (Venice, 1536).

[27] *Emile* 2.141 (B, 113–15).

[28] *Emile* 2.141 (B, 113).

[29] Ibid.

[30] Ibid.

[31] Ibid.

[32] *Emile* 2.141 (B, 113–14).

[33] *Emile* 2.141 (B, 114).

[34] Ibid.

35 Ibid.

36 Ibid.

37 Ibid.

38 Ibid.

39 Ibid.

40 Ibid.

41 Ibid.

42 Ibid.

43 *Emile* 2.141 (B, 115).

44 Ibid.

45 Ibid.

46 Ibid.

47 Private education refers to instruction by the parent or a tutor at home in contrast to education at a school.

48 *Emile* 2.123 (B, 109).

49 *Emile* 2.125 (B, 109).

50 Quintilian, *Instruction of the Orator* (*Institutio oratoria*) Book 10, ch. 1.

51 Paulus Manutius (1512–1574), an influential publisher, devoted to the study of Cicero, was considered one of the finer Latinists of his day. Girolamo Fracastoro (1478–1553) was an Italian physician, scientist, man of letters, and poet. Today he is best known for his discoveries of the nature of infectious diseases. His account of syphilis, published in rhyme, *Syphilis sive morbus Gallicus* (*Syphilis or the French Disease*) (1530), was considered a masterpiece of refined Latin style.

52 Pietro Bembo (1470–1547), secretary to Pope Leo X and cardinal (1539), wrote one of the earliest Italian grammars. In general his scholarly work on the Italian language and his works of Italian poetry were influential in the development of standard Italian. His Latin lyric poetry was renowned for its formal beauty. Jacopo Sadoleto (1477–1547), cardinal, bishop of Carpentras, was a noted classical scholar, a vigorous proponent of reform within the Catholic Church. Besides some minor poetry, he authored *De laudibus philosophiae*.

53 Sigebert of Gembloux (1030–1112), a Benedictine monk, authored *Chronicon ab anno 381 ad 1113*, which was a major source for later historians of the early middle ages.

54 Ludovico Ariosto (1478–1533), authored *Orlando Furioso* (1516), a classic of Italian literature and a signal work of the Italian Renaissance. Giovanni Della Casa (1503–1556), bishop, translator, and author of both Latin and Italian verse, is best known for his popular practical treatise on social manners, *Galateo*.

55 Jean-Baptiste Racine (1639–1699), famous playwright for the French theater, particularly noted for his tragedies and his use of classical themes and characters; *Phèdre* is often considered his masterpiece. Molière (= Jean-Baptiste Poquelin) (1622–1673) is the most famous of French playwrights; among his comedies are *Le Tartuffe* and *Le Misanthrope*. Despreaux (= Nicolas Boileau) (1636–1711), a man of letters whose influential *L'Art poétique* set out the rules of poetic form in the classical tradition. Jacques-Bénigne Bossuet (1627–1704), bishop, popular Parisian preacher, Catholic apologist against the Protestant reform, defender of French national prerogatives against the Ultramontanes, a tutor to the king of France's eldest son, he opposed the political liberalism and was widely admired for his superb command of the French language. François de Salignac de La Mothe Fénelon (1651–1715), archbishop of Cambrai, theologian and defender of Quietism, man of letters, tutor to Louis XIV's heir, had written a treatise on the education of women. His *Les Adventures de Télémaque* (*The Adventures of Telemachus*), composed for the education of his student, the prince of France, was well received and much published. *Telemachus* was the novel that played so important a part in the cultivation of Sophie's romantic ideal; see *Emile* V. 185; 350; (B, 410, 450).

56 Bernard Le Bovier Fontenelle (1657–1757), man of letters and longtime secretary of the French Academy, did much to popularize philosophy and science; his bias against religion, pagan and Christian, comes out in his satire *Relation de l'île de Bornéo* (*Account of the Island of Borneo*).

57 Fracastoro (see endnote 51 above). Jacopo Sannazzaro (1456–1530), poet of both Italian and Latin works, his *Arcadia* is an influential classic of Italian literature. Marco Girolamo Vida (c. 1490–1566), taking Virgil's *Aeneid* as his model, presented Christ as the perfect Aeneas in his *Christias*. After the fashion of Horace, he also wrote a Latin versified defense of poetry, *De arte poetica*. Marc-Antoine de Muret (1526–1585), French classical scholar and poet, was renowned in his day for his excellent Latin. Julius Caesar Scaliger (1484–1558), classical scholar, with

an interest in natural philosophy, his work on Latin grammar and the principles of classical rhetoric and poetry were influential; his Latin poetry was admired.

58 Gilles Ménage (1613–1692), scholar and man of letters, is known for his works in philology and for the literary meetings he sponsored for over 30 years. François-Séraphin de Régnier Des Marais (c. 1632–1713) French man of letters, his Italian poetry was widely appreciated.

59 Voltaire, *Discours a sa réception a l'Académie Française prononcé le lundi 9 mai 1746*, in *Mélange*, Bibliothèque de la Pléiade, Préface par Emmanuel Berl, texte établi et annoté par Jacques van den Heuvel (Dijon: Gallimard, 1965), p. 243: Nous nous sommes interdit nous-mêmes insensiblement presque tous les objets que d'autres nations ont osé peidre. Il n'est rien que le Dante n'exprimât, à l'exemple des anciens: il accoutuma les Italiens à tout dire; mais nous, comment pourrions-nous aujourd'hui imiter l'auteur des *Géorgiques*, qui nomme sans détour tous les instruments de l'agriculture? A peine les connaissons-nous. . . ."

60 Melchior de Polignac, *Anti-Lucretius, sive de Deo et natura libri novem* (Paris: Guerin, 1747), a Latin text noted for its elegant hexameter.

61 *Emile* 2.123 (B, 109).

62 Seneca, *Moral Letters to Lucilius* (*Epistulae Morales ad Lucilium*) 114, "On Style as a Mirror of Character" in *Seneca ad Lucilium Epistulae Morales*, with an English Translation by Richard M Gummere, vol. 3, Loeb Classical Library (Cambridge: Harvard University Press, 1953): "Exactly as each individual man's actions seem to speak, so people's style of speaking often reproduces the general character of the time, if the morale of the public has relaxed and has given itself over to effeminacy. . . . A man's ability cannot possibly be of one sort and his soul of another. If his soul be wholesome, well-ordered, serious, and restrained, his ability also is sound and sober. Conversely, when the one degenerates, the other is also contaminated. . . . Therefore, I say, take care of the soul; for from the soul issue our thoughts, from the soul our words, from the soul our dispositions, our expressions, our very gait. When the soul is sound and strong, the style too is vigorous, energetic, manly; but if the soul loses its balance, down comes all the rest in ruins. (Quemadmodum autem uniuscuiusque actio dicenti similis est, sic genus dicendi aliquando imitatur publicos mores, si disciplina civitatis laboravit et se in delicias dedit. . . . Non potest alius esse ingenio, alius animo color. . . . Ideo ille

[animum] curetur; ab illo sensus, ab illo verba exeunt, ab illo nobis est habitus, vultus, incessus. Illo sano ac valente oratio quoque robusta, fortis, virilis est; si ille procubuit, et cetera ruinam sequuntur)," pp. 300–301, 314–15.

63 *Emile* 1.193 (B, 74).

64 *Emile* 2.123 (B, 109).

65 *Emile* 2.134 (B, 111).

66 *Emile* 2.137 (B, 112).

67 *Emile* 2.128 (B, 110).

68 *Emile* 2.131 (B, 111).

69 *Encyclopédie, ou Dictionnaire raisonné des sciences, des arts et des métiers* (Paris: Briasson, 1751–1765).

70 (See Part Two, endnote 25 above.) Rollin authored historical works: *Histoire ancienne des Égyptiens, des Carthaginois, des Assyriens, des Babyloniens, des Mèdes et des Perses, des Macédoniens, des Grecs . . .* , 13 volumes (Paris, 1730–1738) and *Histoire romaine depuis la fondation de Rome jusqu'à la bataille d'Actium . . .* , left unfinished at 5 volumes (Paris, 1738–1748).

71 *Emile* 2 (B, 156 fn).

72 Cicero, *Letters to Friends* (*Epistulae ad Familiares*), 351 (XVI.26), edited and translated by D. R. Shackleton Bailey, (Cambridge and London: Harvard University Press, 2001), vol. 3, pp. 168–69: ". . . I remember how our mother in the old days used to seal up the empty bottles, so that the bottle drained on the sly could not be included with the empties. . . ."

73 *Emile* 2.126 (B, 109–10).

74 Bernhardus Varenius (1622–1650) authored *Geographia generalis* (Amsterdam, 1650), which became the standard authority in scientific and comparative geography for over a hundred years.

75 *Emile* 2.259, 261 (B, 145).

76 The Abbé de la Chapelle (1710–1792) was a man of various scientific and mathematical achievements. The inventor of the underwater diving suit, he also produced a singular study of ventriloquism.

77 Christian Freiherr Wolff (1679–1754), philosopher, mathematician, and scientist, a major figure of the German Enlightenment, is noted for his penchant for systematizing knowledge. He authored a popular handbook on mathematics, *Anfangsgründe aller mathematischen Wissenschaften* (Halle, 1710).

78 Geminiano Rondelli (= Ronoscalglia) (1652–1735), professor at the University of Bologna, expert in mathematics and hydraulics, published a popular edition of Euclid's *Elements.*

79 *Emile* 2.266 (B, 146).

80 Antoine Arnauld (1612–1694), called the "Great Arnauld," controversial Jansenist, published works in theology, mathematics, science and philosophy, including *Logique ou Art de penser* and *Nouveaux élements de géométrie*; in the latter work Euclidean theorems are reordered so as to cultivate the habits of clarity and procedure in the development of the science.

81 Pierre Varignon (1654–1722), prominent mathematician who was particularly distinguished for his teaching of mechanics and his development of simplicity and order in the organization of mathematical systems, as represented in his *Éléments de mathématiques* (1731) and his *Éclaircissemens sur l'analyse des infiniment petits* (1725). Joseph Sauveur (1653–1716), a man of diverse intellectual accomplishments, made numerous early and enduring contributions to the study of acoustics, published *Géométrie élémentaire* and was the teacher of Prince Eugene of Savoy. Nicholas de Maezieu (1713–1762), another versatile intellectual, published the lessons he had given to noble patrons under the title *Éléments de géométrie de M. le Duc de Bourgogne*. Nicholas-Louis de Lacaille (1713–1762), important contributor to astronomy and geodesy, known as the father of southern astronomy, he authored several successful elementary texts on mechanics, geometrical astronomy, and optics; his *Leçons élémentaires de mathématiques, ou éléments d'algèbre et de géométrie* (1741) was particularly successful.

82 Alexis-Claude Clairaut (1713–1765), a mathematical prodigy, with many contributions to theoretical mathematics and physics, authored *Éléments de géométrie*, in which he promoted a "natural" method of discovering the principles of geometry as it might have been discovered by its inventors, so to speak.

83 Eustachio Manfredi (1674–1739), Gerdil's teacher at Bologna, was a noted astronomer, mathematician and poet.

84 Andreas Tacquet (1612–1660), Belgian Jesuit, was one of the great mathematical pedagogues of his age. He authored the very popular *Elementa geometriae quibus accedunt selecta ex Archimede theoremata*, which was distinguished for the clarity and order in which it developed Euclid

and Archimedes and *Arithmeticae theoria et praxis.*

85 Eugene of Savoy (1663–1736) was among the greatest generals of his era. Napoleon studied his campaigns closely. He was Frederick the Great's teacher. Under his leadership and in the service of the Holy Roman Emperor, the Turkish invaders were forced to withdraw from the European lands along the Danube. In addition to his military brilliance he was noted for his wisdom in seeking political order and peace in the follow-up to his military campaigns.

86 Gerdil refers to the sequence of topics concerned with curricular matters that he began above in sec. 19.

87 Gerdil quotes from *Sermones Fideles, sive Interiora rerum* a Latin translation of Bacon's much-published *Essays or Counsels, Civil and Moral.* The Latin translations, probably produced by many hands, was announced by Bacon in 1625, but only published by his literary executor in 1638, twelve years after his death. See Michael Kieran in *The Essays or Counsels, Civill and Morall* by Sir Francis Bacon, edited, with Introduction and Commentary by Michael Kiernan (Cambridge: Harvard University Press, 1985), p. liii and Brian Vickers in *Francis Bacon. A Critical Edition of the Major Works,* The Oxford Authors, edited by Brian Vickers (Oxford and New York: Oxford University Press, 1996), pp. 711–17. Beside the Latin version which he cites, Gerdil gives a loose paraphrase in French, and sometimes adds a brief comment of his own. We have translated literally Gerdil's paraphrase and in the corresponding footnote quoted from Bacon's original English essay, "On Studies," from Vickers's edition, pp. 439–40.

88 "Studies serve for delight, for ornament, and for ability. Their chief use for delight is in privateness and retiring. . . . To spend too much time in studies is sloth."

89 " . . . [their chief use] for ornament is in discourse . . . [T]o use them too much for ornament is affectation."

90 Claude Fleury (1640–1723), historian, jurist and educator, friend of Bossuet and Fénelon, authored the twenty-volume *Historie ecclésiastique* (1690–1720) and the very popular *Catéchisme historique* (1683) and *Traité du choix et de la méthode des études* (1686), which was widely translated and much reprinted.

91 " . . . and [the chief use] for ability is in the judgment and disposition of business. For expert men can execute, and perhaps judge of particulars,

one by one, but the general counsels, and the plots and marshaling of affairs comes best from those that are learned. . . . [T]o make judgments wholly by the rules [of studies] is the humour of a scholar. They perfect nature, and are perfected by experience . . . and studies themselves do give forth directions too much at large, except they be bounded in by experience."

92 Jean-Charles Folard (1669–1752), as a military strategist promoted the use of infantry columns that soon proved impractical as the technology of fire power advanced. Henri de La Tour d'Auvergne, vicomte de Turenne (1611–1675), distinguished military commander during the reign of Louis XIV, was noted for his "strategic chess moves" and bold opportunism.

93 "Crafty men contemn studies, simple men admire them, and wise men use them; for they teach not their own use; but that is a wisdom without them, and above them, won by observation."

94 "Read not to contradict and confute; nor to believe and take for granted; nor to find talk and discourse; but to weigh and consider."

95 "[S]ome books are to be read only in parts; others to be read, but not curiously; and some few are to be read wholly, and with diligence and attention."

96 Note-taking was a highly formalized activity among Renaissance humanists. See Vickers's "Introduction" (esp. pp. xli–xliv) to *Francis Bacon. A Critical Edition of the Major Works*: "From the first influential school masters in fifteenth-century Italy, those pioneers who did so much to establish humanism as discipline that could be taught in school . . . the notebook played a crucial role in the transmission of knowledge. All educationalists taught that reading was to be carried out with pen in hand, ready to note in the margins metaphors, similes, *exempla*, *sententiae*, apophthegms, proverbs, or any other transportable units of literary composition. These were then copied out into one or more notebooks, divided either alphabetically or by topics, and to be used in one's own writing. . . . The Renaissance was fundamentally a notebook culture. . . ."

97 "Reading maketh a full man; conference a ready man; and writing an exact man. And therefore, if a man write little, he had need have a great memory. . . ."

98 "Histories make men wise; poets witty; mathematics subtile; natural philosophy deep; moral grave; logic and rhetoric ready to contend."

99 "Nay there is no stond [= obstacle] or impediment in the wit but may be wrought out by fit studies: like as diseases of the body may have appropriate exercises."

100 "So if a man's wit be wandering, let him study mathematics; for in demonstrations, if his wit be called away never so little, he must begin again."

101 "If he be not apt to beat over [= reflect upon] matters, and to call up one thing to prove and illustrate another, let him study the lawyers' cases."

102 "If his wit be not apt to distinguish or find differences, let him study the schoolmen, for they are the *cymini sectores*." *Cymini sectores* = splitters of cummin seed, in other words, those who make very fine distinctions. The expression originates from Dio Cassius, *Epitome Dionis*. Epitome of Book 70, describing the character of Roman emperor Antonius Pius: "Antonius is said to have been of an enquiring turn of mind and not to have held aloof from careful investigations of even small and commonplace matters; for this the scoffers called him Cummin-splitter." *Dio's Roman History*, 9 vol. Loeb Classical Library, with an English translation by Earnest Cary (Cambridge: Harvard University Press and London: Heinemann, 1961), vol. 8, p. 471.

103 *La Logique ou l'art de penser* (*Logic or the Art of Thinking*), popularly called *Port-Royal Logic*, was co-authored by Antoine Arnauld and Pierre Nicole, originally published 1662, was used widely in its French, Latin, and English editions in the seventeenth and eighteenth centuries.

104 Gerdil refers to Voltaire's *Lettres Philosophiques, vingt-cinquième: Sur les Pensées de M. Pascal*, in *Mélange*, Bibliothèque de la Pléiade, Préface par Emmanuel Berlé, texte établi et annoté par Jacques van den Heuvel (Dijon: Gallimard, 1965), p. 1351. It is an axiom of logic that two propositions that are in contrary opposition to one another, that is, possessing the logical form "All X are Y" and "No X are Y," can both be false, although both cannot be simultaneously true. And this is so regardless of the subject matter being discussed.

105 Noël Antoine Pluche (1688–1761) in his *La méchanique des langues, e l'art de les enseigner* (Paris: Estienne, 1751) laments the difficulty of learning Latin and attributes it to the faulty method of emphasizing from the beginning mastery of the formal elements of the language rather than learning to speak the language in normal social situations.

106 *Emile* 1.83 (B, 53).

107 *Emile* 1.5 (B, 38).

108 *Emile* 2.115 (B, 106).

109 *Emile* 2.115 (B, 106).

110 *Emile* 1.84–85 (B, 52).

111 It is interesting to note that Descartes opens his *Discourse on the Method for Rightly Conducting One's Reason and for Seeking Truth in the Sciences* with the claim that "good sense [*bon sens*] is the most evenly distributed commodity in the world, . . . [T]he power of judging rightly and of distinguishing the true from the false (which properly speaking, is what people call good sense or reason) is naturally equal in all men;" trans. by Donald A. Cress, (Indianapolis/Cambridge: Hackett, 1980), p. 1.

112 Antoine-François Prévost (1697–1763), *Histoire générale des voyages*, 76 vol. (Paris: Didot, 1749), vol. 3, pp. 109–16.

113 Albrecht von Haller (1708–1777), famous for his work in anatomy, botany, and physiology, is called the father of experimental physiology and the father of modern taxonomy. Toward the end of his life he wrote three novels; his poem *Die Alpen* (1729) on the wonder and beauty of nature had some influence on German literature. Salomon Gessner (1733–1788), Swiss writer, painter, etcher, and publisher, authored the pastoral prose *Idyllen* (1756–1772) and the epic poem, *Der Tod Abels* (1758), works that were much translated and published. Friedrich Gottlieb Klopstock (1724–1803) is especially known for his epic poem *Der Messias*, which marks a break with rationalism in German literature.

114 *On Social Contract* Bk. 3, ch. 5.

115 *On Social Contract* Bk. 3, ch. 9 (tr. Bondanella, Norton ed., 1988; p. 137).

116 *Emile* 1.94 (B, 53).

117 *Emile* 1.14 (B, 39).

118 *Emile* 1.3 fn (B, 37–38).

119 *Emile* 1.87–8 (B, 52).

120 *Spirit of the Laws* Bk. 19, ch.16.

121 Gerdil draws together different passages from Rom 12:10–19.

122 *Emile* 1.109 (B, 56).

123 J.-B. le Rond d'Alembert, *Essai sur la société des gens de lettres et des Grands*.

124 *Emile* 1.23 (B, 40).

[125] Rousseau introduces himself as "citizen of Geneva" on the title pages of both *On Social Contract* and *Discourse on the Origin and Foundations of Inequality among Men.*

[126] *Emile* 1.24 (B, 40–41).

[127] Gerdil undoubtedly has in mind the likes of Vittorio Amedeo II and Carlo Emmanuel II, of the house of Savoy, who sponsored reforms of instruction in the secondary schools. See Marina Roggero, *Scuola e riforma nello stato sabaudo. L'istruzione secndaria dalla ratio studiorum alle constituzioni del 1772* (Torino: Deputazione subalpina de storia patria, 1981).

[128] Charlemagne ordered the establishment of schools in conjunction with the monasteries and cathedrals in his realm. In a circular letter addressed to Bauguld, abbot of Fulda: "We, Charles, by the grace of God king of the Franks and Lombards and patrician of the Romans . . . have deemed it useful that bishoprics and monasteries which through the favor of Christ have been entrusted to us to govern should, in addition to the way of life prescribed by their rule and their practice of holy religion, devote their efforts to the study of literature and to the teaching of it, each according to his ability, to those upon whom God has bestowed the capacity to learn. . . ." *Encyclica de litteris colendis (Karoli epistola de litteris colendis)* in H. R. Loyn and John Percival, *The Reign of Charlemagne: Documents on Carolingian Government and Administration* (New York: St. Martin's, 1975), p. 63. This early step toward public education in Europe was an important part of the Carolingian Renaissance. See Charles Edward Russell, *Charlemagne: First of the Moderns* (Boston and New York: Houghton Mifflin, 1930), pp. 189–201.

[129] Horace, *Epistles*, II. 1, v. 117: "Scribimus indocti, doctique poemata passim (we all write poetry, the unlearned and the learned alike)."

[130] Francis Bacon, "On Atheism," in *Essays or Counsels, Civil and Moral*; in Vickers ed. p. 371.

[131] See Pierre Bayle, *Pensées diverses . . .À l'occasion de la cometè qui parut au mois de Decembre 1680. Addition aux pensées diverses sur les cometes*, 2 vol., 3th ed., (Rotterdam: Reiner Leer, 1699).

[132] In addition to his numerous systematic works in metaphysics, moral and political philosophy, and pedagogy, Gerdil wrote for the use of his students a brief survey of the history of philosophy, entitled *Histoire des sectes des philosophes.*

[133] See, for example, *The Citizen: Philosophical Rudiments concerning Govern-*

ment and Society, I, 9–14; in *Man and Citizen*, edited with an Introduction by Bernart Gert (Garden City, N.Y.: Anchor, 1972), pp. 116–19, and *Leviathan*, Pt. 1, ch. 13.

134 See, for instance, *Spirit of the Laws*, Bk. 1, ch. 2 and Bk. 10, ch. 3.

135 *On Social Contract*, Bk. 1, ch. 3.

136 See esp. Robert Filmer, *Patriarcha. The Naturall Power of Kinges Defended against the Unnatural Liberty of People: By Arguments Theological, Rational, Historical, Legall* [London, 1680], esp. ch. 1, sec. 3 and 10 and ch. 3, sec. 1, in *Patriarcha and Other Writings*, edited by Johann P. Sommerville, Cambridge Texts in the History of Political Thought (Cambridge, New York, Port Chester, Melbourne, Sydney: Cambridge University Press, 1991), who defended the divine right of kings with a theory that roots authority in fatherhood and its political expression in the patriarchy of Noah and Moses.

137 *On Social Contract* Bk. 4, ch.2.

138 Helvetius, *De l'esprit, or Essay on the Mind and Its Several Faculties*, Essay 1, ch. 2; translated from the French (New York: Burt Franklin, 1970; reprint of the1810 edition), pp. 39–43.

139 *Spirit of the Laws* Bk. 1, ch. 1–2.

140 *Spirit of the Laws* Bk. 3, ch.3, 5–6.

141 Voltaire, *Supplément au Siècle de Louis XIV* in his *Le siècles de Louis XIV*, (Dresden: Walther, 1753), II, pp. 81–82.

142 *On Social Contract* Bk. 3, ch., 4.

143 *Spirit of the Laws* Bk. 3, ch. 3.

144 Nicholas Antoine Boulanger in vol. 3 of *Oeuvres de Boulanger* 6 vol. (Amsterdam: [s.n.], 1794), pp, 177–78.

145 *Spirit of the Laws* Bk. 19, ch. 4.

146 *De l'esprit, or Essay on the Mind and Its Several Faculties*, Essay 3, ch. 27; translated from the French (New York: Burt Franklin, 1970; reprint of the1810 edition), esp. pp. 340–42.

147 Pierre Bayle, *Pensées diverses . . .À l'occasion de la cometè qui parut au mois de Decembre 1680. Addition aux pensées diverses sur les cometes*, 2 vol., 3th ed., (Rotterdam: Reiner Leer, 1699){{{ see esp. ch. 145. }}}

148 Montesquieu, *Spirit of the Laws* Bk. 24, ch. 2.

149 Jean Morelly, *Code de la nature ou le véritable esprit de se loix, de tout tems négligé ou méconnu* (Par-Tout [i.e., Netherlands]: Le vrai sage, 1755).

¹⁵⁰ *Emile* 2. 33–36, 50 (B, 84–86, 89).

¹⁵¹ It is interesting to note that Gerdil published works on dueling and lux-ury: *Traité des combats singuliers* (Turin, 1759) and *Discours de la nature et des effets du luxe* (Turin, 1767). In the latter he responds to J.-F. Melon, *Essai politique sur le commerce* (n.p., 1734), who defends the pursuit of luxury as a major spur to a national economy. Montesquieu, *Spirit of the Laws* Bk. 7 thinks that "luxury is singularly appropriate in monarchies" (Cohler-Miller-Stone trans., p. 99).

¹⁵² J.-B le Rond d'Alembert, *Essai sure les élémens de philosophie, ou sur les principes des connaissances humaines.*

¹⁵³ For example, Bernard Mandeville, *Fable of the Bees or Private Vices, Pub-lick Benefits*, 2 vols., with a Commentary Critical, Historical and Ex-planatory by F. B. Kaye (Oxford: Clarendon, 1924; reproduced Indianapolis: Liberty Classics, 1988); see, for example, vol.1, p. 369.

¹⁵⁴ Among Gerdil's many works is his defense of the Catholic understand-ing of matrimony: *Trattato del matrimonio o sia confutazione de' sistemi con-trarî all' autorità della Chiesa circa il matrimonio*, in vol. 15 of the Roman ed. of opera.

¹⁵⁵ Charles-Jean-François Hénault (1685–1770) authored *Abrégé chrono-logique de l'histoire de France jusqu'à la mort du Louis XIV*, which was a great success and went through many editions; Gerdil had recom-mended it in his *Sur la lecture et le choix de livres.*

¹⁵⁶ Francis Bacon, "On Truth," in his *Essays and Counsels, Civil and Moral* (1625), from Vickers's ed., p. 341. Gerdil quotes the Latin translation (see footnote 186 above): Certe sunt qui cogitationum vertigine delec-tantur, ac pro servitute habent fide fixa aut axiomatis constantibus con-stringi; liberi arbitrii usum in cogitando affectantes. Cujusmodi quidem sectae philosophorum licet defecerint, supersunt tamen ingenia quaedam ventosa et discursantia, quibus eaedem omnino venae, licet non pari, cum antiquis, copia sanguinis, repletae.

CONCLUSION

¹ *Emile* 2.129 (B, 110).

Index

Aesop, 71, 73–75, 152
Africa, 28, 123
    see also Negro
Aguesseau, Henri-François d', 26,
    147
Alexander the Great, 98, 106, 122,
    148
America, xvi, xvii, 28, 101, 125, 144
    see also New World
amour propre, xxxiii, 112
ancients, the
    benefits of reading, 89, 94
    imitation of 88–91
    teachings of, 9, 16–17, 61, 85,
        137
Anti-Emile
    addressed to parents, elders,
        educators, xix, 142
    as ordered reflections on edu-
        cation, 2, 5
    current relevance of, xv–xviii
    origin of title, xv
Aquinas, Thomas, xxxvi–xxxvii, 56,
    149
Archimedes, 70, 158
Ariosto, Ludovico, 89, 152
Aristides, 16, 26, 145
Aristotle, xxv, 39, 148
Arnauld, Antoine, 108–9, 157, 160
Arrighi, G. L. xxxii, xxxix, 151
Asia, 28, 100

Augustinian Platonism, xxxix
authority, xix–xx, xxxv–xxxvii, 24–
    25, 30–31, 36, 42, 51, 53–55, 57,
    59, 87, 100, 129, 135–36, 149–
    50, 163
    see also fathers; Rousseau

Bachelet, Silvia Fasciolo, xxxv, xl
Bacon, Francis, xxxvii, 110–18, 134,
    137, 142, 158–59, 162, 164
Bayle, Pierre, 134, 136, 162–63
Being, Supreme, see God
beggars
    wandering, 41
Bembo, Pietro, 88, 153
beneficence, 16, 21
benevolence, xxi–xxii, 35–36
Bible, see Scripture, Holy
Bloom, Allan, xvi, xvii, xx, xxxiii
Boccaccio, Giovanni, 89
Bongie, Laurence L., xxxiv–xxxv
bonum honestum, xxi–xxii, xxxv–
    xxxvi,146
    as intrinsic goodness, 9, 23
Bossuet, Jacques-Benigne, 24–25,
    89, 93, 113, 118, 142, 147, 154,
    158
Boulanger, Nicholas Antoine, 136,
    163

Caesar, Julius, 88–89, 94, 122

catechism, 83
Cato of Utica, 120, 122
Chambliss, J. J., xviii
Chapelle, Abbé de la, 108, 156
Charlemagne
    on public education, 133, 162
Christian
    courage of, 29, 31
    see also Christianity; philosophy
Christianity
    completes philosophy, 133–34
    influence on morality, 17, 130–31, 140
    makes men reasonable, 125
    Rousseau's hostility to, xxi, xxxiv, 1, 17, 128, 140–41
Cicero, xxv, xxxvii, 10, 21–23, 26, 87–89, 93, 102, 118, 142, 144–46, 149, 153, 156
citizen
    and philosophy, 133–38
    and virtue, 18, 24, 55
    as opposite of Rousseau's natural man, xxii–xxiv, 6, 11, 16–18, 141
    character of, xxi, 16–18
    education of, xx–xxi, xxiii, 16–18, 52, 55, 133–38
    Emile's malformation of, xxxiv, 1, 18
    mutual dependence of, 130
Clairaut, Alexis-Claude, 108, 157
Compayré, Gabriel, 16–17
Copleston, Frederick, 35
Corneille, Pierre, 20–21, 146
Corsetti, Carlo, xvi, xxxii, 145, 151
contrariety
    as principal object of education, 10
    of man and citizen, xxiii, xxiv

of reason and inclination, xxi, 7–11, 144
culture, xxxi, 27, 38, 40, 42, 122, 124, 159
    Gerdil's Italian intellectual, xxxiv
    of reason, *see* reason, culture of
    philosophy of, xxxvii
    Western xvi, xvii
curriculum, xix, xxvii, xxxii, 58, 96

D'Alembert, Jean-Baptiste le Rond, 4, 19, 132, 136, 143, 146, 161, 164
Dante, 89, 91, 155
death
    fear of, 27–30
Deioces, 32
Del Noce, Augusto, xxxvii, xxxix
Del Pozzo, Luca, xxxvii
Della Casa, Giovanni, 89, 154
Descartes, René, xxxvi–xxxvii, xxxix, 118, 161
Despreaux, 89, 154
Dewey, John, xvii–xviii
Discourse on the Origin and Foundations of Inequality among Men, 14, 148, 162
disposition, xxxi, 11, 15, 18, 24, 30, 37, 49, 52, 70, 103, 119, 121, 155, 158
    three basic kinds of, 9–10, 11, 17, 144
    see also inclination
Divine Master, *see* God
Divinity, *see* God
dueling, 136, 164
duty, xxv, 14, 17, 26, 41–43, 55, 59, 63, 65, 67, 95, 110, 125, 130, 134, 136–37, 140

education
agents, responsible for, xix, 2,
58, 142
and cultivation of reason, xxvii,
xxxiii, 12, 58, 61, 123–25
and habits, moral, 131
and legislation, 1–2, 52
and nature, 8
and original contrariety, xxi, 10,
144
and religion, 142
and virtue, xviii, 131–32
as art, ministerial, 10, 13
as philosophy's medicine, 10
civil, 14–15, 38
classical, xix, xxv
cooperation of parents in, 56–57
deficiency in, 96, 119
Emile's two stages of, xxiii, 143
Emile's pernicious effects on,
xxxiv, 141
ends of, xviii–xix, xxi, xxiv–xxvii,
xxxii–xxxiii, 8, 10, 62, 95, 117,
125
for one's self, xxv, xxxviii, 1, 11,
13–14, 16–17
for others, xxv, xxxviii, 1, 11,
13–14, 16–17
fosters judgment, xxxiii, 48, 129
fosters sociability, xviii, xxiv–xxv,
xxxiii, 12, 14–15
importance of reading and study
in, 110–17
law as conditions of, 33, 38
methods of, xvi, 67, 142
of the poor, 129–32, 139, 141
of the wealthy, 132
philosophy of, xv, xx, xxiv, xxviii,
xxxii, xxxviii, 10
point of departure for, 61

principles of, xvi, xxxiii, 1–2, 7,
43
private, 67, 85, 153
progressive, xvii
public, 133, 162
Rousseau's impractical plan for,
5
society as condition of, 12, 33,
38
theory of, xvii–xviii, xxiv, xxxviii,
1–2
Rousseau's three kinds of, 8, 11,
143
see also citizen, education of
eloquence, 4, 21, 93
Rousseau's, xxxiii, 4–5, 139
Emile (the book)
and *On Social Contract*, xx, xxiv, 1
controversy over, xv–xvi
influence of, xvi–xxi, xxvi–xxxvii
main narrative lines of, xxii–xxiii
Emile (the student)
an unreal abstraction, xxii–xxiii,
5–6
empiricism, xxxv
Epictetus, 26, 129
Epicureanism, xxxvi, 22, 146
Euclid, xxix, xxxi, 108–9, 157
Eugene of Savoy, Prince, 110, 158
Europe, xxxiv–xxxv, 5, 7, 16, 20, 26–
28, 41, 52, 100–102, 122–25,
130, 158, 162
evil, 6–7, 9, 24, 29, 34, 36, 40, 57,
90, 101, 119, 130, 137
original, 10; *see also* perversity
child's discernment of, 45–47,
59, 63, 65, 67
see also wicked

fable, 102, 121

and reflection, 84
child's ability to understand, 71–73, 76, 84
Fox and Crow: an exemplar, 77–84
literary style for, 73–76, 152
Rousseau's objection to, 64, 71
useful in teaching morality, *see* moral reasoning
Fabricus, 16
family, 22, 36, 55, 94, 101, 130, 149
forms a natural society, xxxv, 23, 146
peace in, 2, 54–55
united by utility, 36
united in benevolence, 36
united in fear, 36
father, 17, 25, 52, 64–67, 104, 106, 127, 130, 151
affection for, 52–54
and authority, 2, 44–45, 51–59, 136, 150, 163
and citizenship, 17
and mother, xix, 53–57, 95, 136, 142
and obedience , 54, 65
duty to, 55, 136
Gerdil's address to, xix, 142
negligence of, 71
fear
motive for association, xxii, 35–36
of death, 27–30
of God, xxxi, 42, 48–51, 54, 66, 103
of punishment, 37, 41
Febronism, xxxv
Fénelon, François de Salignac de La Mothe, 89, 113, 142, 154, 158

Filmer, Robert, 136, 163
fitness
of objects, 9–10, 12, 39–40, 80
Fleury, Claude, 113, 158
Folard, Jean-Charles, 114, 159
Fontenelle, Bernard Le Bovier, 90, 113, 154
Fracastoro, Girolamo, 88, 91, 153–54
freedom, xii, xxxviii, xxxix, 28, 31–33, 38, 52, 90, 137, 139, 151
see also liberty

Galen, 39, 148–49
Galileo Galilei, 89, 114, 118
Gassendi, Pierre, 118
geography, xxix, 67, 104–110, 156
scientific vs historical, 105–6
tied to history, 106
use of maps, 105–6
geometry, xxix–xxxi, 19, 67, 69–70, 105, 107–110
experiential vs scientific, 107–8
methods of, xxix–xxx, 108–10
Gerdil
body of work of, xxxix–xli
chronology, xli
modernity of, xxxvi–xxxix
rhetorical style of, xv–xvi
influence of, xxxiv–xxxv
Gessner, Salomon, 124, 161
God, xxvi, xxxi, xxxiii, xxxvi, 23, 29–30, 42, 54–55, 60–61, 65–66, 103, 130, 140–41, 162
duty to, 43
fear of, *see* fear, of God
idea of, *see* God, knowledge of
knowledge of, xxxvi, xl, 48–51, 140–41
law of, 45, 66,

love of, xxxi, xxxiii, 31, 103
neglect of, 140–41
people of, 103,
providence of, xxi, xxvi, 13, 56,
    103
sight of, 45,
the Creator, 49, 103, 141
wisdom of, xxxvi, 23
word of, 45; *see* also Scripture,
    Holy
goodness
intrinsic, *see bonum honestum*
grammar, 93, 95, 118
and logic, 86
Grotius, Hugo, 56, 118

Haller, Albrecht von, 124, 161
Helvetius, 136, 145, 163
Hegel, Georg Wilhelm Friedrich,
    xxxvii
Hénault, Charles-Jean-François,
    137, 164
Hobbes, Thomas, 34, 136, 148,
    162–63,
history
ancient. 101–2
epochs of, 100–101
natural, 78
mastering facts, 96–97
modern, 100
study of relations, xxx, 98–99
salvation, xxxi, 102–3
Holy Spirit, 54
Homer, 75, 103
honor, 7, 18–21, 23–24, 38, 42, 54,
    61, 74, 76, 79, 128, 131, 132, 142
and the idea of perfection, 18–21
Horace, 46, 59, 67, 74, 89, 148,
    150–51, 154, 162
Hottentot, 41

human condition, 6, 144
Hume, David, xxxiv–xxxv, xxxvii
Huron, 41

idea, *passim*
and child's capacity for, 47– 48,
    53, 58–61, 67–71, 84, 67–70
and reason's combining of,
    xxvii, xxx, 58–59, 96, 99,
    111, 117, 121, 123
as a notion determined by
    relations, xxvii, xxx, 38, 40,
    59–61, 69, 96–97, 106 148
of happiness and perfection,
    9–10, 12, 18–21, 40, 144
immortality, xxxv, 27, 147
inclination, xvii, xxi–xxii, xxiv, 9, 10,
    35, 40, 71, 134;
see also: dispositions
Indians, 14–15, 123–24
injustice, *see* justice
instinct, 121, 134
man's want of, 12, 15, 38–39,
    47–48
institutions
social, xx, xxiii–xxiv, xxxiii–xxxiv,
    xxxviii, 1, 5–6, 11, 17, 25, 41, 42,
    101, 130, 133, 139, 141–42, 145

Jansenism, 35
Josephism, 35
joy
child's experience of, 81
justice, xxi, 14, 16, 22, 25, 31, 34,
    45–47, 49, 55, 72, 119, 128–29,
    132, 136, 141, 145
virtue of, xxxv, 5, 18, 21

Klopstock, Friedrich Gottlieb, 124,
    161

La Fontaine, 71, 73, 75–76
Lacaille, Nicholas-Louis de, 108, 157
languages
    study of, xxix, 67, 85–96
    form the mind, 15–16, 74–75, 93–95
Lantura, Antonio, xxxv, xxxix–xl
Laplander, 122–24
Lapponi, Massimo, xxxv, xl
Latin
    study of, 87–88, 91–93, 160
    and cultivation of taste, 87–90
law, xxxix, 31, 41, 44, 79, 84, 100, 128, 137–38, 140
    and authority, 36, 57
    and civil order, 36
    and education, 38
    and freedom, xxxviii, 32
    and God, *see* God, law of
    and society, xxxviii, 1–2, 25–26, 33–34, 37–38, 40, 42, 127, 141
    natural, xxi, 66, 128, 136
    Rousseau's reductive view of, xxxviii, 1–2, 25–26, 30–34,141
Lawgiver, Divine, *see* God
Leibniz, Gottfried Wilhelm, 118
libertinism, 35
liberty
    natural, 24, 42, 45, 52, 127, 141
    personal, 31–32, 100, 141
    premature, 57
    see also freedom
Livy, 89
Locke, John, xl, 58, 62–63, 67, 142, 147, 150–51
logic
    and grammar, 86
    study of, 117–19, 159–60
Lycurgus, 26, 38

Maezieu, Nicholas de, 108, 157
Malebranche, Nicolas, xxvi, xxxvi–xxxvii, xxxix–xl
man
    as relational being, xxii–xxiv xxxiii, 6–8, 11–13
Mandeville, Bernard, 137, 154
Manfredi, Eustachio, 109, 157
Manutius, Paulus, 88, 153
Marcus Aurelius, 7, 26
materialism, 27–29, 39, 145
Ménage, Gilles, 91, 151
metaphysics, xxxv–xxxvi, xxxix, xl, 64, 162
Molière, 89, 154
Montesquieu, Charles-Louis de Secondat, 136, 163
moral reasoning,
    and use of fables, 71–84
    with children, 43–48, 60–67
morality, xxxvi, xxxix, 22, 30, 101, 105, 129
    and fables, *see* fables
    child capable of, 43, 46–47, 59, 61–62, 64, 66
    Emile contrary to, xv, 2, 4
    principles of, 42, 136
Morelly, Jean, 136, 163
mother, *see* father, and mother
Muret, Marc-Antoine de, 91, 154

national ethos
    formation of, xxi, 133–38
natural man, 11–12, 14, 145
    as a fiction, 16, 139
nature
    endows talent without discrimination, 131
    state of, 1, 23–24, 33–34, 36–41
Negro, 122–24

New World, 14
  see also America
Newman, John Henry, xxxiv
Newton, Issac, 26, 52, 70, 105, 118, 151
Nicole, Pierre, 118

obedience, 24, 31–33, 44–45, 51, 54–55, 59, 63, 65–66, 136
On Duties; 26, 144–46
  see also Cicero
On Social Contract, xx, xxiv, 1, 6, 125, 140, 143, 146–47, 149, 151, 161–63
On the Laws; 23, 143
  see also Cicero
order
  civic, *see* order, social
  idea of, xxii, xl, 35, 141
  in geometry, 108–9, 111
  love of, xxii, 35–36
  of ideas, xxvii, xxix–xxx, xxvii, 96–97
  of reality, xxiv, xxxi, 34–35
  of religion, 29
  providential, xxvi, 23, 31
  social, xii, xx–xxi, xxxvi, 1, 12–13, 30, 32–34, 36–37, 40–42, 57, 127, 134
  see also reason, *facultas ordinatrix*
original sin; *see* contrariety
Ovid, 85

paradox, *see* Rousseau, paradoxes
Pascal, Blaise, 93, 117, 122, 160
patriotism, xxxiii, 135, 137
Paul, St., 31, 45, 130, 147
penmanship, 62
perfection, *see* idea, of happiness and perfection

Perry, Ralph Barton, xxxviii
perversity, 119
  original, 43
  see also contrariety
Peter, St., 31
Petrarch, 89
Phaedo, 147, 152
  see also Plato
Phaedrus, 73–75, 152
philosophy, xi, xxvi, 4, 10, 17, 26, 54, 66, 73, 75, 83, 89, 115, 118, 139, 141, 145, 154–55, 157, 159
  and nation's ethos, *see* national ethos
  and religion, xi, xxii, 103, 135
  Christian, xxxix, 23, 26
  conflicting systems of, 136–37
  history of, xix, xx, xxxv, xxxvii, 162
  in legislation, 137–38
  limitation of, 133–38
  modern, xvii, xix, xxxiv–xxxix
  social and political, xxii, xxxv, xxxvii, xl, 162
  see also education, philosophy of
Pincianus, 75, 152
Pius VI, Pope, xxxv, xli
Pius VII, Pope, xxxv
pleasure
  sensual, 18–21
  see also sensibility
Plato, xvi, xviii, xxv, 9, 71, 142
Plautus, 93
Pluche, Noël Antoine, 118, 160
poor
  and their need of education, 129–30
Pope, Alexander, 122
Prévost, Antoine-François, 124, 161

Providence, *see* God, providence of
prudence, 56, 113–15, 131
Pyrrhus, King, 17, 145

Quintilian, 73–75, 87, 142, 152, 153

Racine, Jean-Baptiste, 89, 154
reading
    and precise language, 112–13
    Bacon's observations on, 110–
        14, 159
    inspire taste for, xxviii, 110–11
    see also study, of ancients
reason
    and Christianity, 125
    and education, xxiv–xxvi, xxvii,
        xxxiii, 12, 15, 57, 61–62, 68,
        96, 123–25
    and geometry, xxx, 69–70
    and grammar, 87
    and ideas of perfection and
        happiness, 9, 12, 18, 40, 144
    and judgment, xxx, 48
    and logic, 117–19
    and philosophy, xviii, xxi–xxii
    and virtue, xvii
    as foundation of arts, 12,
    as rule, xxxvii–xxxviii
    as social faculty, xxiv–xxv, xxxii–
        xxxiii, 12–14, 41
    as universal art, 39
    common to all men, 123–24
    compensates want of instinct,
        12, 38–43, 56–57
    cool monotony of, 5
    culture of, 40–42
    duties to God as end of, 43
    enlarged by reading and study,
        xxix, xxxi
    enlightened by prudence, 56

facultas ordinatrix, xxx, 58
    faculty for combining ideas,
        xxx, 38, 58–61, 99
    faculty for ordering ideas,
        xxvii, xxx, 58, 96
    Horace as poet of, 46
    restrains sensibility, xvii, 10–11,
        48, 57
    strong, xxv, 14
    wisdom as end of, 43
    see also moral reasoning
*Reflections on the Theory and Practice
    of Education against the Principles
    of Rousseau, see Anti-Emile*
Régnier Des Marais, François-
    Séraphin de, 91, 155
relation
    as object of reason, xxvii, xxix–
        xxxi, 38, 40, 60–61, 69, 72,
        96–98, 103, 106–7, 109, 117
    see also man, as relational being
religion
    and courage, 69
    and morality, 42, 130–31
    and philosophy, xl, 23, 26, 83,
        84, 133, 135,
    and public virtue, xxi, xxxiii–
        xxxiv, 136–37, 162
    and virtue, 128, 135
    Rousseau's hostility to, xv–xvi,
        2, 4, 139–42
    transcends self-interest, xxii,
        xxxiii
Republic, xvi, 152
    see also Plato
revelation, 10, 25, 135, 140
    see also Scripture, Holy
revolution, xvi, xx, xxxv, 1, 52, 89,
    97, 99–101
Richelieu, Cardinal, 20–21, 146

Robinson Crusoe, 32, 41, 148
Rollin, Charles, 73–74, 101, 113, 142, 152, 156
Rondelli, Geminiano, 108, 157
Rorty, Richard, xxi
Rousseau, Jean-Jacques, *passim*
  aversion to Christianity, xxi, xxxiv, 1, 17, 128, 140–41
  aversion to authority, xvii, 51–52, 56, 140–42, 149,
  his eloquence, 4–5
  paradoxes of, 1–2, 4, 45, 83, 87, 137

Sacks, Oliver, xxxi
Sadoleto, Jacopo, 88, 153
Saint-Pierre, Abbé de, 1, 21, 143, 146
Sallust, 89
Sannazzaro, Jacopo, 91, 154
Sauveur, Joseph, 108, 157
savages, 1, 26, 28, 30, 41, 125–26, 128, 141
Savoyard Vicar, 141
Scaliger, Julius Caesar, 91, 154
Scotus, John Duns, xxvi
Scripture, Holy, 30, 45, 140, 147
  see also revelation
secularism, xxxv
self
  autonomy of, xviii, xxvi
  Gerdil's connected, xxvi
  Rousseau's unalienated, xxvi
self-expression, xxvii
self-interest
  as insufficient foundation for society, 17–18
Seneca, 73, 75, 93, 142, 152, 155
sensibility, xxxvi, 10, 17, 145
  see also pleasure, sensual

sentiment, xxi, xl, 19–23, 27–29, 36, 38, 42, 45–48, 51–54, 60–61, 72, 81, 94, 103, 131, 140
Sigebert of Gembloux, 88, 153
Simonides, 48
Slade, Francis, xxxvii–xxxviii
sociability
  as inherent perfection, xviii, xxiv–xxvii, xxxiii, 12–13
  see also reason, as social faculty
social contract, 2, 31, 144
society
  ends of, 127
  state of, xxv, 14, 23–24, 33, 36–37
Socrates, 16, 26, 28, 129, 142, 152
solitary man, xxvi, 8, 12, 139
  see also natural man
Solon, 26
Sparta
  unjust to innocents, 127
Spinoza, Baruch, xxxvii
Spirit of the Laws, 149, 161, 163–64
  see also Montesquieu
Stella, Pietro, xli
study
  and logic, *see* logic, study of
  and its two advantages, 114
  as hard work, 111
  Bacon's observations on, 110–14, 159–60
  of the ancients, 88–91
style
  literary; *see* fables, literary styles for

Tacquet, Andreas, 109, 157–58
taste
  cultivation of, *see* Latin
  for reading, xxviii, 111

Terence, 93
Terrasson, Jean, 70, 152
Themistocles, 16
Turenne, Henri de La Tour
   d'Auvergne, 26, 114, 147, 159
Turk, 128, 158

Ulloa, Don George Juan de and
   Don Antonio de, 14–16, 144–45
utility
   as a category of good, xxii,
   xxviii, xxxvi, 9, 18, 20, 22, 35–
   36, 102, 106, 108, 114, 144

Valebrega, Roberto, xxxii, xxxiii,
   xxxiv
Varen (=Bernhardus Varenius), 105,
   156
Varignon, Pierre, 108, 157
vice, *see* virtue
Vida, Marco Girolamo, 91, 154
Virgil, 75, 87–89, 93, 154

virtue
   and citizenship, 18, 136
   and religion, xxi, 23, 128, 135
   attraction to, 23–24, 59, 61, 73,
      99, 134, 150
   classical concept of, xvii–xviii,
      xxv
   intrinsic good of, xxxvi, 23, 135,
      148–49
   Rousseau's concept of, xvii–
      xviii, 18, 23, 146
   satisfaction of, 21–23
   teaching children, 73, 99, 131–
      32, 134
   see also fables, useful in teaching
Voltaire, 91, 136, 146, 155, 160, 163

wicked people, 28, 34, 36, 49, 59,
   80
wickedness, 134
   see also evil
Wolff, Christian Freiherr, 108, 156